INTERMEDIATE

ILLUSTRATED COURSE GUIDES

MICROSOFT® OFFICE 365™

WORD 2016

MICROSOFT® OFFICE 365™

WORD 2016

DUFFY + CRAM

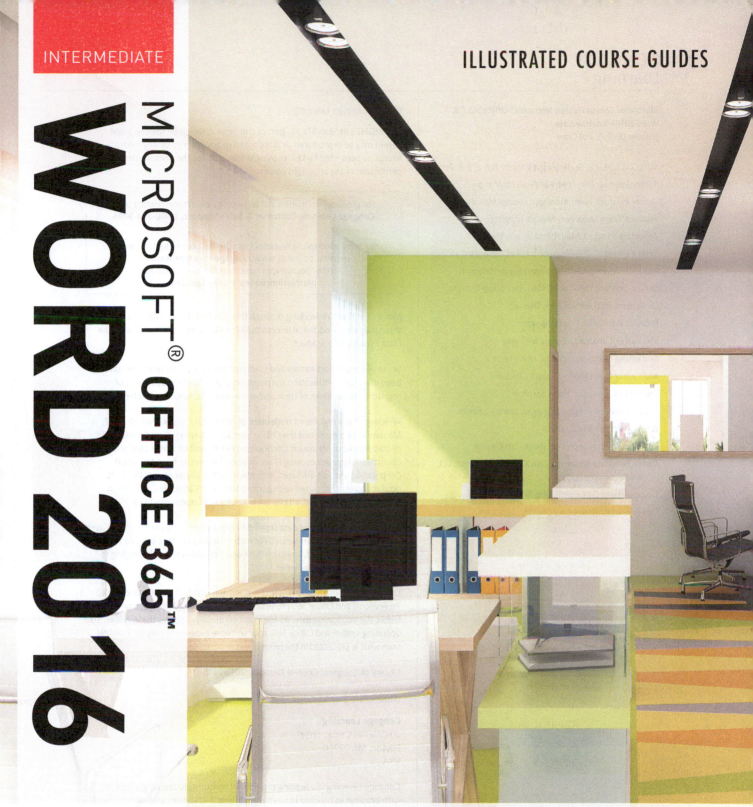

For Microsoft® Office updates, go to sam.cengage.com

CENGAGE
Learning·

Australia • Brazil • Mexico • Singapore • United Kingdom • United States

CENGAGE
Learning®

**Illustrated Course Guides: Microsoft® Office 365™ &
Word 2016—Intermediate**
Jennifer Duffy/Carol Cram

SVP, GM Science, Technology & Math: Balraj S. Kalsi

Senior Product Director: Kathleen McMahon

Senior Product Team Manager: Lauren Murphy

Product Team Manager: Andrea Topping

Associate Product Manager: Melissa Stehler

Senior Director, Development: Julia Caballero

Product Development Manager: Leigh Hefferon

Senior Content Developer: Christina Kling-Garrett

Developmental Editor: Pam Conrad

Product Assistant: Erica Chapman

Marketing Director: Michele McTighe

Marketing Manager: Stephanie Albracht

Marketing Coordinator: Cassie Cloutier

Production Director: Patty Stephan

Senior Content Project Manager: Stacey Lamodi

Art Director: Diana Graham

Text Designer: Joseph Lee, Black Fish Design

Cover Template Designer: Lisa Kuhn, Curio Press, LLC
www.curiopress.com

Composition: GEX Publishing Services

Cover Image: irisdesign / ShutterStock.com

Mac users: If you're working through this product using a Mac, some of the
steps may vary. Additional information for Mac users is included with the
Data Files for this product.

Some of the product names and company names used in this book have
been used for identification purposes only and may be trademarks or
registered trademarks of their respective manufacturers and sellers.

Windows® is a registered trademark of Microsoft Corporation. © 2012
Microsoft. Microsoft and the Office logo are either registered trademarks
or trademarks of Microsoft Corporation in the United States and/or other
countries. Cengage Learning is an independent entity from Microsoft
Corporation and not affiliated with Microsoft in any manner. Microsoft
product screenshots used with permission from Microsoft Corporation.
Unless otherwise noted, all clip art is courtesy of openclipart.org.

Disclaimer: Any fictional data related to persons or companies or URLs used
throughout this text is intended for instructional purposes only. At the time
this text was published, any such data was fictional and not belonging to
any real persons or companies.

Disclaimer: The material in this text was written using Microsoft Windows 10
Professional and Office 365 Professional Plus and was Quality Assurance tested
before the publication date. As Microsoft continually updates the Windows 10
operating system and Office 365, your software experience may vary slightly
from what is presented in the printed text.

Library of Congress Control Number: 2016943583

ISBN: 978-1-305-87855-6

Cengage Learning
20 Channel Center Street
Boston, MA 02210
USA

Cengage Learning is a leading provider of customized learning solutions
with employees residing in nearly 40 different countries and sales in more
than 125 countries around the world. Find your local representative at
www.cengage.com

Cengage Learning products are represented in Canada by
Nelson Education, Ltd.

For your course and learning solutions, visit **www.cengage.com**

Purchase any of our products at your local college store or at our
preferred online store **www.cengagebrain.com**

Printed at EPAC, 07-16

Brief Contents

Contents

Illustrating Documents with Graphics

CASE ▸ You are preparing a flyer advertising Reason2Go add-on destination tours in Mexico. You use the graphics features in Word to illustrate the flyer.

Module Objectives

After completing this module, you will be able to:

- Insert a graphic
- Size and scale a graphic
- Position a graphic
- Create a text box

- Create WordArt
- Draw shapes
- Create a chart
- Finalize page layout

Files You Will Need

WD 6-1.docx	Playa.jpg
WD 6-2.docx	Stone Barn.jpg
WD 6-3.docx	

Insert a Graphic

Learning Outcomes
• Insert a bitmap graphic
• Add a shadow
• Wrap text

You can insert graphic images, including photos taken with a digital camera, scanned art, and graphics created in other graphics programs, into a Word document. To insert a graphic file into a document, you use the Pictures command in the Illustrations group on the Insert tab. Once you insert a graphic, you can apply a Picture style to it to enhance its appearance. **CASE** *You have written and formatted the text for the Mexico add-ons flyer, and now you want to add a photograph. You insert a photo file in the document, apply a shadow to the photo, and then wrap text around it to make it a floating graphic.*

STEPS

1. **Start Word, open the file WD 6-1.docx from the location where you store your Data Files, save it as WD 6-Volunteer Mexico, change the zoom level to 120%, click the Show/Hide ¶ button ¶ in the Paragraph group to display formatting marks, read the flyer to get a feel for its format and contents, then press [Ctrl][Home]**

   The flyer is divided into five sections. It includes a hard page break and several inline graphics. The second and fourth sections are formatted in three columns.

2. **Click the Insert tab, then click the Pictures button in the Illustrations group**

   The Insert Picture dialog box opens. You use this dialog box to locate and insert graphic files. Most graphic files are **bitmap graphics**, which are often saved with a .bmp, .png, .jpg, .tif, or .gif file extension.

3. **Navigate to the location where you store your Data Files, click the file Playa.jpg, then click Insert**

   The photo is inserted as an inline graphic at the location of the insertion point. When a graphic is selected, white circles, called **sizing handles**, appear on the sides and corners of the graphic, a white **rotate handle** appears at the top, and the Picture Tools Format tab appears on the Ribbon. You use this tab to size, crop, position, wrap text around, format, and adjust a graphic.

4. **Click the Picture Effects button in the Picture Styles group, point to Shadow, move the pointer over the shadow styles in the gallery to preview them in the document, then click Offset Diagonal Bottom Right in the Outer section**

   A drop shadow is applied to the photo. You can use the Picture Effects button to apply other visual effects to a graphic, such as a glow, soft edge, reflection, bevel, or 3-D rotation.

5. **Click the Picture Effects button, point to Shadow, then click Shadow Options**

   The Format Picture pane opens with the Effects category active and the Shadow section expanded, as shown in **FIGURE 6-1**. You use this pane to adjust the format settings applied to graphic objects.

6. **Click the Distance up arrow four times until 7 pt appears, then click the Close button in the task pane**

   The distance of the shadow from the picture is increased to 7 points. Notice that as you adjust the settings in the Format Picture pane, the change is applied immediately in the document.

7. **Click the Wrap Text button in the Arrange group, then click Tight**

   The text wraps around the sides of the graphic, as shown in **FIGURE 6-2**, making the graphic a floating object. You can also use the Layout Options button to change the text wrapping style applied to a graphic. A floating object is part of the drawing layer in a document and can be moved anywhere on a page, including in front of or behind text and other objects. Notice the anchor that appears in the upper-left corner of the photo. The anchor indicates the floating graphic is **anchored** to the nearest paragraph, in this case the Volunteer Mexico paragraph, which means the graphic moves with the paragraph if the paragraph is moved. The anchor is a non-printing symbol that appears when an object is selected.

8. **Deselect the graphic, then click the Save button 🖫 on the Quick Access toolbar**

Illustrating Documents with Graphics

FIGURE 6-1: Format Picture pane

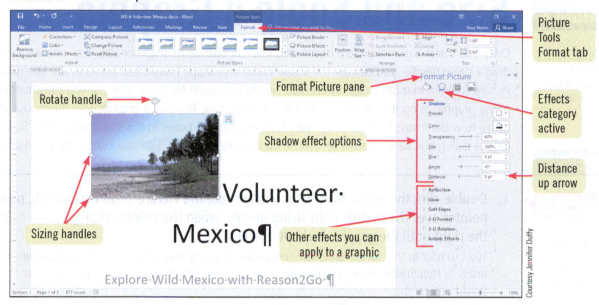

Picture Tools Format tab

Rotate handle

Format Picture pane

Effects category active

Shadow effect options

Distance up arrow

Sizing handles

Other effects you can apply to a graphic

Volunteer·
Mexico¶

Explore·Wild·Mexico·with·Reason2Go·¶

Courtesy Jennifer Duffy

FIGURE 6-2: Floating graphic

Photo is anchored to the paragraph next to it

Layout Options button; use to change the text-wrapping style of the graphic

Text wraps around the shape of the graphic

Volunteer·
Mexico¶

Explore·Wild·Mexico·with·Reason2Go·¶
Reason2Go ● Adventure·travel·that·makes·a·difference ● www.R2G.com¶

Courtesy Jennifer Duffy

Correcting pictures, changing colors, and applying artistic effects

The Corrections command in the Adjust group allows you to adjust a picture's relative lightness (**brightness**), alter the difference between its darkest and lightest areas (**contrast**), and change the sharpness of an image. To make these adjustments, select the image and then click the Corrections button to open a gallery of preset percentages applied to the selected picture. Point to an option in the gallery to preview it in the document; click an option in the gallery to apply it. You can also fine-tune brightness, contrast, or sharpness by clicking Picture Corrections Options in the Corrections gallery, and then using the sliders in the Picture Corrections section of the Format Picture pane to adjust the percentage.

The Color command in the Adjust group is used to change the vividness and intensity of color in an image (**color saturation**), and to change the "temperature" of a photo by bringing out the cooler blue tones or the warmer orange tones (**color tone**). The Color command is also used to recolor a picture to give it a stylized effect, such as sepia tone, grayscale, or duotone (using theme colors). To make changes to the colors in a picture, select it, click the Color button, and then select one of the color modes or variations in the gallery that opens, or click Picture Color Options to fine tune color settings using the Picture Format pane.

The Artistic Effects command in the Adjust group allows you to make a photo look like a drawing, a painting, a photocopy, a sketch (see **FIGURE 6-3**), or some

other artistic medium. To experiment with applying an artistic effect, select a photo, click the Artistic Effects button, and then point to each effect to preview it applied to the photo.

After you adjust a picture, you can undo any changes by clicking the Reset Picture button in the Adjust group. This command discards all formatting changes made to a picture, including size, cropping, borders, and effects.

FIGURE 6-3: Artistic effect applied to a photograph

Courtesy Jennifer Duffy

Word 2016

Size and Scale a Graphic

Once you insert a graphic into a document, you can change its shape or size. You can use the mouse to drag a sizing handle, you can use the Shape Width and Shape Height text boxes in the Size group on the Picture Tools Format tab to specify an exact height and width for the graphic, or you can change the scale of the graphic using the Size tab in the Layout dialog box. Resizing a graphic with the mouse allows you to see how the image looks as you modify it. Using the text boxes in the Size group or the Size tab in the Layout dialog box allows you to set precise measurements. **CASE** ▶ *You enlarge the photograph.*

STEPS

1. **Double-click the photo to select it and activate the Picture Tools Format tab, place the pointer over the middle-right sizing handle, when the pointer changes to ⬌, drag to the right until the graphic is about 5" wide**

   You can refer to the ruler to gauge the measurements as you drag. When you release the mouse button, the image is stretched to be wider. Dragging a side, top, or bottom sizing handle changes only the width or height of a graphic.

2. **Click the Undo button ↺ on the Quick Access toolbar, place the pointer over the lower-right sizing handle, when the pointer changes to ⬊, drag down and to the right until the graphic is about 2¾" tall and 4" wide, then release the mouse button**

   The image is enlarged. Dragging a corner sizing handle resizes the photo proportionally so that its width and height are reduced or enlarged by the same percentage. **TABLE 6-1** describes ways to resize objects using the mouse.

3. **Click the launcher 🔲 in the Size group**

   The Layout dialog box opens with the Size tab active, as shown in **FIGURE 6-4**. The Size tab allows you to enter precise height and width measurements for a graphic or to scale a graphic by entering the percentage you want to reduce or enlarge it by. When a graphic is sized to **scale** (or scaled), its height to width ratio remains the same.

4. **Select the measurement in the Height text box in the Scale section, type 150, then click the Width text box in the Scale section**

   The scale of the width changes to 150% and the Absolute measurements in the Height and Width sections increase proportionally. When the Lock aspect ratio check box is selected, you need to enter only a height or width measurement. Word calculates the other measurement so that the resized graphic is proportional.

5. **Click OK**

   The photo is enlarged to 150% of its original size.

6. **Type 4.6 in the Shape Width text box in the Size group, press [Enter], then save your changes**

   The photo is enlarged to be 4.6" wide and close to 3.06" tall, as shown in **FIGURE 6-5**. Because the Lock aspect ratio check box is selected on the Size tab in the Layout dialog box for this graphic, the photo is sized proportionally when you adjust a setting in either the Shape Height or the Shape Width text box.

TABLE 6-1: Methods for resizing an object using the mouse

do this	to
Drag a corner sizing handle	Resize a clip art or bitmap graphic and maintain its proportions
Press [Shift] and drag a corner sizing handle	Resize any graphic object and maintain its proportions
Press [Ctrl] and drag a side, top, or bottom sizing handle	Resize any graphic object vertically or horizontally while keeping the center position fixed
Press [Ctrl] and drag a corner sizing handle	Resize any graphic object diagonally while keeping the center position fixed
Press [Shift][Ctrl] and drag a corner sizing handle	Resize any graphic object while keeping the center position fixed and maintaining its proportions

Illustrating Documents with Graphics

FIGURE 6-4: Size tab in the Layout dialog box

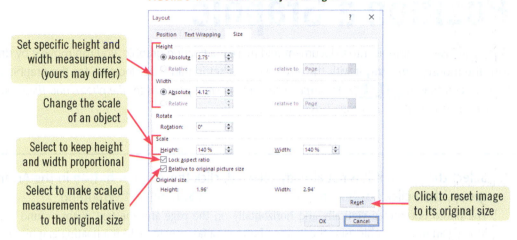

Set specific height and width measurements (yours may differ)

Change the scale of an object

Select to keep height and width proportional

Select to make scaled measurements relative to the original size

Click to reset image to its original size

FIGURE 6-5: Enlarged photo

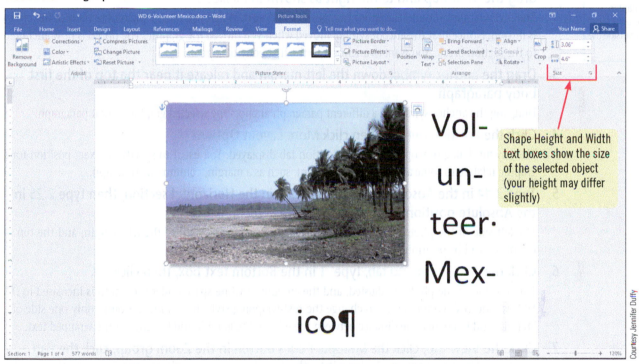

Shape Height and Width text boxes show the size of the selected object (your height may differ slightly)

Cropping graphics

If you want to use only part of a picture in a document, you can **crop** the graphic to trim the parts you don't want to use. To crop a graphic, select it, then click the Crop button in the Size group on the Picture Tools Format tab. Cropping handles (solid black lines) appear on all four corners and sides of the graphic. To crop one side of a graphic, drag a side cropping handle inward to where you want to trim the graphic. To crop two adjacent sides at once, drag a corner cropping handle inward to the point where you want the corner of the cropped image to be.

When you finish adjusting the parameters of the graphic, click the Crop button again to turn off the crop feature.

You can also crop a graphic to fit a shape, such as an oval, a star, a sun, or a triangle, or you can crop a graphic to conform to a certain aspect ratio, so that its height and width are proportionate to a ratio, such as 3:5. To apply one of these cropping behaviors to a graphic, select it, click the Crop list arrow in the Size group, point to Crop to Shape or to Aspect Ratio on the menu that opens, and then select the option you want.

Position a Graphic

Learning Outcomes
• Change text wrapping
• Move an anchor

Once you insert a graphic into a document and make it a floating graphic, you can move it by dragging it with the mouse, **nudging** it with the arrow keys, or setting an exact location for the graphic using the Position command. **CASE** *You experiment with different positions for the photo, and then you move an inline graphic from page 2 to page 1 using Cut and Paste.*

STEPS

1. **Select the photo if it is not already selected, click the Position button in the Arrange group, then click Position in Middle Center with Square Text Wrapping**

   The photo is centered vertically and horizontally on the page and the text wraps around the graphic. Moving an inline graphic using the Position button is a fast way to make it a floating graphic and position it so it is centered or aligned with the margins.

2. **Scroll to position the section break at the top of your screen, then use the ⟨⟨⟨ pointer to drag the photo up and to the right as shown in FIGURE 6-6**

   The text wrapping around the photo changes as you drag it. When you release the mouse button, the photo is moved. Notice that the anchor symbol moved when you moved the graphic. The photo is now anchored to the section break. You want to anchor it to the first body paragraph.

3. **Drag the anchor symbol down the left margin and release it near the top of the first body paragraph**

   Dragging the anchor symbol to a different paragraph anchors the selected graphic to that paragraph.

4. **Click the Position button, then click More Layout Options**

   The Layout dialog box opens with the Position tab displayed. You use it to specify an exact position for a graphic relative to some aspect of the document, such as a margin, column, or paragraph.

5. **Type 2.44 in the Absolute position text box in the Horizontal section, then type 2.25 in the Absolute position text box in the Vertical section**

   The left side of the photo will be positioned exactly 2.44" to the right of the left margin, and the top of the photo will be positioned precisely 2.25" below the top margin.

6. **Click the Text Wrapping tab, type .1 in the Bottom text box, then click OK**

   The position of the photo is adjusted, and the amount of white space under the photo is increased to .1". You use the Text Wrapping tab to change the text-wrapping style, to wrap text around only one side of a graphic, and to change the distance between the edge of the graphic and the edge of the wrapped text.

7. **Click the View tab, click the Multiple Pages button in the Zoom group, click the flag photo at the top of page 3, drag it to the blank paragraph above the Reason2Go Mexico… heading in the first column on the first page, then release the mouse button**

   The inline graphic is moved to the bottom of column 1 on page 1, and the document changes to two pages.

8. **Double-click the flag photo, click the Position button, click Position in Bottom Left with Square Text Wrapping, then drag the anchor symbol to the margin left of the first body paragraph in the column**

   The flag photo becomes a floating graphic aligned in the lower-left corner of the first page and anchored to the first body paragraph. Dragging the anchor symbol to a different paragraph anchors the selected graphic to that paragraph. Both photos are now anchored to the same paragraph.

9. **Click the Playa photo, click the Home tab, click the Format Painter button in the Clipboard group, click the flag photo with the ⟨⟨ pointer, then click 🖫**

   The shadow format settings are copied from the Playa photo to the flag photo, as shown in **FIGURE 6-7**.

FIGURE 6-6: Dragging a graphic to move it

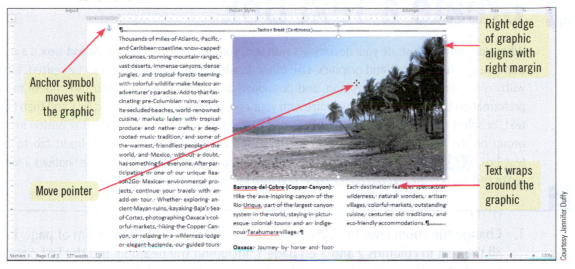

Anchor symbol moves with the graphic

Move pointer

Right edge of graphic aligns with right margin

Text wraps around the graphic

Courtesy Jennifer Duffy

FIGURE 6-7: Repositioned photos

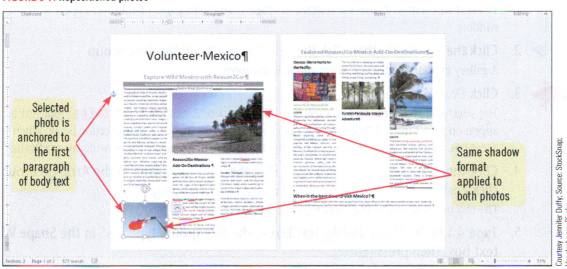

Selected photo is anchored to the first paragraph of body text

Same shadow format applied to both photos

Courtesy Jennifer Duffy; Source: StockSnap; Unsplash.com; Pixabay

Removing the background from a picture

When you want to call attention to a detail in a picture or remove a distracting element, you can use the Remove Background command to remove all or part of the picture background. To do this, select the picture, then click the Remove Background button in the Adjust group on the Picture Tools Format tab. The background of the photo is highlighted automatically in pink, four marquee lines appear on the photo in the shape of a rectangle, and the Picture Tools Background Removal tab is activated. You can drag a handle on the marquee lines to indicate the areas of the photo you want to keep. The area within the marquee lines is the area that will be kept when the pink background is removed, and the area outside the marquee lines will be removed. To fine-tune the background area (the pink area) you use the Mark Areas to Keep and Mark Areas to Remove commands in the Refine group on the Picture Tools Background Removal tab. Clicking these buttons activates a pointer that you use to click an area of the picture to mark for removal (make it pink) or keep (remove the pink). When you are finished, click Keep Changes in the Close group to remove the background. **FIGURE 6-8** shows a photo of a sea turtle and the same photo with the background removed.

FIGURE 6-8: Background removed from photo

Source: Unsplash.com

Illustrating Documents with Graphics

Create a Text Box

Learning Outcomes
• Draw a text box
• Format a text box
• Add a drop cap

When you want to illustrate your documents with text, you can create a text box. A **text box** is a container that you can fill with text and graphics. Like other drawing objects, a text box can be resized, formatted with colors, lines, and text wrapping, and positioned anywhere on a page. You can choose to insert a preformatted text box that you customize with your own text, draw an empty text box and then fill it with text, or select existing text and then draw a text box around it. You use the Text Box button in the Text group on the Insert tab, or the Shapes button in the Illustrations group on the Insert tab to create a text box. **CASE** *You draw a text box around the Reason2Go Mexico Add-on Destinations information, resize and position the text box on the page, and then format it using a text box style.*

STEPS

1. **Change the zoom level to 100%, scroll to see all the text at the bottom of page 1, select all the text in columns 2 and 3 on page 1, including the heading and the last paragraph mark before the section break, click the View tab, then click the Multiple Pages button in the Zoom group**

   The text in columns 2 and 3 is selected on page 1, and both pages of the flyer appear in the document window.

2. **Click the Insert tab, then click the Text Box button in the Text group**

   A gallery of preformatted text boxes and sidebars opens.

3. **Click Draw Text Box**

   The selected text is formatted as a text box on a new page 2, as shown in **FIGURE 6-9**. Your text box might appear on page 1 instead. In either case, notice the text box is anchored to the section break. When you draw a text box around existing text or graphics, the text box becomes part of the drawing layer (a floating object).

4. **Click the Drawing Tools Format tab, click the Position button in the Arrange group, then click Position in Bottom Right with Square Text Wrapping**

   The text box is moved to the lower-right corner of the page.

5. **Type 4.1 in the Shape Height text box in the Size group, type 4.65 in the Shape Width text box, then press [Enter]**

   The text box is resized to be exactly 4.1" tall and 4.65" wide.

6. **Locate the anchor symbol next to the section break, then drag the anchor symbol to the left margin of the first body paragraph on the first page**

   The text box is anchored to the first body paragraph and is located in the lower-right corner of page 1.

7. **Click the More button ▼ in the Shape Styles group, then click Subtle Effect – Gray-50%, Accent 3**

   A style that includes gray shading and a thin gray border is applied to the text box. You can also create your own designs using the Shape Fill and Shape Outline buttons in the Shape Styles group.

8. **Place the insertion point in the first body paragraph above the flag photo, click the Insert tab, click the Drop Cap button in the Text group, click Dropped, then deselect the drop cap**

   A drop cap is added to the paragraph.

9. **Click the Home tab, click the Show/Hide ¶ button ¶ in the Paragraph group, then save your work**

   Compare your document to **FIGURE 6-10**.

FIGURE 6-9: Text formatted as a text box

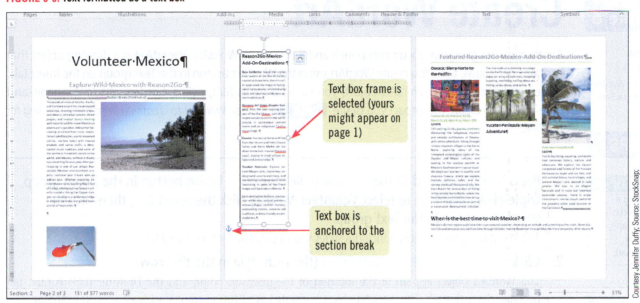

Text box frame is selected (yours might appear on page 1)

Text box is anchored to the section break

FIGURE 6-10: Formatted text box and drop cap in flyer

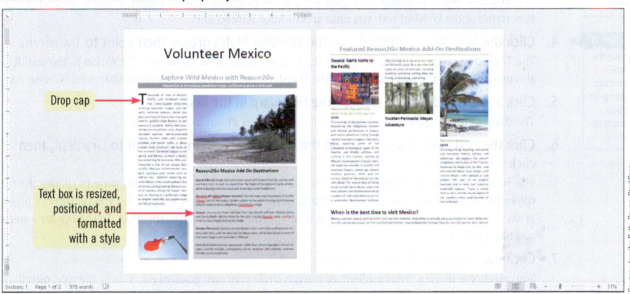

Drop cap

Text box is resized, positioned, and formatted with a style

Linking text boxes

If you are working on a longer document, you might want text to begin in a text box on one page and then continue in a text box on another page. By creating a **link** between two or more text boxes, you can force text to flow automatically from one text box to another, allowing you to size and format the text boxes any way you wish. To link two or more text boxes, you must first create the original text box, fill it with text, and then create a second, empty text box. Then, to create the link, select the first text box, click the Create Link button in the Text group on the Drawing Tools Format tab to activate the pointer, and then click the second text box with the pointer. Any overflow text from the first text box flows seamlessly into the second text box. As you resize the first text box, the flow of text adjusts automatically between the two linked text boxes. If you want to break a link between two linked text boxes so that all the text is contained in the original text box, select the original text box, and then click the Break Link button in the Text group.

Illustrating Documents with Graphics

Create WordArt

Another way to give your documents punch and flair is to use WordArt. **WordArt** is a drawing object that contains decorative text. You create WordArt using the WordArt button in the Text group on the Insert tab. Once you have created a WordArt object, you can change its font, colors, borders, shadows, shape, and other effects to create the impact you desire. **CASE** ▶ *You use WordArt to create an impressive heading for the flyer.*

STEPS

1. **Press [Ctrl][Home], click the View tab, click the Page Width button in the Zoom group, triple-click Volunteer to select Volunteer Mexico, click the Insert tab, then click the WordArt button in the Text group**

   The WordArt Gallery opens. It includes styles you can choose for your WordArt.

2. **Click Fill – Gold, Accent 4, Soft Bevel (the fifth style in the first row)**

   The WordArt object appears at the location of the insertion point, and the Drawing Tools Format tab becomes the active tab. The WordArt object is inserted as a floating graphic with square text wrapping.

3. **Type 1.3 in the Shape Height text box in the Size group, type 7 in the Shape Width text box, then press [Enter]**

   The WordArt object is enlarged to span the page between the left and right margins. To change the appearance of the WordArt text, you must apply format settings to it.

4. **Click the Text Effects button Ⓐ in the WordArt Styles group, then point to Transform**

   The Text Effects button is used to apply a shadow, reflection, glow, bevel, or 3-D rotation to the text. It is also used to change the shape of the text. The Transform gallery shows the available shapes for WordArt text.

5. **Click Square in the Warp section (the first warp in the first row)**

   The shape of the WordArt text changes to fill the object, as shown in **FIGURE 6-11**.

6. **Click the Text Fill list arrow Ⓐ ▾ in the WordArt Styles group, point to Gradient, then click More Gradients**

   The Format Shape pane opens with the Text Fill options expanded. You use this pane to change the fill colors and effects of WordArt and other graphic objects. Using the Text Fill options, you can select a preset gradient effect or choose colors and shading styles to create your own gradient effect. You will create a green and blue gradient.

7. **Click the Gradient fill option button**

   You can choose to use a preset gradient, or you can create your own gradient effect using the type, direction, angle, color, and other options available in the Text Fill section of the Format Shape pane. The Stop 1 of 4 slide is selected on the Gradient stops slide. You can create a custom gradient by adding, removing, or changing the position or color of a gradient stop.

8. **Click the Color list arrow, click Blue, Accent 5, click the Stop 4 of 4 slide on the Gradient stops slide, click the Color list arrow, click Green, Accent 6, click the Stop 3 of 4 slide, click the Remove gradient stop button, click the Stop 2 of 3 slide, click the Color list arrow, click Green, Accent 6, Lighter 40%, then drag the Stop 2 of 3 slide right to approximately the 90% position on the Gradient stops slide**

   The customized gradient settings and the new fill effects applied to the WordArt are shown in **FIGURE 6-12**.

9. **Close the Format Shape pane, deselect the object, then save your changes**

FIGURE 6-11: WordArt object

FIGURE 6-12: Format Shape pane and completed WordArt object

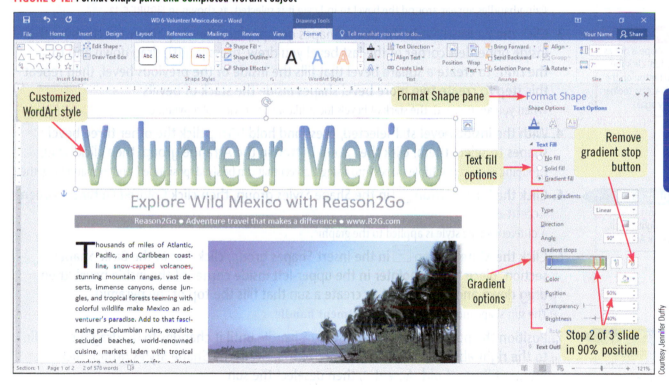

Word 2016

Enhancing graphic objects with styles and effects

Another fun way to give a document personality and flair is to apply a style or an effect to a graphic object. To apply a style, select the object and then choose from the style options in the Styles group on the active Format tab for that type of object. Styles include a preset mixture of effects, such as shading, borders, shadows, and other settings. The Effects command in the Styles group on the active Format tab gives you the power to apply a customized variety of effects to an object, including a shadow,

bevel, glow, reflection, soft edge, or 3-D rotation. To apply an effect, select the object, click the Effects command for that type of object, point to the type of effect you want to apply, and then select from the options in the gallery that opens. To further customize an effect, click the Options command for that type of effect at the bottom of the gallery to open the Format Shape pane. The best way to learn about styles and effects is to experiment by applying them to an object and seeing what works.

Draw Shapes

One way you can create your own graphics in Word is to draw shapes. **Shapes** are the rectangles, ovals, lines, callouts, block arrows, stars, and other drawing objects you can create using the Shapes command in the Illustrations group on the Insert tab. Once you draw a shape, you can add colors, borders, fill effects, shadows, and three-dimensional effects to it. **CASE** ▶ *You use the Shapes feature to draw a Mayan pyramid in the document.*

STEPS

1. **Press [Ctrl][End], click the Insert tab, click the Shapes button in the Illustrations group, then click Bevel in the Basic Shapes section of the Shapes menu**

   The Shapes menu contains categories of shapes and lines that you can draw. When you click a shape in the Shapes menu, the pointer changes to ┼. You draw a shape by clicking and dragging with this pointer.

   > **QUICK TIP**
   > To draw a circle, click the Oval, then press [Shift] while you drag with the pointer.

2. **Position the ┼ pointer in the blank area at the bottom of the page, press [Shift], then drag down and to the right to create a square bevel that is approximately 2" tall and wide**

   Pressing [Shift] as you drag creates a bevel that is perfectly square. When you release the mouse button, sizing handles appear around the bevel to indicate it is selected, as shown in **FIGURE 6-13**.

   > **TROUBLE**
   > If the shape is not as expected, click the Undo button on the Quick Access toolbar and try again.

3. **Click the Bevel shape in the Insert Shapes group, place the ┼ pointer exactly over the inside upper-left corner of the last bevel you drew, press [Shift], drag down and to the right to create a square bevel that fills the inside of the previous bevel, then repeat this step to create two more bevel shapes inside the stack of bevels**

   When you are finished, the stack of bevels looks like an aerial view of a pyramid.

4. **With the inside bevel still selected, press and hold [Ctrl], click the other three bevel shapes to select them, click the Group button in the Arrange group, then click Group**

   Grouping converts multiple shapes into a single object that can be sized, positioned, and formatted together.

   > **QUICK TIP**
   > To add text to a shape, right-click it, then click Add Text.

5. **Click the More button ⏷ in the Shape Styles group, then click Colored Outline – Green, Accent 6**

   A different shape style is applied to the graphic.

6. **Click the More button ⏷ in the Insert Shapes group, click Sun in the Basic Shapes section, place the ┼ pointer in the upper-left inside corner of the inside bevel, then drag down and to the right to create a sun that fills the top of the pyramid**

   The sun shape includes a yellow **adjustment handle**.

   > **QUICK TIP**
   > Drag an adjustment handle to modify the shape, but not the size, of a drawing object.

7. **Position the pointer over the adjustment handle until it changes to ▷, drag the handle to the right about 1/8", click the More button ⏷ in the Shape Styles group, click Intense Effect – Gold, Accent 4, then deselect the sun**

   The sun shape becomes yellow with a shadow, as shown in **FIGURE 6-14**.

8. **Double-click the grouped bevel shape to select it, press and hold [Ctrl], click the sun shape to select it, click the Group button, then click Group**

   The pyramid shape and the sun shape are grouped into a single object.

   > **QUICK TIP**
   > Use the Bring Forward and Send Backward list arrows to shift the order of the layers in a stack of graphic objects.

9. **Click the Rotate button in the Arrange group, then click Rotate Right 90°**

   The pyramid drawing is rotated 90°. You can also rotate a graphic by dragging the white rotate handle.

10. **Change the zoom level to 100%, drag the pyramid drawing up to position it temporarily over the third column of text, as shown in FIGURE 6-15, then save your changes**

    The drawing object is automatically formatted as a floating graphic with the In Front of Text wrapping style applied, making it part of the drawing layer. You will finalize the object's position in a later lesson.

FIGURE 6-13: Bevel shape

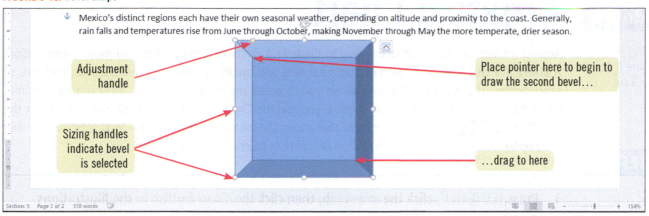

FIGURE 6-14: Sun added to pyramid

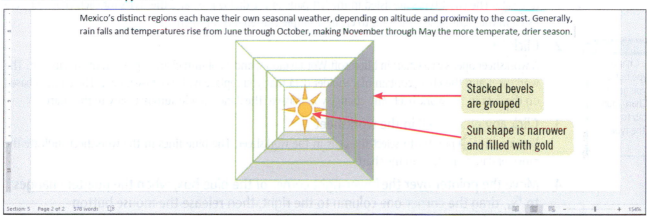

FIGURE 6-15: Rotated drawing in new position

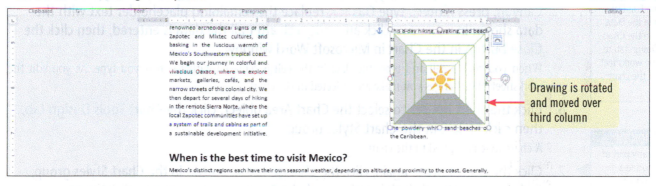

Creating an illustration in a drawing canvas

A **drawing canvas** is a workspace for creating your own graphics. It provides a framelike boundary between an illustration and the rest of the document so that the illustration can be sized, formatted, and positioned like a single graphic object. If you are creating an illustration that includes multiple shapes, such as a flow chart, it is helpful to create the illustration in a drawing canvas. To draw shapes or lines in a drawing canvas, click the Shapes button in the Illustrations group on the Insert tab, click New Drawing Canvas to open a drawing canvas in the document, and then create and format your illustration in the drawing canvas. When you are finished, right-click the border of the drawing canvas and then click Fit to resize the drawing canvas to fit the illustration. You can then resize the illustration by dragging a border of the drawing canvas. Once you have resized a drawing canvas, you can wrap text around it and position it. By default, a drawing canvas has no border or background so that it is transparent in a document, but you can add fill and borders to it if you wish.

Create a Chart

Adding a chart can be an attractive way to illustrate a document that includes numerical information. A **chart** is a visual representation of numerical data and usually is used to illustrate trends, patterns, or relationships. The Word chart feature allows you to create many types of charts, including bar, column, pie, area, and line charts. To create a chart, you use the Chart button in the Illustrations group on the Insert tab. **CASE** *You create a chart that shows the average temperature for each season in the four geographic areas where R2G Mexico Add-On Destinations tours are located.*

STEPS

1. **Press [Ctrl][End], click the Insert tab, then click the Chart button in the Illustrations group**

   The Insert Chart dialog box opens. You use this dialog box to select the type and style of chart you intend to create. The chart types are listed in the left pane of the dialog box, and the styles for each chart type are listed in the right pane. You want to create a simple clustered column chart.

2. **Click OK**

   A worksheet opens in a Chart in Microsoft Word window, and a column chart appears in the document. The worksheet and the chart contain placeholder data that you replace with your own data. The chart is based on the data in the worksheet. Any change you make to the data is made automatically to the chart.

3. **Click any empty cell in the worksheet**

   You use the ✛ pointer to select the cells in the worksheet. The blue lines in the worksheet indicate the range of data to include in the chart.

4. **Move the pointer over the lower-right corner of the blue box, when the pointer changes to ↖, drag the corner one column to the right, then release the mouse button**

   The range is enlarged to include five columns and five rows.

5. **Click the Category 1 cell, type Baja California, click the Category 2 cell, type Copper Canyon, press [Enter], type Oaxaca, replace the remaining placeholder text with the data shown in FIGURE 6-16, click an empty cell after all the data is entered, then click the Close button in the Chart in Microsoft Word window**

   When you click a cell and type, the data in the cell is replaced with the text you type. As you edit the worksheet, the changes you make are reflected in the chart.

6. **Click the chart border to select the Chart Area object, click the Chart Tools Design tab, then click Style 2 in the Chart Styles group**

   A chart style is applied to the chart.

7. **Click the chart border again, click the Change Colors button in the Chart Styles group, click Color 4 in the Colorful section, click the Chart Tools Format tab, click the More button ▼ in the Shape Styles group, then click Colored Outline – Green, Accent 6**

   The chart colors change and a green border is added to the chart object.

8. **Select the Chart Area object, type 2.5 in the Shape Height text box in the Size group, type 4.1 in the Shape Width text box in the Size group, press [Enter], then deselect the chart**

   The chart object is resized. You can click any chart element to select it, or use the Chart Elements list arrow in the Current Selection group on the Chart Tools Format tab to select a chart element.

9. **Click the Chart Title object to select it, select the text CHART TITLE, click the Decrease Font Size button ꓮ on the Mini toolbar two times, type Average Temperature (Celsius), then save your changes**

   The font size of the chart title is reduced. The completed chart is shown in **FIGURE 6-17**.

Illustrating Documents with Graphics

FIGURE 6-16: Chart object and worksheet in Word

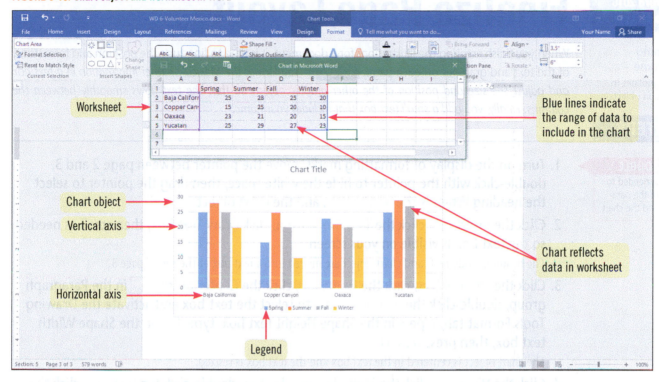

Worksheet

Blue lines indicate the range of data to include in the chart

Chart object

Vertical axis

Horizontal axis

Chart reflects data in worksheet

Legend

FIGURE 6-17: Completed chart

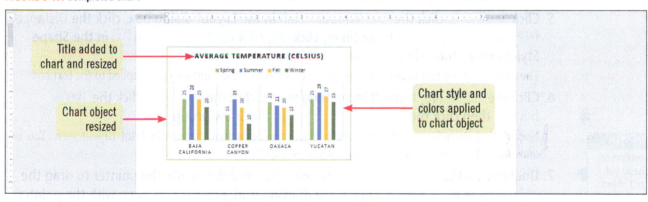

Title added to chart and resized

Chart object resized

Chart style and colors applied to chart object

Creating SmartArt graphics

Diagrams are another way to illustrate concepts in your documents. The powerful Word **SmartArt** feature makes it easy for you to quickly create and format many types of diagrams, including pyramid, process, cycle, and matrix diagrams, as well as lists and organization charts. To insert a SmartArt graphic in a document, click the SmartArt button in the Illustrations group on the Insert tab to open the Choose a SmartArt Graphic dialog box. In this dialog box, select a diagram category in the left pane, select a specific diagram layout and design in the middle pane, preview the selected diagram layout in the right pane, and then click OK. The SmartArt object appears in the document with placeholder text, and the SmartArt Tools Design and Format tabs are enabled. These tabs contain commands and styles for customizing and formatting the SmartArt graphic and for sizing and positioning the graphic in the document.

Finalize Page Layout

When you finish creating the illustrations for a document, it is time to fine-tune the position and formatting of the text and graphics on each page. **CASE** ▶ *You format the Mexico weather information in a text box and adjust the size and position of the other graphic objects so that the text flows smoothly between the columns. Finally, you add a small text box that includes your name.*

STEPS

1. **Turn on the display of formatting marks, move the pointer between page 2 and 3, double-click with the pointer to hide the white space, then drag the pointer to select the heading When is the best time..., and the chart object**

2. **Click the Insert tab, click the Text Box button, click Draw Text Box, then scroll as needed so the text box is visible on your screen**

   The heading, body text, and chart object are moved into a text box at the top of page 3.

3. **Click the chart object, click the Home tab, click the Center button ☰ in the Paragraph group, double-click the text box frame to select the text box and activate the Drawing Tools Format tab, type 4 in the Shape Height text box, type 4.65 in the Shape Width text box, then press [Enter]**

   The chart object is centered in the text box and the text box is resized.

4. **Click the View tab, click the Multiple Pages button, double-click the text box, click the Position button in the Arrange group, click Position in Bottom Left..., then click the Layout Options button over the text box**

   The text box is moved to the lower-left corner of page 2. The Layout Options button provides quick access to the most commonly used text wrapping commands.

5. **Click See more, click the Text Wrapping tab in the Layout dialog box, click the Distance from text Top up arrow three times, click OK, click the More button ▼ in the Shape Styles group, then click Subtle Effect – Gray-50%, Accent 3**

   The distance of the text wrapping above the text box is increased and a style is applied to the text box.

6. **Click the Home tab, turn off formatting marks, click the View tab, click the 100% button, then click the Gridlines check box in the Show group**

   Nonprinting **drawing gridlines** appear within the document margins in Print Layout view. You use drawing gridlines to help you size, align, and position objects.

7. **Double-click the pyramid drawing to select it, scroll down, use the pointer to drag the object down onto a blank area of the drawing grid, press [Shift], then with the pointer, drag the lower-left sizing handle up and to the right until the object is about 1" square**

   Use the ruler and the gridlines to help judge the size of the object as you drag.

8. **Drag the object to position it as shown in** FIGURE 6-18

   You can nudge the drawing with the arrow keys if necessary to position it more precisely on the grid.

9. **Click the Draw Text Box button in the Insert Shapes group, then, with the pointer, draw a text box under the pyramid similar to the one shown in Figure 6-18, type Contact: followed by your name in the text box, click the More button ▼ in the Shape Styles group, then click Subtle Effect – Blue, Accent 1**

   Figure 6-18 shows the pyramid drawing reduced and repositioned and the new text box.

10. **Click the View tab, click the Gridlines check box, click the Multiple Pages button, save your changes, submit a copy to your instructor, then close the file and exit Word**

    The completed document is shown in FIGURE 6-19.

FIGURE 6-18: Repositioned object and new text box

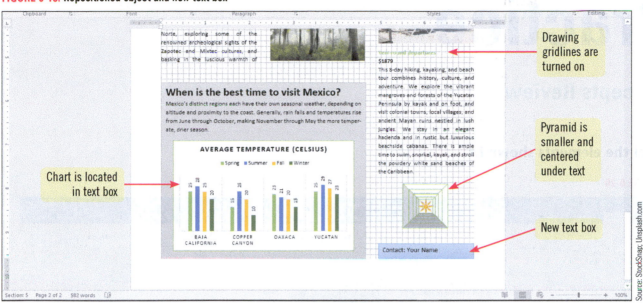

Chart is located in text box

Drawing gridlines are turned on

Pyramid is smaller and centered under text

New text box

FIGURE 6-19: Completed flyer

Word 2016

Inserting online videos and online pictures in a document

You can also illustrate your documents with graphics and media found on the web. The Online Video command in the Media group on the Insert tab allows you to insert and play videos found on the web into your Word documents, and the Online Pictures command in the Illustrations group allows you to insert online images. To search the web for videos or images to add to a document, click the appropriate command on the Insert tab to open the Insert Video or Insert Pictures window, type a keyword or phrase in the search box for the website you want to search, and then press [Enter]. Select the video or image you want to insert from the search results, click Insert to add it to the document, and then format the item as you would any other graphic object. Videos inserted in a document include a play button that you can click to view the video right in Word.

Practice

Concepts Review

Label the elements shown in FIGURE 6-20.

FIGURE 6-20

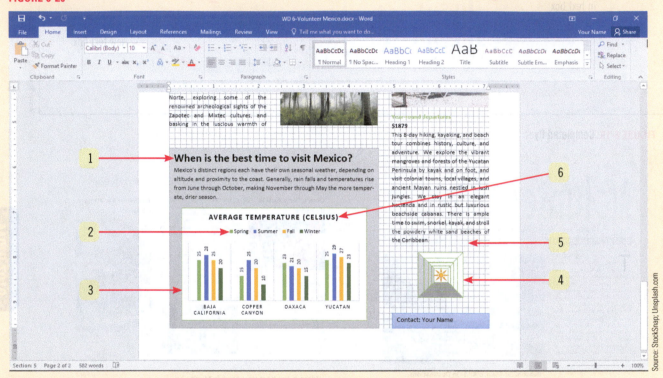

Source: StockSnap; Unsplash.com

Match each term with the statement that best describes it.

7. **Drawing gridlines**
8. **Contrast**
9. **Text box**
10. **Brightness**
11. **WordArt**
12. **Drawing Canvas**
13. **Chart**
14. **Floating graphic**

a. Nonprinting lines that are used to align, size, and position objects
b. A workspace for creating graphics
c. A graphic that a text-wrapping style has been applied to
d. A visual representation of numerical data
e. The relative lightness of a picture
f. A graphic object composed of specially formatted text
g. A graphic object that is a container for text and graphics
h. The difference between the darkest and lightest areas in a picture

Select the best answer from the list of choices.

15. **Which button is used to change a photograph to a pencil sketch?**
   a. Artistic Effects
   b. Corrections
   c. Color
   d. Picture Effects

16. **Which button is used to change an inline graphic to a floating graphic?**
    a. Crop
    b. Change Picture
    c. Corrections
    d. Layout Options

17. **What style of text wrapping is applied to a graphic by default?**
    a. Square
    b. In line with text
    c. In front of text
    d. Tight

18. **Which method do you use to nudge a picture?**
    a. Select the picture, then press an arrow key.
    b. Select the picture, then drag it to a new location.
    c. Select the picture, then drag a top, bottom, or side sizing handle.
    d. Select the picture, then drag a corner sizing handle.

19. **Which is not an example of a Picture Effect?**
    a. Glow
    b. Paintbrush
    c. Bevel
    d. Shadow

20. **What do you drag to change a drawing object's shape, but not its size or dimensions?**
    a. Sizing handle
    b. Adjustment handle
    c. Rotate handle
    d. Cropping handle

Skills Review

1. **Insert a graphic.**
   a. Start Word, open the file WD 6-2.docx from the drive and folder where you store your Data Files, then save it as **WD 6-Stone Barn CSA**.
   b. Display formatting marks, scroll down, read the document to get a feel for its contents and formatting, then press [Ctrl][Home].
   c. Select the colorful mixed vegetables photo on page 1, apply square text wrapping, apply the picture style Simple Frame, Black to the photo, then use the Format Painter to copy the picture style settings from the mixed vegetables photo to the photo of the carrots on page 2 and the photo of the beans on page 3.
   d. Press [Ctrl][Home], then apply square text wrapping to the photo of the carrots.
   e. Scroll down, place the insertion point at the top of page 2, insert the file Stone Barn.jpg from the location where you store your Data Files, then save your changes.

2. **Size and scale a graphic.**
   a. With the Stone Barn photo still selected, click the Crop button in the Size group.
   b. Drag the bottom-middle cropping handle up approximately 1", drag the top-middle cropping handle down approximately .7", verify that the photo is approximately 2.8" tall, adjust if necessary using the cropping handles, then click the Crop button again.
   c. Deselect the photo, then scroll to page 1.
   d. Resize the mixed vegetables photo proportionally so that it is about **2.7"** high and **1.8"** wide.
   e. Resize the photo of the carrots proportionally so that it is about **1.7"** high and **1.1"** wide.
   f. Scroll to page 2, then resize the photo of the beans proportionally to be precisely **2.7"** high.
   g. Press [Ctrl][Home], then save your changes.

3. **Position a graphic.**
   a. Drag the mixed vegetables photo up so its top is aligned with the first line of body text and its right side is aligned with the right margin.
   b. Change the view to Multiple Pages, then use the Position command to position the photo of the carrots so it aligns with the middle left.
   c. On page 2, use the Position command to align the beans photo with the bottom and right margins, then save your changes.

Skills Review (continued)

4. Create a text box.

    a. Change the zoom level to 120%, then scroll to the top of page 1.

    b. Add a drop cap using the default settings for the Dropped option to the first body paragraph.

    c. Select the What does Stone Barn Community Farm do? heading, the paragraph under it, and the two paragraph marks above the page break, then insert a text box.

    d. Delete the paragraph mark after 7 p.m. in the last line of the How does it work? paragraph on page 1, then select the text box.

    e. Apply the shape style Colored Outline – Green, Accent 6 to the text box, use the Position command to align it with the bottom and right margins, click the Layout Options button, click the Fix Position on Page option button, resize the text box to be approximately **3.3"** high and **4.5"** wide, change to multiple pages view, then drag the anchor symbol up to the How does it work? heading. (*Hint*: The blue anchor symbol might be over the photo of the carrots.)

    f. Return to page width view, scroll to page 2, then draw a text box that covers the bottom of the Stone Barn photo. The text box should span the width of the photo and be approximately **.4"** high.

    g. Type **Welcome to Stone Barn Community Farm – A USDA Certified Organic Farm** in the text box, center the text, change the font to 12-point Arial Rounded MT Bold, then change the font color to Orange, Accent 2.

    h. Remove the shape fill from the text box, adjust the placement of the text box as necessary so the text is attractively placed over the bottom of the photo, then remove the border from the text box.

    i. Scroll down, select all the green text, then insert a text box.

    j. Turn off paragraph marks, resize the text box to be **2.8"** tall and **5.4"** wide, then align it with the lower-left corner of the page.

    k. Remove the border from the text box, then save your changes.

5. Create WordArt.

    a. Press [Ctrl][Home], triple-click to select Stone Barn Community Farm, insert a WordArt object, then select the style Fill - White, Outline - Accent 1, Shadow (in the first row).

    b. Resize the WordArt object to be **7.3"** wide and **1"** tall.

    c. Click the Text Effects button in the WordArt Styles group, point to Transform, then click the Square warp.

    d. Change the Text Fill color to Green, Accent 6, Darker 25%.

    e. Change the Text Outline color to Green, Accent 6, Darker 50%.

    f. Change the shadow color to Green, Accent 6, Lighter 40%, close the Format Shape pane, then save your changes. (*Hint*: Use the Shape Effects button.)

6. Draw shapes.

    a. Scroll down to the middle of page 2, select the three-line address, then draw a text box around it.

    b. Move the text box approximately ¾" to the right.

    c. Click the Shapes button, then click the Sun shape.

    d. In a blank area, draw a sun that is approximately .5" tall and wide.

    e. Fill the sun with Gold, Accent 4, Darker 25% apply the gradient style From Center in the Light Variations section, change the shape outline color to Gold, Accent 4.

    f. Move the sun left of the address text box if necessary, then remove the shape outline from the address text box.

    g. Click the Shapes button in the Illustrations group on the Insert tab, then click Rectangle.

    h. Draw a rectangle around the sun and the address, remove the fill, then change the shape outline to Green, Accent 6.

    i. Adjust the size of the rectangle to resemble an address label, then save your changes.

7. Create a chart.

    a. Scroll up, place the insertion point in the text box at the bottom of page 1, press [↓] as many times as necessary to move the insertion point to the second blank line under the text in the text box.

    b. Insert a chart, select Bar chart, select Clustered Bar for the style, then click OK.

c. Type the information shown in **FIGURE 6-21**, adjust the range to include just the columns and rows that include data, then close the Chart in Microsoft Word window.

FIGURE 6-21

	A	B
2	CSA	0.41
3	U-Pick	0.11
4	Farm Stand	0.21
5	Farmers' Market	0.18
6	Other	0.09

d. Select the text box, use the Position command to align it with the bottom and right margins, select the chart, resize it to be approximately **2"** high and **4.1"** wide, center it in the text box, change the colors to Color 4, then apply the Style 2 chart style to the chart.

e. Select the chart title Series 1, type **Harvest Sales**, change the font of the title to 12-point Arial Rounded MT Bold, remove the bold formatting, then change the font color to Green, Accent 6. (*Hint*: To replace and then format the chart title text, select the chart title object, and then start typing.)

f. Select the legend, then press [Delete] to remove the legend from the chart.

g. Select the Horizontal (Value) Axis, click the Format Selection button, scroll down the Format Axis pane, expand the Number section, then scroll again as needed to see the categories.

h. Click the Category list arrow, select Percentage in the Category list, change the number of decimal places to 0, press [Enter], then close the Format Axis pane.

i. Resize the chart object to be approximately **2"** tall and **3.5"** wide, center the chart object in the text box, select the text box, apply the Intense Effect - Green, Accent 6 shape style, then save your changes.

8. Finalize page layout.

a. Resize the text box that includes the chart to be approximately **3.2"** tall and **4.7"** wide, change the font size of the heading in the text box to 14 points, change the font color to Green, Accent 6, Darker 50%, then center the heading.

b. Turn on the gridlines in the Show group on the View tab, then change the view to Multiple Pages. (*Note*: The gridlines show the margins.)

c. Resize and shift the position of the photographs and the text box until all the text fits on page 1 and the layout of page 1 of the flyer looks similar to the completed flyer, which is shown in two-page view in **FIGURE 6-22**. Your flyer does not need to match exactly.

d. Type your name in the document footer, save your changes, submit a copy to your instructor, close the file, then exit Word.

FIGURE 6-22

Source: Pixabay, Courtesy Jennifer Duffy

Independent Challenge 1

Your company just completed a major survey of its customer base, and your boss has asked you to prepare a summary of the results for your colleagues. You create a chart for the summary that shows the distribution of customers by gender and age.

a. Start Word, then save a blank document as **WD 6-Age and Gender** to the location where you store your Data Files.

b. Type **Prepared by** followed by your name at the top of the document, press [Enter] twice, then insert a clustered column chart object into the document.

FIGURE 6-23

c. Enter the data shown in **FIGURE 6-23** into the worksheet. To begin, delete the data in rows 4 and 5 of the worksheet, and then adjust the range to include 5 columns and 3 rows. When you are finished, close the Chart in Microsoft Word window.

	A	B	C	D	E
1		18-34	35-49	50-64	65+
2	Female	0.22	0.18	0.13	0.07
3	Male	0.17	0.14	0.16	0.05

d. Click the Select Data button in the Data group on the Chart Tools Design tab, then click Switch Row/Column button in the Select Data Source dialog box that opens to switch the data so the age groups appear on the horizontal axis.

e. Apply chart style 6 to the chart, then add the title **Customers by Age and Gender** above the chart.

f. Add the Primary Horizontal axis title **Age Range**. (*Hint:* Use the Add Chart Element button.)

g. Select the Vertical Value Axis, then click the launcher in the Shape Styles group on the Chart Tools Format tab to open the Format Axis pane. Click Axis Options to expand the axis options, scroll down, Expand the Number section, change the Category to Percentage, change the number of decimal places to **0**, press [Enter], then close the Format Axis pane.

h. Use the Change Chart Type button in the Type group on the Chart Tools Design tab to change to a different type of column chart, taking care to choose an appropriate type for the data, then format the chart with styles, fills, colors, outlines, and other effects so it is attractive and readable.

i. Save your changes, submit a copy of the chart to your instructor, close the file, then exit Word.

Independent Challenge 2

You design ads for bestvacations.com, a company that specializes in custom vacation packages. Your next assignment is to design a full-page ad for a travel magazine. Your ad needs to contain three photographs of vacation scenes, such as the photo shown in **FIGURE 6-24**, the text "Your vacation begins here." and the web address "www.bestvacations.com."

FIGURE 6-24

Source: Pixabay

a. Start Word, then save a blank document as **WD 6-Vacations Ad** to the drive and folder where your Data Files are located.

b. Change all four page margins to .7".

c. Using keywords such as beach, snowboard, fishing, or some other vacation-related word, find and insert at least three appropriate online photographs into the document.

d. Using pencil and paper, sketch the layout for your ad.

e. Change the photos to floating graphics, then format them. You can crop, resize, move, and combine them with other design elements, or enhance them with styles, shapes, borders, and effects.

f. Using text effects or WordArt, add the text **Your vacation begins here.** and the web address **www.bestvacations.com** to the ad.

g. Adjust the layout, design, and colors in the ad as necessary. When you are satisfied with your ad, type your name in the document header, save your changes, submit a copy to your instructor, close the document, then exit Word.

Illustrating Documents with Graphics

Independent Challenge 3

You are a graphic designer. The public library has hired you to design a bookmark for Earth Day. Their only request is that the bookmark includes the words Earth Day. You'll create three different bookmarks for the library.

a. Start Word, then save a blank document as **WD 6-Earth Day** to the location where you store your Data Files.

b. Change all four page margins to .7", change the page orientation to landscape, and change the zoom level to Whole Page.

c. Draw one text box. Resize the text box to be approximately 6.5" tall x 2.5" wide. Copy and paste the text box two times for a total of three text boxes, then move the text boxes so they do not overlap. Each text box will become a bookmark.

d. Use clip art, WordArt or text effects, and a photograph (either a personal photograph or one you find on the web) at least one time as you create the bookmarks. (*Hints*: When you insert a graphic in a text box, you cannot wrap text around it, so you must design bookmarks that use inline graphics. Alternatively, you can insert an online image in the document and then crop it and resize it to be the shape and size of a bookmark. You can also nest text boxes inside text boxes.)

e. Format the bookmarks with fills, colors, borders, styles, shadows, and other picture effects. Be sure to add the words **Earth Day** to each bookmark.

f. Type your name in the document header, save your changes, submit a copy to your instructor, close the document, then exit Word.

Independent Challenge 4: Explore

One way to find graphic images to use in your documents is to download them from the web. Many websites feature images that are in the public domain, which means they have no copyright restrictions and permission is not required to use the images. You are free to download these images and use them in your documents, although you must acknowledge the artist or identify the source. Other websites include images that are copyrighted and require written permission, and often payment, to use. Before downloading and using graphics from the web, it's important to research and establish their copyright status and permission requirements. In this exercise, you download photographs from the web and research their copyright restrictions.

a. Start Word, then save a blank document as **WD 6-Copyright Images** to the drive and folder where you store your Data Files.

b. Type your name at the top of the page, press [Enter], then create a table with four rows and three columns. Type the following column headings in the header row: **Photo**, **URL**, **Copyright Restrictions**. You will fill this table with photos you find on the web and the copyright restrictions for those photos.

c. Use your favorite search engine to search the web for photographs that you might use for your work or a personal project. Use the keywords **free photo archives** or **free public domain photos**. You can also add a keyword that describes the subject of the photos you want to find.

d. Find at least three websites that contain photos you could use in a document. Save a photo from each website to your computer. To save an image from a webpage, right-click the image, then click the appropriate command on the shortcut menu.

e. Go to your Word document, and insert each photo you saved from the web in the Photo column of the table. Resize the photos proportionally so that they are about 1.5" tall or 1.5" wide. Wrap text around the photos, and center them in the table cells.

f. For each photo in column 1, enter its URL in column 2 and its copyright restrictions in column 3. In the Copyright Restrictions column, indicate if the photo is copyrighted or in the public domain, and note the requirements for using that photo in a document.

g. Adjust the formatting of the table so it is easy to read, save your changes, submit a copy to your instructor, close the file, then exit Word.

Visual Workshop

Using the file WD 6-3.docx (located where you store your Data Files), create the flyer shown in **FIGURE 6-25**. (*Hints*: Change the margins to .8". For the WordArt object, use the Fill - Blue, Accent 1, Outline - Background 1, Hard Shadow, Accent 1 style, apply a Square warp and apply a gradient effect using shades of Blue, Accent 1.) Type your name in the footer, save the flyer as **WD 6-Surf Safe**, then submit a copy to your instructor.

FIGURE 6-25

Surf Safe, Surf Fun
Safety Tips for Surfers

Recognize a rip current

A rip current is a volume of water moving out to sea: the bigger the surf, the stronger the rip. Indicators of rips include:

- Brown water from stirred up sand
- Foam on the surface of the water that trails past the break
- Waves breaking on both sides of a rip current
- A rippled appearance between calm water
- Debris floating out to sea

Follow the rules

All surfers need to follow basic safety rules before heading into the waves. The key to fun and safe surfing is caution and awareness.

Study the surf

Always study the surf before going in. Select a safe beach with waves under 1 meter, and pick waves that are suitable for your ability. Be aware of rocks and other obstructions that might be under water.

Use a safe surfboard

A safe surfboard is a surfboard that suits your ability. Beginners need a big, thick surfboard for stability.

Dress appropriately and wear sunscreen

Wear a wet suit that is appropriate for the water temperature or a rash vest to help protect against UV rays. Wear at least SPF 30 broad spectrum sunscreen, and reapply it frequently. Zinc cream also prevents sunburn and guards against UV rays.

Learn how to escape rips

If you are dragged out by a rip, don't panic! Stay calm and examine the rip conditions before trying to escape the current. Poor swimmers should ride the rip out from the beach and then swim parallel to the shore for 30 or 40 meters. Once you have escaped the rip, swim toward the shore where the waves are breaking or probe with your feet to feel if a sand bar has formed near the edge of the rip. Strong swimmers should swim at a 45 degree angle across the rip.

Your Name

Source: Pixabay

Working with Themes and Building Blocks

> **CASE** You are preparing a project summary report for a new R2G project in Kenya. You create a customized theme for the report and simplify the process of designing the layout by using predesigned building blocks. Once the project report is finished, you save the theme and several reusable pieces of customized content to use in other project reports.

Module Objectives

After completing this module, you will be able to:

- Apply styles to text
- Apply a theme
- Customize a theme
- Insert a sidebar

- Insert Quick Parts
- Add a cover page
- Create building blocks
- Insert building blocks

Files You Will Need

WD 7-1.docx	WD 7-7.docx
WD 7-2.docx	WD 7-8.docx
WD 7-3.docx	WD 7-9.docx
WD 7-4.docx	WD 7-10.docx
WD 7-5.docx	Cheetah.jpg
WD 7-6.docx	R2G Logo.jpg

Apply Styles to Text

Learning Outcomes
• Apply a style
• Modify text formatted with a style

Applying a style to text allows you to apply multiple format settings to text in one easy step. A **style** is a set of format settings, such as font, font size, font color, paragraph spacing, and alignment, that are named and stored together. Word includes many **Style sets**—groups of related styles that share common fonts, colors, and formats, and are designed to be used together in a document—that you can use to give your documents a polished and cohesive look. Each Style set includes styles for a title, subtitle, headings, body text, lists, quotes, and other text elements. **CASE** *You apply styles to the project summary report to help organize the text attractively and make the report easy to read at a glance.*

STEPS

1. **Start Word, open the file WD 7-1.docx from the drive and folder where you store your Data Files, save it as WD 7-Kenya Project, scroll the document to get a feel for its contents, then press [Ctrl][Home]**

   The three-page document includes text, photographs, and a chart.

2. **Select Savannah Conservation and Safari, click the More button ⥥ in the Styles group, then move the pointer over the styles in the Styles gallery**

   As you move the pointer over a style in the gallery, a preview of that style is applied to the selected text.

3. **Click Title**

   The Title style is applied to the selected text.

4. **Select Four weeks, Nairobi to Mombasa, click Subtitle in the Styles group, click the Font Color list arrow [A▾] in the Font group, then click Blue, Accent 5, Darker 25%**

   The Subtitle style is applied to the paragraph under the title, and then the font color is changed to blue. You can modify the format of text to which a style has been applied without changing the style itself.

5. **Select Project Highlights, click Heading 1 in the Styles group, then deselect the text**

   The Heading 1 style is applied to the Project Highlights heading, as shown in **FIGURE 7-1**.

6. **Apply the Heading 1 style to each red heading in the document, scrolling down as needed**

   The Heading 1 style is applied to the Project Highlights, Project Summary, Planning Your Trip, and What to Bring headings in the report.

7. **Scroll to page 2, select Climate, then click Heading 2 in the Styles group**

   The Heading 2 style is applied to the Climate subheading. The style seems too similar to the Heading 1 style for your purposes.

8. **Select Climate if necessary, click Heading 3 in the Styles group, click the Font Color list arrow [A▾], click Orange, Accent 2, then deselect the text**

   The Heading 3 style is applied to the Climate subheading, and the font color is changed to Orange, Accent 2, as shown in **FIGURE 7-2**.

9. **Use the Format Painter to apply the Heading 3 style and the Orange, Accent 2 font color to each purple subheading in the document, scrolling down as needed, then save your changes**

   The Heading 3 style and the Orange, Accent 2 font color are applied to the Climate, Visa and Vaccination Requirements, Luggage, Clothing and Footwear, and Equipment subheadings in the report.

FIGURE 7-1: Styles applied to the report

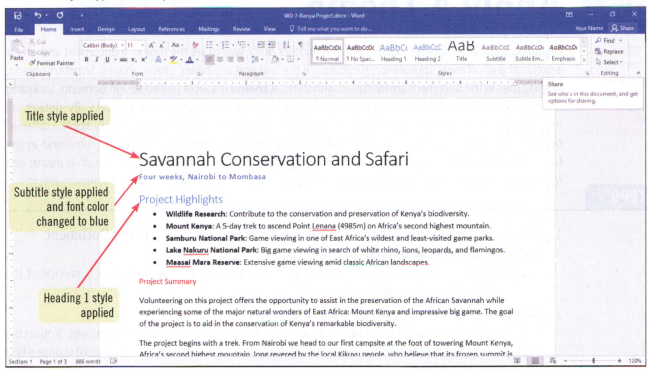

Title style applied

Subtitle style applied and font color changed to blue

Heading 1 style applied

FIGURE 7-2: Heading 3 style applied and modified

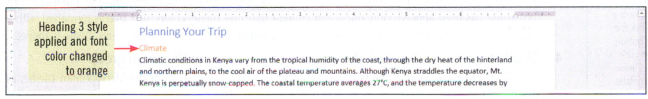

Heading 3 style applied and font color changed to orange

Saving a document as a webpage

Creating a webpage and posting it on the Internet or an intranet is a powerful way to share information with other people. You can design a webpage from scratch in Word, or you can use the Save As command to save an existing document in HTML format so it can be viewed with a browser. When you save an existing document as a webpage, Word converts the content and formatting of the Word file to HTML and displays the webpage in Web Layout view, which shows the webpage as it will appear in a browser. Any formatting that is not supported by web browsers is either converted to similar supported formatting or removed from the webpage. For example, if you save a document that contains a floating graphic in HTML format, the graphic will be left- or right-aligned on the webpage. In a document you plan to save as a webpage, it's best to create a table in the document, and

then insert text and graphics in the table cells in order to be able to position text and graphics precisely.

To save a document as a webpage, open the Save As dialog box, and then select a Web Page format in the Save as type list box. You have the option of saving the document in Single File Web Page (.mht or .mhtml) format, or in Web Page or Web Page, Filtered (.htm or .html) format. In a single file webpage, all the elements of the webpage, including the text and graphics, are saved together in a single MIME encapsulated aggregate HTML (MHTML) file, making it simple to publish your webpage or send it via e-mail. By contrast, if you choose to save a webpage as an .htm file, Word automatically creates a supporting folder in the same location as the .htm file. This folder has the same name as the .htm file plus the suffix_files, and it houses the supporting files associated with the webpage, such as graphics.

Apply a Theme

Changing the theme applied to a document is another quick way to set the tone of a document and give it a polished and cohesive appearance, particularly if the text and any tables, charts, shapes, SmartArt objects, or text boxes in the document are formatted with styles. A **theme** is a set of unified design elements, including theme colors, theme fonts for body text and headings, and theme effects for graphics. By default, all documents that you create in Word are formatted with the Office theme, but you can easily apply a different built-in theme to a document. To apply a theme to a document, you use the Themes command in the Document Formatting group on the Design tab. **CASE** *You experiment with different built-in themes and then apply a theme that more closely suits the message you want to convey with the project summary report.*

STEPS

1. **Press [Ctrl][Home], click the Design tab, click the Themes button in the Document Formatting group, then point to Facet**

   A gallery of built-in themes opens. When you point to the Facet theme in the gallery, a preview of the theme is applied to the document, as shown in FIGURE 7-3.

2. **Move the pointer over each theme in the gallery**

   When you point to a theme in the gallery, a preview of the theme is applied to the document. Notice that the font colors and the fonts for the body text and headings to which a style has been applied change when you preview each theme.

3. **Scroll down, then click Metropolitan**

   A complete set of new theme colors, fonts, styles, and effects is applied to the document. Notice that while the font of the body text changed, the bold formatting applied to the text under the Project Highlights heading at the top of page 1 remains. Changing the document theme does not affect the formatting of text to which font formatting has been applied. Only document content that uses theme colors, text that is formatted with a style (including default body text), and table styles and graphic effects change when a new theme is applied.

4. **Click the View tab, then click the Multiple Pages button in the Zoom group**

   The fill effect in the chart at the bottom of the last page is a fill effect from the Metropolitan theme, as shown in FIGURE 7-4.

5. **Click the Design tab, click the Themes button, then point to each built-in theme in the gallery**

   Notice how each theme affects the formatting of the chart, and, in some cases, the pagination of the document. It's important to choose a theme that not only mirrors the tone, content, and purpose of your document, but also meets your goal for document length.

6. **Click Wisp**

   The Wisp theme is applied to the document.

7. **Click the View tab, click the 100% button in the Zoom group, press [Ctrl][Home], then save your changes**

Changing the style set

Applying a different style set is another quick way to change the look of an entire document. Style sets include font and paragraph settings for headings and body text so that when you apply a new style set to a document, all the body text and all the headings that have been formatted with a style change to the format settings for the active style set. You apply styles to a document using the styles available in the Styles group on the

Home tab. You apply a style set using the style sets available in the Document Formatting group on the Design tab.

You can also save a group of font and paragraph settings as a new style set. To do this, click the More button in the Document Formatting group, and then click Save as a New Style Set. If you want to return a document to its original style set, click the More button, and then click Reset to the (default) Style Set.

FIGURE 7-3: Facet theme previewed in document

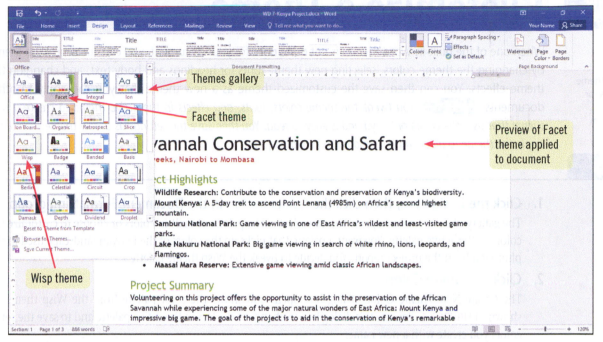

FIGURE 7-4: Metropolitan theme applied to document

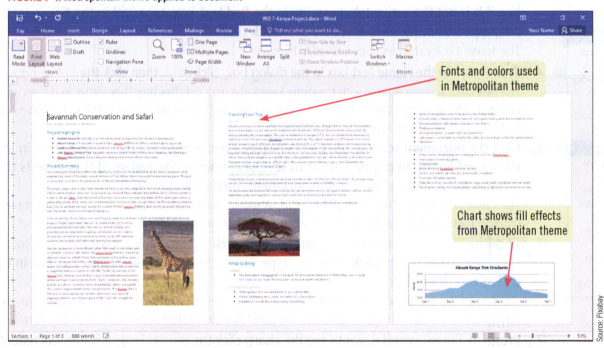

Source: Pixabay

Changing the default theme

By default, all new documents created in Word are formatted with the Office theme, but you can change your settings to use a different theme as the default. To change the default theme to a different built-in theme, press [Ctrl][N] to open a new blank document, click the Themes button in the Document Formatting group on the Design tab, and then click the theme you want to use as the default. If you want to customize the theme before saving it as the new default, use the Colors, Fonts, and Effects buttons in the Document Formatting group to customize the settings for theme colors, fonts, and effects. Alternatively, click the More button in the Document Formatting group and then select a new style set to use in the new default theme. When you are satisfied with the settings for the new default theme, click the Set as Default button in the Document Formatting group. The Themes gallery will be updated to reflect your changes.

Customize a Theme

Learning
Outcomes
• Customize theme
  colors, fonts, or
  effects
• Save a custom
  theme

When one of the built-in Word themes is not quite right for your document, you can customize the theme by changing the theme colors, selecting new theme fonts for headings and body text, and changing the theme effects. You can then save the customized theme as a new theme that you can apply to other documents. **CASE** *You tweak the theme colors, fonts, and effects in the active theme to create a new theme that uses the colors of Kenya and is easy to read. You then save the settings as a new theme so you can apply the theme to all documents related to Kenya projects.*

STEPS

1. **Click the Design tab, then click the Colors button in the Document Formatting group**

   The gallery of theme colors opens. You can select a new palette of built-in colors or choose to customize the colors in the active palette. You want a palette that picks up the colors of the Kenyan landscape used in the photographs in the project report. You decide to tweak the Wisp theme palette.

2. **Click Customize Colors**

   The Create New Theme Colors dialog box opens and shows the color palette from the Wisp theme, as shown in **FIGURE 7-5**. You use this dialog box to change the colors in the active palette and to save the set of colors you create with a new name.

3. **Click the Accent 1 list arrow, click More Colors, click the Custom tab in the Colors dialog box if it is not the active tab, type 146 in the Red text box, type 169 in the Green text box, type 185 in the Blue text box, then click OK**

   The Accent 1 color changes from dark red to blue-gray.

QUICK TIP
To remove a custom
color scheme from
the gallery, right-click
the scheme, then
click Delete.

4. **Type Kenya in the Name text box in the dialog box, click Save, then click the Colors button**

   The new color scheme is saved with the name Kenya, the dark red (Heading 1) headings in the document change to blue-gray, and the Kenya color scheme appears in the Custom section in the Colors gallery. The Kenya colors can now be applied to any document.

QUICK TIP
To change the line
and paragraph
spacing applied to
a document, click
the Paragraph
Spacing button in
the Document
Formatting group,
and then click a
Built-In style or click
Custom Paragraph
Spacing to enter
custom settings in
the Manage Styles
dialog box.

5. **Click the document to close the Colors gallery if necessary, click the Fonts button in the Document Formatting group, point to several options in the gallery of theme fonts to preview those fonts applied to the document, then click Customize Fonts**

   The Create New Theme Fonts dialog box opens, as shown in **FIGURE 7-6**. You use this dialog box to select different fonts for headings and body text, and to save the font combination as a new theme font set.

6. **Click the Heading font list arrow, scroll down, click Trebuchet MS, click the Body font list arrow, scroll down, click Perpetua, type Project Reports in the Name text box in the dialog box, then click Save**

   The font of the headings in the report changes to Trebuchet MS, the font of the body text changes to Perpetua, and the Project Reports theme font set is added to the Custom section of the Fonts gallery.

7. **Press [Ctrl][End], scroll down to see the chart, click the Effects button in the Document Formatting group, point to each effect in the gallery to see it previewed in the chart, then click Milk Glass**

   The Milk Glass effect is applied to the document.

8. **Click the Themes button, click Save Current Theme, type Kenya Project Report in the File name text box in the Save Current Theme dialog box, then click Save**

   The Kenya theme colors, Project Reports theme fonts, and theme effects from the Milk Glass theme are saved together as a new theme called Kenya Project Report in the default location for document themes.

QUICK TIP
To remove a custom
theme from the
gallery, right-click
the theme, then
click Delete.

9. **Save your changes, then click the Themes button**

   The new theme appears in the Custom section of the Themes gallery, as shown in **FIGURE 7-7**.

Working with Themes and Building Blocks

FIGURE 7-5: Create New Theme Colors dialog box

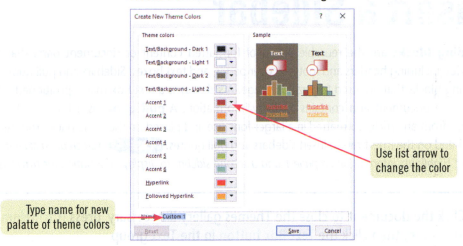

Type name for new palatte of theme colors

Use list arrow to change the color

FIGURE 7-6: Create New Theme Fonts dialog box

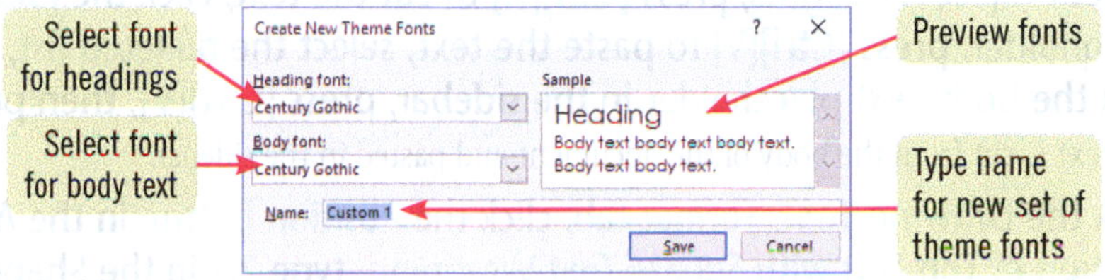

Select font for headings

Select font for body text

Preview fonts

Type name for new set of theme fonts

FIGURE 7-7: Custom theme in the Themes gallery

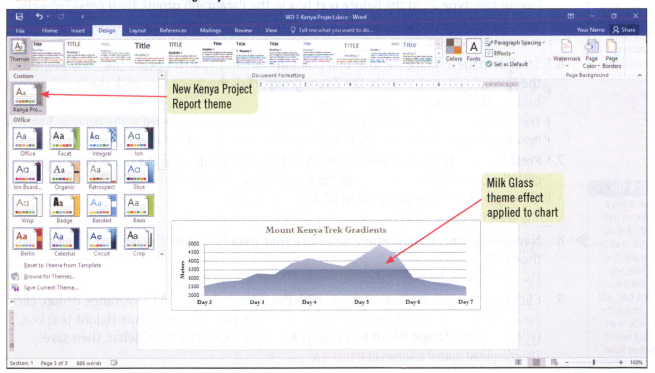

New Kenya Project Report theme

Milk Glass theme effect applied to chart

Insert a Sidebar

Learning Outcomes
• Format a sidebar
• Insert a text file
• Position a sidebar

Building blocks are the reusable pieces of formatted content or document parts that are stored in galleries, including headers and footers, cover pages, and text boxes. Sidebars and pull quotes are text box building blocks that are used to jazz up a page. A **sidebar** is a text box that is positioned adjacent to the body of a document and contains auxiliary information. A **pull quote** is a text box that contains an excerpt from an article, formatted in a larger font size and placed on the same page. You use the Text Box command on the Insert tab to insert sidebars and pull quotes. **CASE** ▶ *You create a sidebar to display the Project Highlights information on page 1 and a second sidebar to display information for travelers on page 2.*

STEPS

1. **Click the document to close the Themes gallery if necessary, press [Ctrl][Home], click the Insert tab, then click the Text Box button in the Text group**
   The Text Box gallery opens. It includes built-in styles for sidebars and pull quotes.

   QUICK TIP
   The sidebar is anchored to the paragraph where the insertion point is located.

2. **Scroll down the gallery, then click the Retrospect Sidebar**
   The Retrospect Sidebar is inserted on the right side of the page. It is composed of an orange text box and a blue-gray shadow. You can type to replace the placeholder text, or you can paste text into the text box.

3. **Select Project Highlights, press [Ctrl][X] to cut the text, click the [Sidebar Title] placeholder, press [Ctrl][V] to paste the text, select the bulleted list, press [Ctrl][X], click the body text placeholder in the sidebar, press [Ctrl][V], then press [Backspace]**
   The text is cut from the body of the document and pasted in the sidebar.

4. **Click the Drawing Tools Format tab, click the Position button in the Arrange group, click Position in Top Left with Square Text Wrapping, type 2.1 in the Shape Height text box in the Size group, type 6.9 in the Shape Width text box, then press [Enter]**
   The sidebar moves to the upper left corner of the page and, after resizing, spans the width of the page at the top.

   QUICK TIP
   You can change the format of a sidebar by applying a shape style or by using the other commands on the Drawing Tools Format tab.

5. **Select Project Highlights, click the Font Color list arrow [A▾] on the Mini toolbar, click Blue-gray, Accent 1, Darker 50%, click the title Savannah Conservation..., click the Layout tab, type 20 in the Before text box in the Paragraph group, then press [Enter]**
   The font color of Project Highlights changes to a darker blue-gray and the spacing above the title is increased, as shown in **FIGURE 7-8**.

6. **Scroll to page 2, place the insertion point in Planning Your Trip, click the View tab, click the Multiple Pages button in the Zoom group, click the Insert tab, click the Text Box button, then click Retrospect Sidebar**
   The Retrospect Sidebar is inserted on the right side of the page and anchored to the Planning Your Trip heading paragraph. Rather than type text in the sidebar, you will insert text from a file.

7. **Press [Delete] twice to delete the Sidebar Title placeholder and the blank paragraph, click the body text placeholder in the new sidebar, click the Insert tab, click the Object list arrow in the Text group, then click Text from File**
   The Insert File dialog box opens. You use this dialog box to select the file you want to insert in the sidebar.

   QUICK TIP
   When you insert a text file into a text box, verify that all the text fits. If all the text does not fit in the text box, you must adjust the size of the text box, edit the text, or link the full text box to an empty text box so that the text flows.

8. **Navigate to the location where you store your Data Files, click the file WD 7-2.docx, then click Insert**
   The content of the file WD 7-2.docx is inserted in the sidebar.

9. **Click the Drawing Tools Format tab, click the Position button in the Arrange group, click Position in Top Left with Square Text Wrapping, type 9.1 in the Shape Height text box, type 2.7 in the Shape Width text box, press [Enter], deselect the sidebar, then save**
   The completed sidebar is shown in **FIGURE 7-9**.

FIGURE 7-8: Retrospect sidebar at top of page

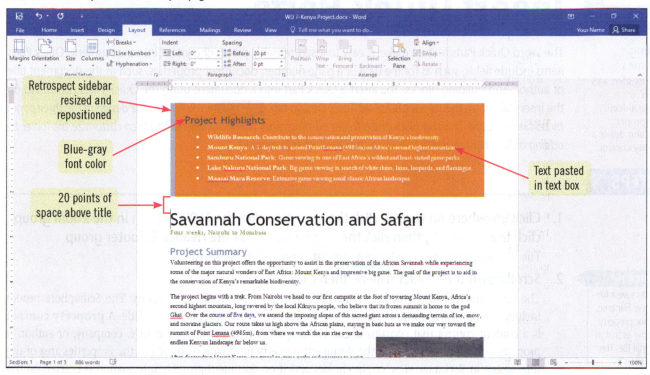

Retrospect sidebar resized and repositioned

Blue-gray font color

20 points of space above title

Text pasted in text box

FIGURE 7-9: Retrospect sidebar on page 2

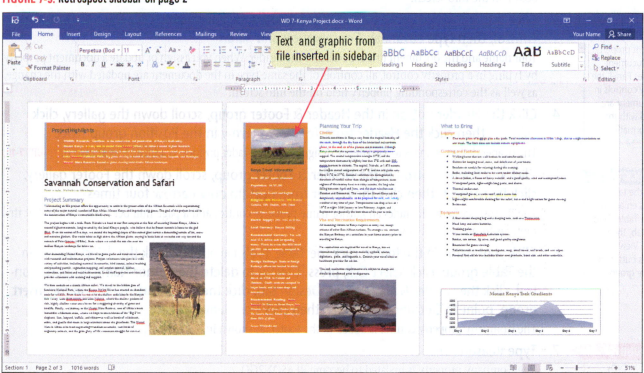

Text and graphic from file inserted in sidebar

Source: Pixabay

Insert Quick Parts

The Word Quick Parts feature makes it easy to insert reusable pieces of content into a document. Quick Parts items include fields, such as for the date or a page number; document properties, such as the document title or author; and building blocks. You insert a Quick Part into a document using the Quick Parts command on the Insert tab or on the Header & Footer Tools Design tab. **CASE** ▶ *You finalize the design of the three pages by adding a header building block and a footer building block to the document. You then customize the footer by adding a document property to it using the Quick Parts command.*

STEPS

1. **Click anywhere on page 2, click the View tab, click the 100% button in the Zoom group, click the Insert tab, then click the Header button in the Header & Footer group**

   The Header gallery opens and displays the list of predesigned headers.

2. **Scroll down the Header gallery, then click Semaphore**

   The Semaphore header is added to the document and the Header area opens. The Semaphore header includes two property controls: one for the Author and one for the Document Title. A **property control** is a content control that contains document property information, such as title, company, or author. A property control contains either the document property information entered in the Properties area of the Info screen in Backstage view, or placeholder text if no document property information is entered on the Info screen. The text in the Author property control is the name entered in the Word Options dialog box or the Microsoft user account name on the computer on which the document was created. You can assign or update a document property by typing directly in a property control or by typing in the Properties text boxes on the Info screen.

3. **Click the Author property control if necessary, type your name, click the Title property control, then type Savannah Conservation and Safari**

   Your name and the document title are added to the header. When you assign or update a document property by typing in a property control, all controls of the same type in the document are updated with the change, as well as the corresponding property field on the Info screen.

4. **Click the Header button in the Header & Footer group, scroll down the gallery, click Filigree, then click the Header from Top down arrow in the Position group twice**

   The header design changes to the Filigree design, and the header position is adjusted, as shown in **FIGURE 7-10**.

5. **Click the Footer button in the Header & Footer group, scroll down the Footer gallery, click Retrospect, then click the Footer from Bottom down arrow four times**

   The Retrospect footer includes an author name property control and a page number field. Notice that this footer is formatted as a table.

6. **Click your name in the footer, click the Table Tools Layout tab, click the Select button in the Table group, click Select Cell, press [Delete] to delete the Author Name property control, click the Header & Footer Tools Design tab, click the Quick Parts button in the Insert group, point to Document Property, then click Company**

   The Company property control is added to the footer, as shown in **FIGURE 7-11**.

7. **Type Reason2Go**

   The Company property is updated to become REASON2GO.

8. **Move the pointer over the footer, click the Table move handle ⊞ to select the table, click the Font Color button ⚊ on the Mini toolbar, close the Footer area, then save your changes**

   Dark blue-gray is applied to the text in the footer. The customized footer is shown in **FIGURE 7-12**.

FIGURE 7-10: Header formatted using the Filigree header style

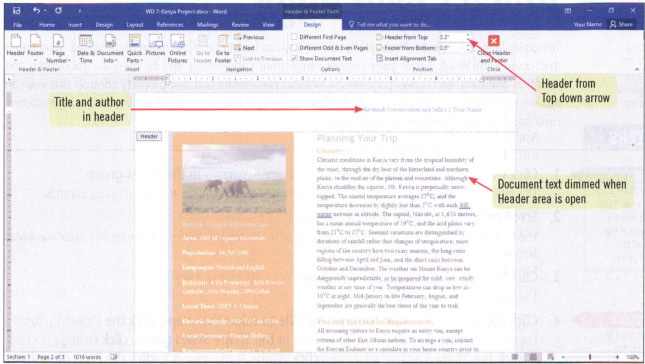

Title and author in header

Header from Top down arrow

Document text dimmed when Header area is open

Source: Pixabay

FIGURE 7-11: Company property control in Retrospect footer

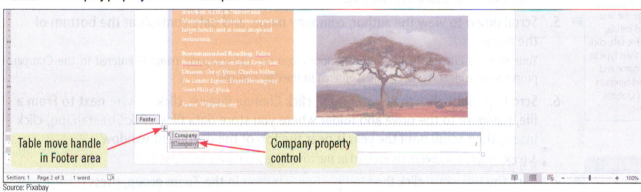

Table move handle in Footer area

Company property control

Source: Pixabay

FIGURE 7-12: Customized footer

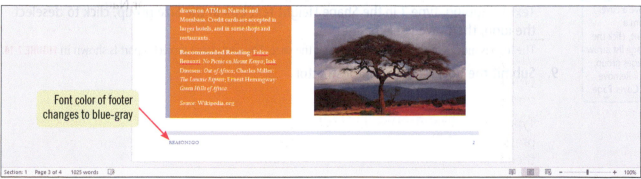

Font color of footer changes to blue-gray

Source: Pixabay

Working with Themes and Building Blocks

Add a Cover Page

To quickly finalize a report with simplicity or flair, you can insert one of the many predesigned cover pages that come with Word. Cover page designs range from conservative and business-like to colorful and attention grabbing. Each cover page design includes placeholder text and property controls that you can replace with your own information. **CASE** ▶ *You finalize the project report by inserting an eye-catching cover page that mirrors the design of the report.*

STEPS

1. **Click the Insert tab, then click the Cover Page list arrow in the Pages group**

   The gallery of cover pages opens. Each page design includes placeholder text and property controls.

2. **Scroll down the gallery, then click Motion**

   The Motion cover page is added at the beginning of the document. Notice that the project name was added automatically to the Title property control.

3. **Click the Year property control, click the Year list arrow, click Today**

   The year changes to the current year.

4. **Click the black shape that contains the title to select the shape, click the Drawing Tools Format tab, click the Shape Fill list arrow in the Shape Styles group, click Orange, Accent 2, click the Shape Outline list arrow, click White, Background 1, click the light blue shape to the right of the word Safari to select the entire light blue shape, click the Shape Fill list arrow in the Shape Styles group, then click Blue-gray, Accent 1**

   The fill color of the title shape changes to orange with a white outline, and the fill color of the shape that includes the year changes to blue-gray.

5. **Scroll down to view the author, company name, and date controls at the bottom of the page**

   Your name is entered in the Author property control, the company name is entered in the Company property control, and today's date is entered in the date control.

6. **Scroll up, right-click the photograph, click Change Picture, click Browse next to From a file, navigate to the drive and folder where you store data files, click Cheetah.jpg, click Insert, then scroll until the year is near the top of the document window**

   A photograph of a cheetah is inserted in the cover page, as shown In **FIGURE 7-13**.

7. **Click the View tab, click the Multiple Pages button in the Zoom group, press [Ctrl][Home], click the Insert tab, click the Pictures button in the Illustrations group, navigate to the location where you store your Data Files, click the file R2G Logo.jpg, then click Insert**

   The R2G logo is added to the cover page.

8. **Click the Position button in the Arrange group, click Position in Bottom Left with Square Text Wrapping, type 1 in the Shape Height text box in the Size group, click to deselect the logo, then save your changes**

   The logo is moved to the lower-left corner of the page. The completed project report is shown in **FIGURE 7-14**.

9. **Submit the document to your instructor**

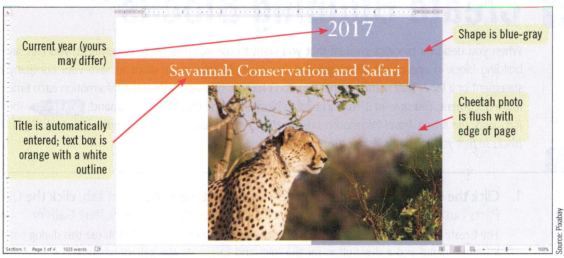

2017

Shape is blue-gray

Current year (yours may differ)

Savannah Conservation and Safari

Title is automatically entered; text box is orange with a white outline

Cheetah photo is flush with edge of page

Section: 1   Page 1 of 4   1025 words

Source: Pixabay

FIGURE 7-14: Completed project report

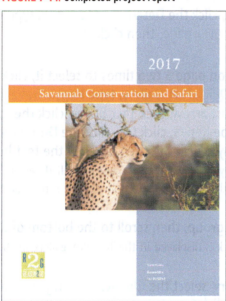

Source: Pixabay

Working with Themes and Building Blocks

Create Building Blocks

Learning Outcomes
• Save a custom building block
• Create a category for building blocks

When you design a piece of content that you want to use again in other documents, you can save it as a building block in one of the Word galleries. For example, you might want to save your company mission statement or a list of staff names so that you don't have to type and format the information each time you use it in a document. You save an item as a building block using the Quick Parts command. **CASE** *You save the R2G logo, the Kenya Travel Information sidebar, the Climate heading and paragraph, and the footer as building blocks so that you can easily include them in other project reports.*

STEPS

1. **Click the logo at the bottom of page 1 to select it, click the Insert tab, click the Quick Parts button in the Text group, then click Save Selection to Quick Part Gallery**

   The Create New Building Block dialog box opens, as shown in **FIGURE 7-15**. You use this dialog box to enter a unique name and a description for the item and to specify the gallery where you want it to appear. You want the logo to appear in the Quick Part gallery.

2. **Type R2G Logo in the Name text box, click the Description text box, type R2G Logo in bottom-left corner of project report cover page, then click OK**

   The logo is added to the Quick Part gallery.

   > **TROUBLE**
   > If the Save Selection ... option is dimmed, close the gallery, and select the sidebar again by clicking the edge two times.

3. **Click the edge of the orange sidebar on page 3 two times to select it, click the Quick Parts button, click Save Selection to Quick Part Gallery, type Kenya Travel Info Sidebar in the Name text box, click the Gallery list arrow, click Text Boxes, click the Category list arrow, click Create New Category, type Kenya, click OK, click the Description text box, type Generic info for travelers to Kenya, click OK, then deselect the text box**

   You added the sidebar to the Text Box gallery and created a new category called Kenya. It's a good idea to assign a descriptive category name to a building block item so that you can sort, organize, and find your building blocks easily.

   > **QUICK TIP**
   > A text building block can also be saved to the AutoText gallery.

4. **Click the Text Box button in the Text group, then scroll to the bottom of the gallery**

   The Kenya Travel Info Sidebar building block is displayed in the Text Box gallery in the Kenya category, as shown in **FIGURE 7-16**.

   > **QUICK TIP**
   > To store paragraph formatting with a building block, make sure to also select the final paragraph mark.

5. **Click the document to close the gallery, select the Climate heading and paragraph on page 3, click the Quick Parts button, click Save Selection to Quick Part Gallery, type Kenya Climate Info in the Name text box, click the Category list arrow, click Create New Category, type Kenya, click OK, then click OK**

   The Climate heading and paragraph are saved in the Quick Part gallery in the Kenya category.

   > **TROUBLE**
   > If a ScreenTip does not appear, continue with step 7.

6. **Click the Quick Parts button to verify that the item was added to the gallery, then point to the R2G Logo item in the gallery**

   The gallery includes the R2G Logo item in the General category and the Kenya Climate Info item in the Kenya category. When you point to the R2G Logo item in the gallery, the name and description appear in a ScreenTip, as shown in **FIGURE 7-17**.

7. **Double-click the footer to open it, click the Table move handle ⊞ to select the table in the footer, click the Footer button in the Header & Footer group on the Header & Footer Tools Design tab, then click Save Selection to Footer Gallery**

   The Create New Building Block dialog box opens with Footers automatically selected as the gallery.

   > **TROUBLE**
   > Save the building blocks if prompted to do so.

8. **Type Project Report Footer in the Name text box, click OK, then save and close the document without closing Word**

   The footer is added to the Footer gallery under the General category. In the next lesson, you will insert the building blocks you created into a different project report document.

FIGURE 7-15: Create New Building Block dialog box

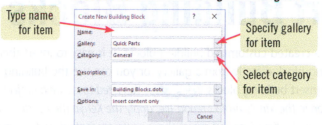

Type name for item

Specify gallery for item

Select category for item

FIGURE 7-16: New building block in Text Box gallery

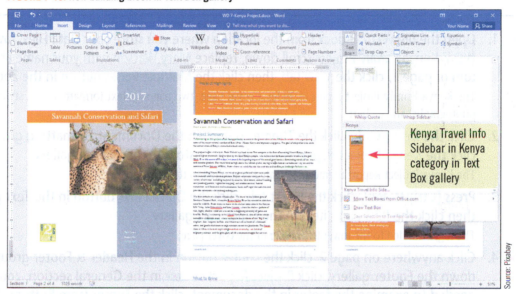

Kenya Travel Info Sidebar in Kenya category in Text Box gallery

FIGURE 7-17: Items in Quick Part gallery

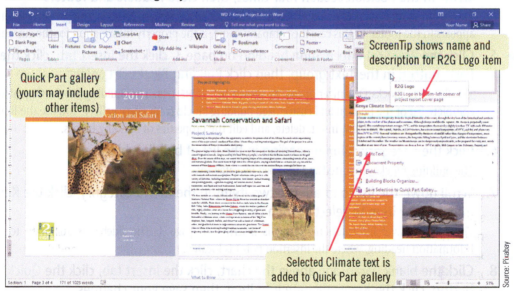

ScreenTip shows name and description for R2G Logo item

Quick Part gallery (yours may include other items)

Selected Climate text is added to Quick Part gallery

Renaming a building block and editing other properties

You can edit the properties of a building block at any time, including changing its name, gallery location, category, and description. To modify building block properties, simply right-click the item in a gallery, and then click Edit Properties. In the Modify Building Block dialog box that opens, edit the item's name or description, or assign it to a new gallery or category. When you are finished, click OK, and then click Yes in the warning box that opens. You can also modify the properties of a building block by selecting the item in the Building Blocks Organizer, and then clicking Edit Properties.

Insert Building Blocks

Learning Outcomes
• Insert custom building blocks using the Building Blocks Organizer

Once you have created customized building blocks, it is easy to insert them in your documents. You can insert a building block directly from a gallery, or you can use the Building Blocks Organizer to search for, organize, and insert building blocks. **CASE** ▸ *You need to create a project report for a different R2G project in Kenya. You open the family project report file, apply the Kenya theme, and then insert the building blocks you created so that all the Kenya project reports have common content and a consistent look and feel.*

STEPS

QUICK TIP
Zoom in as needed to replace the author name.

1. **Open the file WD 7-3.docx from the location where you store your Data Files, save it as WD 7-Kenya Family Project scroll down, replace Mary Watson with your name at the bottom of page 1, click the View tab, then click the Multiple Pages button in the Zoom group**

   The Kenya Family Project report includes a cover page, two pages of text formatted with styles, a sidebar, photographs, and a chart.

2. **Click the Design tab, click the Themes button in the Document Formatting group, then click the Kenya Project Report theme in the Custom section of the gallery**

   The Kenya Project Report theme you created is applied to the document.

3. **Press [Ctrl][Home], click the Insert tab, click the Quick Parts button in the Text group, then click the R2G Logo item in the Quick Part gallery**

   The logo is added to the lower-left corner of the cover page.

TROUBLE
If the insertion point is located on the cover page, the footer will appear on the cover page only.

4. **Click anywhere on page 2, click the Footer button in the Header & Footer group, scroll down the Footer gallery, click Project Report Footer in the General section, zoom as needed to examine the footer in the document, click the Footer from Bottom down arrow in the Position section four times, then close headers and footers**

   The custom footer you created is added to the Footer area on pages 2 and 3. The property information that appears in the footer, in this case the company name, is the property information for the current document.

QUICK TIP
To edit the content of a building block, insert the item in a document, edit the item, then save the selection to the same Quick Part gallery using the same name.

5. **Click the Practical Information heading on page 3, click the Insert tab, click the Quick Parts button in the Text group, then click Building Blocks Organizer**

   The Building Blocks Organizer opens, as shown in **FIGURE 7-18**. The Building Blocks Organizer includes a complete list of the built-in and customized building blocks from every gallery. You use the Building Blocks Organizer to sort, preview, insert, delete, and edit the properties of building blocks.

6. **Click the Category column heading in the list of building blocks**

   The building blocks are sorted and grouped by category.

QUICK TIP
To delete a building block, select it in the Building Blocks Organizer, then click Delete.

7. **Scroll down the list to locate the two items in the Kenya category, click the Kenya Travel Info Sidebar item to select it, then click Insert**

   The Kenya Travel Information sidebar is inserted on page 3. The sidebar is anchored to the Practical Information heading, where the insertion point is located.

8. **Click the blank paragraph above the chart, click the Insert tab, click the Quick Parts button, click the Kenya Climate Info item, then save your changes**

   The Climate heading and associated paragraph are inserted above the chart. The completed Kenya Family Project report is shown in **FIGURE 7-19**.

TROUBLE
If you are working on your personal computer and you want to save the building blocks you created, click Yes to save the Building Blocks.dotx file.

9. **Submit the document, close the file, exit Word, then click Don't Save in the warning box that opens**

   You removed the customized building blocks you created in this session from the Building Blocks Organizer. If you wanted to use the customized building blocks at a later time, you would save them when prompted when exiting Word.

FIGURE 7-18: Building Blocks Organizer

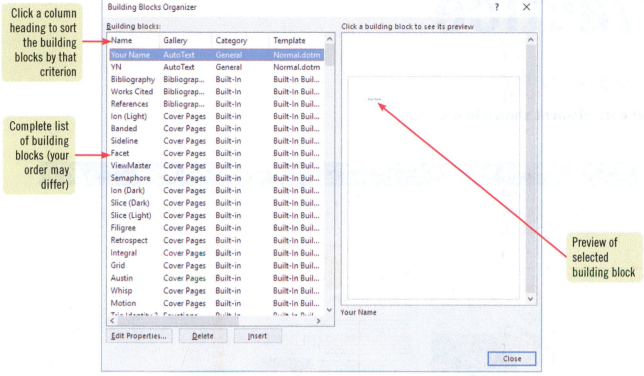

Click a column heading to sort the building blocks by that criterion

Complete list of building blocks (your order may differ)

Preview of selected building block

FIGURE 7-19: Completed Kenya Family Project report

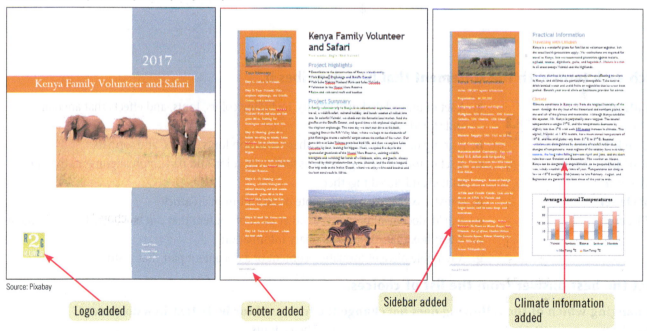

Source: Pixabay

Logo added

Footer added

Sidebar added

Climate information added

Word 2016

Practice

Concepts Review

Label each element shown in FIGURE 7-20.

FIGURE 7-20

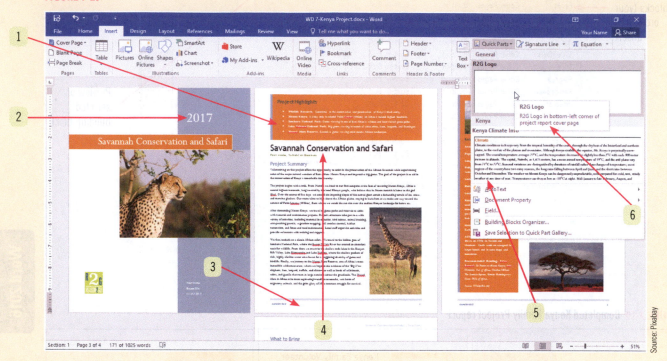

Match each term with the statement that best describes it.

7. Pull quote

8. Style

9. Quick Part

10. Building Block

11. Sidebar

12. Style set

13. Theme

a. A set of unified design elements, including colors, fonts, and effects that are named and stored together

b. A group of related styles that share common fonts, colors, and formats

c. A set of format settings, such as font, font color, and paragraph alignment, that are named and stored together

d. A text box that contains a quote or excerpt from an article

e. A field, document property, or other piece of content that can be inserted in a document

f. A text box that contains auxiliary information

g. A reusable piece of formatted content or a document part that is stored in a gallery

Select the best answer from the list of choices.

14. Changing which of the following does *not* change the font used for body text in a document?

  a. Theme

  b. Style set

  c. Theme fonts

  d. Theme effects

15. Which of the following is *not* an example of a building block?

  a. Footer

  b. Document property

  c. Pull quote

  d. Cover page

Working with Themes and Building Blocks

16. **Which of the following elements uses theme effects?**
   a. Tables
   b. Styles
   c. Charts
   d. Headers and footers

17. **Which of the following is _not_ a design element included in a theme?**
   a. Effects
   b. Colors
   c. Fonts
   d. Picture styles

Skills Review

1. **Apply styles to text.**
   a. Start Word, open the file WD 7-4.docx from the location where you store your Data Files, save it as **WD 7-Green Home**, set the view to page width, read the document, then press [Ctrl][Home].
   b. Apply the Title style to the Greening Your Home heading, click the Increase Font Size button twice, then change the font color to Green, Accent 6.
   c. Apply the Subtitle style to the Reducing your personal greenhouse gas emissions heading, click the Increase Font Size button twice, then change the font color to Blue, Accent 1, Darker 25%.
   d. Apply the Heading 1 style and Green, Accent 6 font color to the red headings: "Small Steps to Take in Your Home and Yard" and "Use Green Power".
   e. Apply the Heading 3 style to the purple subheadings, then save your changes.

2. **Apply a theme.**
   a. Change the view to Multiple Pages, then change the Style Set to Basic (Simple). (_Hint_: Use the Style Set gallery in the Document Formatting group on the Design tab.)
   b. Open the Themes gallery, apply the Slice theme, then zoom in to view page 3.
   c. Apply the Wisp theme, scroll to see it applied to all the pages, zoom out to 50%, then save your changes.

3. **Customize a theme.**
   a. Click the Theme Colors button, then change the theme colors to Green Yellow.
   b. Click the Theme Colors button again, click Customize Colors, click the Accent 3 list arrow, click More Colors, click the Custom tab if it is not the active tab, type **5** in the Red text box, type **102** in the Green text box, type **153** in the Blue text box, then click OK. The Accent 3 color is now dark blue.
   c. Name the palette of new theme colors **Green Earth**, then save it.
   d. Change the theme fonts to Corbel, scroll to the end, then change the theme effects to Subtle Solids.
   e. Change the paragraph spacing to Open, then save the current theme with the name **Green Earth**.
   f. Press [Ctrl][Home], change the font color of the Title and the Heading 1 headings to Dark Blue, Accent 3, then save your changes.

4. **Insert a sidebar.**
   a. Place the insertion point in the title, then insert the Ion Quote (Dark) text box.
   b. Zoom in to 100%, select the second paragraph of body text on page 1, cut it, paste it in the sidebar, click the Paste Options button, click Merge Formatting (M), press [Backspace], select the pasted text, then click the Increase Font Size button on the Mini toolbar.
   c. Click the Cite your source here placeholder, then type **Environmental Protection Agency**.
   d. Select the sidebar if it is not already selected, click the Drawing Tools Format tab, change the Shape Height to 2.5", change the Shape Width to 3", position the pull quote in the top right with square text wrapping, then drag it straight down so that the Title and Subtitle are each on one line.
   e. Apply the Moderate Effect, Green, Accent 2 shape style to the shape, then change the view to One Page.
   f. Click the Be green in your yard subheading on page 2, insert the Grid Sidebar, press [Delete] twice to delete the Sidebar Title placeholder, apply the Moderate Effect, Lime, Accent 1 shape style, change the position to top right with square text wrapping, then change the shape height to 9" and the shape width to 2.5".
   g. Insert the text file WD 7-5.docx from the drive and folder where you store your Data Files, in the sidebar, then zoom in to make sure all the text fits.

Skills Review (continued)

h. Scroll to page 3, click the Use Green Power heading, insert the Grid Sidebar, change the position to top left with square text wrapping, change the shape height to 9", change the shape width to 2.5", then press [Delete] twice to delete the Sidebar Title placeholder.

i. Click the body text placeholder in the sidebar, insert the text file WD 7-6.docx from the location where you store your Data Files, apply the Moderate Effect, Dark Blue, Accent 3 shape style to the shape, then save your changes. (*Hint*: If all the text does not fit, adjust the sidebar height.)

5. **Insert Quick Parts.**

a. Change the view to 100%, insert the Sideline header from the Header gallery, click the Title property control, type **Greening Your Home**, then press [End] to move the insertion point out of the control.

b. Press [Spacebar], insert a small bullet symbol of your choice, press [Spacebar], insert an Author property control, then add your name to the control as the author.

c. Insert the Sideline footer from the Footer gallery, click the Footer from Bottom down arrow twice, close headers and footers, then save your changes.

6. **Add a cover page.**

a. Change the view to Multiple Pages, press [Ctrl][Home], insert the Whisp cover page, zoom in, click the Subtitle control, then type **Reducing your personal greenhouse gas emissions**.

b. Scroll down, verify that your name appears in the Author control, then right-click the remaining content controls and click Remove Content Control to delete them.

c. Zoom out, select the whisp shape, use the More button in the Shape Styles group to change the Shape Fill to Colored Fill - Green, Accent 2, change the font color of the title to Dark Blue, Accent 3, save your changes, then submit the document to your instructor. The completed document is shown in **FIGURE 7-21**.

FIGURE 7-21

Source: Pixabay

7. **Create building blocks.**

a. Change the view to Multiple Pages, click the edge of the pull quote on page 2 two times to select it, click the Insert tab, then use the Quick Parts button to save the selection as a Quick Part. (*Note*: Sizing handles and solid borders appear around the green box when the sidebar is selected.)

b. Name the building block **Intro Pull Quote**, assign it to the Text Boxes gallery, create a category called **Green Reports**, and then click OK twice.

c. Select the sidebar on page 4, save it as a Quick Part, name the building block **Measure Your Impact Sidebar**, assign it to the Text Box gallery, assign it to the Green Reports category, and then click OK.

d. Zoom in, open the Header area, click to the left of the header text to select the entire header, then save the header to the Header Gallery, using the name **Green Reports header**, creating a **Green Reports** category, then clicking OK.

e. Close the Header area, save your changes, then close the file without exiting Word.

8. **Insert building blocks.**

a. Open the file WD 7-7.docx from the drive and folder where you store your Data Files, save it as **WD 7-Green Work**, then apply the Green Earth theme.

b. Scroll to page 2, then insert the Green Reports header from the Green Reports category in the Header gallery and replace the information in the Author control with your name if necessary.

Skills Review (continued)

c. Insert the Sideline footer in the document, then close headers and footers.

d. Click the title on page 2, open the Text Box gallery, then insert the Intro Pull Quote from the Green Reports category. Adjust the position of the pull quote so that it is flush with the right margin and below the title and subtitle.

e. Zoom in, select the second body paragraph in the document, cut it, select all the pull quote text in the pull quote except for the final period, paste the text, click the Paste Options button, click Merge Formatting, then press [Backspace] twice to delete the extra line and period.

f. Scroll to page 3, click On the Road, then open the Building Blocks Organizer.

g. Click the Category heading to sort the items by category, scroll to locate the items in the Green Reports category, click the Measure Your Impact Sidebar, then click Insert.

h. Adjust the size and placement of items so that all the text fits on three pages, save your changes, then print your document. Pages 2 and 3 of the completed document are shown in **FIGURE 7-22**.

i. Close the file and exit Word, not saving changes to the Building Blocks.dotx file if prompted.

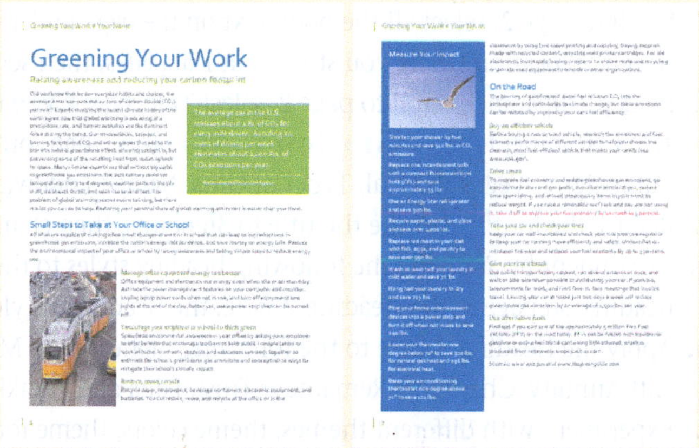

FIGURE 7-22

Source: Pixabay

Independent Challenge 1

You volunteer for an organization that promotes literacy in your community. You have written the text for a literacy fact sheet and now want to format it quickly and attractively. You decide to format the fact sheet using styles, themes, and preformatted building blocks.

a. Start Word, open the file WD 7-8.docx from the location where you store your Data Files, save the file as **WD 7-Facts on Literacy**, then read the document to get a feel for its contents.

b. Apply the Title style to the Facts on Literacy title.

c. Apply the Heading 2 style to the Literacy and Poverty, Literacy and Children, and How Can You Help? headings.

d. Press [Ctrl][Home], then add a Slice Sidebar (Dark) Sidebar to the document.

e. Select the paragraphs under the How Can You Help? heading, press [Ctrl][X], click the Sidebar body text placeholder, press [Ctrl][V], then select the How Can You Help? heading, cut it, and paste it into the Sidebar Title placeholder by applying the Keep Text Only formatting when you paste the text.

f. Increase the width of the sidebar so that all the text fits in it. (*Hint*: Deselect the sidebar, then click it once to select it again.)

g. Add the Facet (Odd Page) footer to the document. Type your name in the Title property control, then **For more information, call 555-8799** in the Subtitle property control.

h. Preview several themes and style sets applied to the document, then select an appropriate theme and style set.

i. If the text flows onto page two or does not all fit in the sidebar, change the theme fonts or adjust the paragraph spacing to allow the text to fit on one page and in the sidebar. Delete the blank page 2 if necessary.

j. Change the theme colors applied to the document elements and adjust other formatting elements as necessary to make the document attractive and readable.

k. Save your changes, submit the document to your instructor, then close the file and exit Word, not saving changes to the Building Blocks.dotx file if prompted.

Independent Challenge 2

You work for the Community Relations Department at your local hospital. You have written the text for a report on annual giving, and now you need to format the report. You decide to start with a report template and then customize the report with a preformatted text box, a sidebar, a new cover page, and theme elements.

a. Start Word, create a new document using the Report design (blank) template, then save it as **WD 7-Annual Report**.

b. Insert a Filigree cover page. Type **Chester Community Hospital Annual Giving** in the Title property control, then type **Invitation to Donors** in the Subtitle property control.

c. Type your name in the Company property control, then remove the Date and Address property controls.

d. Scroll to page 2, select all the body text on the page under the Heading heading, insert the text file WD 7-9.docx from the location where you store your Data Files, then scroll down to view the format and content of the report.

e. Press [Ctrl][Home], scroll to page 2, select Title, type **Chester Community Hospital Annual Giving**, select Heading, type **Invitation to Donors**, then format the following headings in the Heading 1 style: Capital Campaign Exceeds Its Goal, Types of Gifts, Named Endowments Leave Lasting Impressions, and Richard Society.

f. Reduce the font size of the the title to 36 points, then change the style set of the document to Lines Stylish.

g. Experiment by applying the following heading styles to the Annual Fund Gifts subheading under the Types of Gifts heading on page 3: the Heading 2 style, the Heading 3 style, and then the Heading 4 style.

h. Apply the Heading 4 style to the following subheadings: Memorial or Tribute Gifts, Charitable Bequests, Charitable Gift Annuity, Charitable Remainder Trust, Edna and Franklin Richard Society Members.

i. Experiment with different themes, theme colors, theme fonts, theme effects, and paragraph spacing, and then use these tools to customize the look of the report.

j. Scroll to page 2, click the Capital Campaign Exceeds Its Goal heading, insert a pull quote of your choice, select the last paragraph of text under the Capital Campaign Exceeds Its Goal heading, copy the paragraph, paste the text in the pull quote, use the Paste Options button to merge the formatting, delete the Cite your source placeholder if necessary, adjust the text box as needed to fit all the text, then reposition the text box as needed so the page is attractive.

k. Scroll to page 4, click the Richard Society heading, insert a sidebar of your choice, then cut the Edna and Franklin Richard Society Members heading and the list that follows it from the body text, paste it in the sidebar, then use the Paste Options button to merge the formatting.

l. Using the Cover Page command, remove the current cover page, then use the Cover Page command again to insert a different cover page for the report from the Built-in category. Update or remove the content and property controls as necessary. (*Hint*: Scroll as needed to see the Built-in options.)

m. Add a footer to the report that includes a page number and your name.

n. Adjust the elements of the report as necessary to make sure each page is attractive and the text fits comfortably on four pages. **FIGURE 7-23** shows a sample finished report.

o. Save your changes to the document, submit the document to your instructor, close the document, then exit Word.

FIGURE 7-23

Independent Challenge 3

You are in charge of publicity for the Sydney Triathlon 2017 World Cup. One of your responsibilities is to create a two-page flyer that captures the spirit of the event and provides the basic details. You format the flyer using styles, themes, and building blocks. **FIGURE 7-24** shows one possible design, but you will create your own two-page design.

a. Start Word, open the file WD 7-10.docx from the location where you store your Data Files, read it, then save it as **WD 7-Triathlon**.

FIGURE 7-24

Source: Pixabay

b. Apply the Title style to the title and the Heading 1 style to these headings: The Triathlon, The Course, Best Views, Public Transport and Road Closures, and The Athletes. Apply other styles to the text as you see fit.

c. Change the Style Set, apply an appropriate theme, then change the theme colors or theme fonts.

d. Add a continuous section break before The Athletes, then format the second section in two columns using the default column settings.

e. Add a manual page break before the Public Transport and Road Closures heading.

f. Click The Triathlon heading on page 1, insert a sidebar of your choice on page 1, then cut the Best Views heading and paragraphs from the document, including the photo of the Sydney Opera House, and paste it in the sidebar. (*Hint*: Do not cut the page break.) Keep the source formatting for the selection.

g. Click The Athletes heading on page 2, insert a sidebar of your choice on page 2, then cut the Public Transport and Road Closures heading and paragraphs from the document and paste them in the sidebar. Keep the source formatting for the selection.

h. Adjust the size, color, alignment, text wrapping, and position of the sidebar text boxes and the photographs so that the layout of each page is attractive.

i. Adjust the font and paragraph formatting of the document text so that the text is readable and the overall layout of the flyer is harmonious. All the text should now fit on two pages.

j. Add your name to the header or footer, save your changes, submit the document to your instructor, close the file, then exit Word.

Independent Challenge 4: Explore

In this Independent Challenge, you will design and save at least one building block for your work or personal use. Your building block might be the masthead for a newsletter, a cover page for your reports, a header or footer that includes your logo, a SmartArt object, a letterhead, a mission statement, or some other item that you use repeatedly in documents.

a. Determine the building block(s) you want to create, start Word, then save a blank document as **WD 7-Building Block 1** to the drive and folder where you store your Data Files.

b. Create your first building block. Whenever possible, insert fields and property controls as appropriate. Format the item using themes, styles, fonts, colors, borders, fill effects, shadows, and other effects, as necessary.

c. When you are satisfied with the item, select it, including the final paragraph mark, and then save it as a new building block. Give it a meaningful name, description, and category, and save it to the appropriate gallery.

d. Repeat Steps b and c to create as many building blocks as necessary for your documents.

e. Type your name at the top, and then save the document, submit it to your instructor, and close the document.

f. Open a blank document, and then save it as **WD 7-Building Block 2** to the location where you store your Data Files. Type your name, insert the building block(s) you created, and then adjust them appropriately.

g. Save the document, submit it to your instructor, and then close the file and exit Word. If you want to save the building blocks you created for future use, save the Building Blocks.dotx file when prompted.

Visual Workshop

Create the flyer shown in **FIGURE 7-25** using the Integral cover page design, the Metropolitan theme, and the Marquee colors. Replace the photograph with an online photograph similar to the one shown in the figure, or another kind of image that illustrates flight. Replace the placeholder text with the text shown in the figure. The font size of the title is 36 points, the font size of the subtitle and the dates is 16 points, the font size of the text in the Abstract control and the text in the Course control is 12 points, and the font size of the text in the Author control is 14 points. Add your name to the footer. Save the document as **WD 7-Art of Flight**, then submit the document to your instructor. *(Note: To complete these steps your computer must be connected to the Internet.)*

FIGURE 7-25

AUGUST 2 – NOVEMBER 14, 2017
Artists explore the beauty and power of flight through photographs, sculpture, film, and mixed media. The Mason Museum of Art and Science is open daily 10 a.m. to 6 p.m.

Mason Museum of Art and Science
www.mason-museum-art-science.org

THE ART OF

FLIGHT

Mason Museum of Art and Science

Source: Pixabay

Merging Word Documents

> **CASE** ▶ You need to send a letter to people who recently booked an R2G migratory bird conservation project confirming their reservation and receipt of their nonrefundable deposit. You also need to send a general information packet to all participants in upcoming R2G projects. You use mail merge to create a personalized form letter for those who recently booked an R2G bird project and mailing labels for the information packet.

Module Objectives

After completing this module, you will be able to:

- Understand mail merge
- Create a main document
- Design a data source
- Enter and edit records
- Add merge fields
- Merge data
- Create labels
- Sort and filter records

Files You Will Need

WD 8-1.docx   WD 8-3.docx

WD 8-2.mdb   WD 8-4.mdb

Understand Mail Merge

Learning Outcomes
- Identify the elements of a mail merge
- State the benefits of performing a mail merge

When you perform a **mail merge**, you merge a standard Word document with a file that contains customized information for many individuals or items. The standard document is called the **main document**. The file with the unique data for individual people or items is called the **data source**. Merging the main document with a data source results in a **merged document** that contains customized versions of the main document, as shown in **FIGURE 8-1**. The Mail Merge pane steps you through the process of setting up and performing a mail merge. You can also perform a mail merge using the commands on the Mailings tab. **CASE** ▶ *You decide to use the Mail Merge pane to create your form letters and the commands on the Mailings tab to create your mailing labels. Before beginning, you explore the steps involved in performing a mail merge.*

DETAILS

- ### Create the main document

  The main document contains the text—often called **boilerplate text**—that appears in every version of the merged document. The main document also includes the merge fields, which indicate where the customized information is inserted when you perform the merge. You insert the merge fields in the main document after you have created or selected the data source. You can create a main document using one of the following: a new blank document, the current document, a template, or an existing document.

- ### Create a data source or select an existing data source

  The data source is a file that contains the unique information for each individual or item, such as a person's name. It provides the information that varies in every version of the merged document. A data source is composed of data fields and data records. A **data field** is a category of information, such as last name, first name, street address, city, or postal code. A **data record** is a complete set of related information for an individual or an item, such as one person's name and address. It is easiest to think of a data source file as a table: the header row contains the names of the data fields (the **field names**), and each row in the table is an individual data record. You can create a new data source, or you can use an existing data source, such as a data source created in Word, an Outlook contact list, an Access database, or an Excel worksheet.

- ### Identify the fields to include in the data source and enter the records

  When you create a new data source, you must first identify the fields to include, such as first name, last name, and street address if you are creating a data source that will include addresses. It is also important to think of and include all the fields you will need (not just the obvious ones) before you begin to enter data. For example, if you are creating a data source that includes names and addresses, you might need to include fields for a person's middle name, title, apartment number, department name, or country, even if some records in the data source will not include that information. Once you have identified the fields and set up your data source, you are ready to enter the data for each record.

- ### Add merge fields to the main document

  A **merge field** is a placeholder that you insert in the main document to indicate where the data from each record should be inserted when you perform the merge. For example, you insert a ZIP Code merge field in the location where you want to insert a ZIP Code. The merge fields in a main document must correspond with the field names in the associated data source. Merge fields must be inserted, not typed, in the main document. The Mail Merge pane and the Mailings tab provide access to the dialog boxes you use to insert merge fields.

- ### Merge the data from the data source into the main document

  Once you have established your data source and inserted the merge fields in the main document, you are ready to perform the merge. You can merge to a new file, which contains a customized version of the main document for each record in the data source, or you can merge directly to a printer or e-mail message.

FIGURE 8-1: Mail merge process

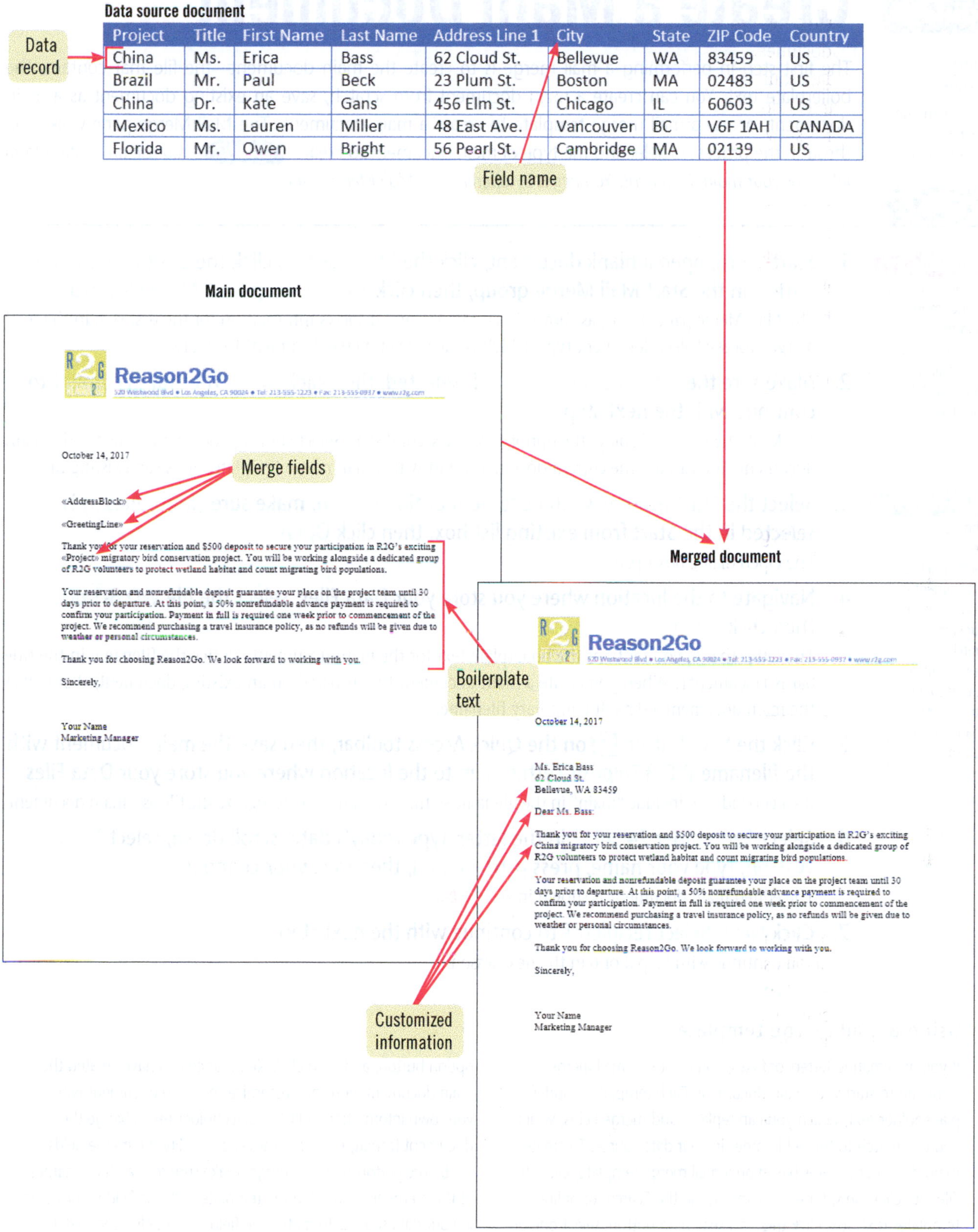

Data source document

	Project	Title	First Name	Last Name	Address Line 1	City	State	ZIP Code	Country
Data record →	China	Ms.	Erica	Bass	62 Cloud St.	Bellevue	WA	83459	US
	Brazil	Mr.	Paul	Beck	23 Plum St.	Boston	MA	02483	US
	China	Dr.	Kate	Gans	456 Elm St.	Chicago	IL	60603	US
	Mexico	Ms.	Lauren	Miller	48 East Ave.	Vancouver	BC	V6F 1AH	CANADA
	Florida	Mr.	Owen	Bright	56 Pearl St.	Cambridge	MA	02139	US

Field name

Main document

R2G Reason2Go
520 Westwood Blvd • Los Angeles, CA 90024 • Tel: 213-555-1223 • Fax: 213-555-0937 • www.r2g.com

October 14, 2017

Merge fields

«AddressBlock»

«GreetingLine»

Thank you for your reservation and $500 deposit to secure your participation in R2G's exciting «Project» migratory bird conservation project. You will be working alongside a dedicated group of R2G volunteers to protect wetland habitat and count migrating bird populations.

Your reservation and nonrefundable deposit guarantee your place on the project team until 30 days prior to departure. At this point, a 50% nonrefundable advance payment is required to confirm your participation. Payment in full is required one week prior to commencement of the project. We recommend purchasing a travel insurance policy, as no refunds will be given due to weather or personal circumstances.

Thank you for choosing Reason2Go. We look forward to working with you.

Sincerely,

Your Name
Marketing Manager

Boilerplate text

Merged document

R2G Reason2Go
520 Westwood Blvd • Los Angeles, CA 90024 • Tel: 213-555-1223 • Fax: 213-555-0937 • www.r2g.com

October 14, 2017

Ms. Erica Bass
62 Cloud St.
Bellevue, WA 83459

Dear Ms. Bass:

Thank you for your reservation and $500 deposit to secure your participation in R2G's exciting China migratory bird conservation project. You will be working alongside a dedicated group of R2G volunteers to protect wetland habitat and count migrating bird populations.

Your reservation and nonrefundable deposit guarantee your place on the project team until 30 days prior to departure. At this point, a 50% nonrefundable advance payment is required to confirm your participation. Payment in full is required one week prior to commencement of the project. We recommend purchasing a travel insurance policy, as no refunds will be given due to weather or personal circumstances.

Thank you for choosing Reason2Go. We look forward to working with you.

Sincerely,

Your Name
Marketing Manager

Customized information

Create a Main Document

Learning Outcomes
• Start a mail merge
• Create a letter main document

The first step in performing a mail merge is to create the main document—the file that contains the boilerplate text. You can create a main document from scratch, save an existing document as a main document, or use a mail merge template to create a main document. The Mail Merge pane walks you through the process of selecting the type of main document to create. **CASE** ▶ *You use an existing form letter for your main document. You begin by opening the Mail Merge pane.*

STEPS

TROUBLE
A document, blank or otherwise, must be open in the program window for the commands on the Mailings tab to be available.

1. **Start Word, open a blank document, click the Mailings tab, click the Start Mail Merge button in the Start Mail Merge group, then click Step-by-Step Mail Merge Wizard**

   The Mail Merge pane opens, as shown in **FIGURE 8-2**, and displays information for the first step in the mail merge process: Select document type, which is the type of merge document to create.

2. **Make sure the Letters option button is selected, then click Next: Starting document to continue with the next step**

   The Mail Merge pane displays the options for the second step: Select starting document, which is the main document. You can use the current document, start with a mail merge template, or use an existing file.

QUICK TIP
If you choose "Use the current document" and the current document is blank, you can create a main document from scratch. Either type the boilerplate text at this step, or wait until the Mail Merge pane prompts you to do so.

3. **Select the Start from existing document option button, make sure (More files...) is selected in the Start from existing list box, then click Open**

   The Open dialog box opens.

4. **Navigate to the location where you store your Data Files, select the file WD 8-1.docx, then click Open**

   The letter that opens contains the boilerplate text for the main document. Notice the filename in the title bar is Document1. When you create a main document that is based on an existing document, Word gives the main document a default temporary filename.

5. **Click the Save button 🔳 on the Quick Access toolbar, then save the main document with the filename WD 8-Deposit Letter Main to the location where you store your Data Files**

   It's a good idea to include "main" in the filename so that you can easily recognize the file as a main document.

6. **Select September 24, 2017 in the letter, type today's date, scroll down, select Mary Watson, type your name, press [Ctrl][Home], then save your changes**

   The edited main document is shown in **FIGURE 8-3**.

7. **Click Next: Select recipients to continue with the next step**

   You continue with Step 3 of 6 in the next lesson.

Using a mail merge template

If you are creating letters or faxes, you can use a mail merge template to start your main document. Each template includes placeholder text, which you can replace, and merge fields, which you can match to the field names in your data source. To create a main document that is based on a mail merge template, click the File tab, click New, type "mail merge" in the Search for online templates text box, click the Start searching button, select one of the mail merge templates to use as your main document, and then click Create. You can then use the Mail Merge pane or the Ribbon to begin a mail merge using the current document. In the Step 2 of 6 Mail Merge pane, click the Use the current document option button, and then click Next. Once you have created the main document, you can customize the main document with your own information: edit the placeholder text; change the document format; or add, remove, or modify the merge fields.

Before performing the merge, make sure to match the names of the merge fields used in the template with the field names used in your data source. To match the field names, click the Match Fields button in the Write & Insert Fields group on the Mailings tab, and then use the list arrows in the Match Fields dialog box to select the field name in your data source that corresponds to each address field component in the main document.

FIGURE 8-2: Step 1 of 6 Mail Merge task pane

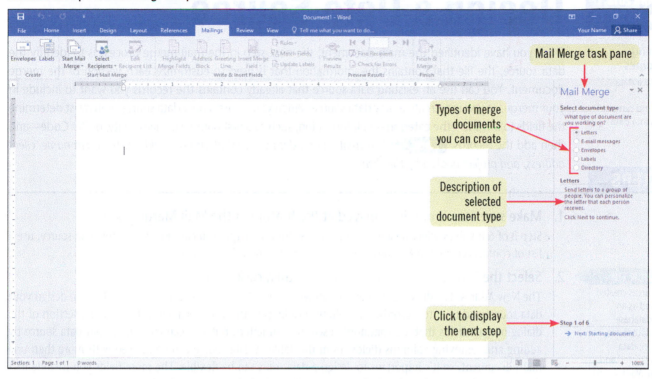

FIGURE 8-3: Main document with Step 2 of 6 Mail Merge task pane

Design a Data Source

Learning Outcomes
- Create a data source
- Add and remove fields in a data source

Once you have identified the main document, the next step in the mail merge process is to identify the data source, the file that contains the information that is used to customize each version of the merge document. You can use an existing data source that already contains the records you want to include in your merge, or you can create a new data source. When you create a new data source, you must determine the fields to include—the categories of information, such as a first name, last name, city, or ZIP Code—and then add the records. **CASE** *You create a new data source that includes fields for the client name, client address, and project booked by the client.*

STEPS

1. **Make sure Step 3 of 6 is displayed at the bottom of the Mail Merge pane**

   Step 3 of 6 involves selecting a data source to use for the merge. You can use an existing data source, use a list of contacts created in Microsoft Outlook, or create a new data source.

QUICK TIP

Data sources created and saved as an Access database use the .accdb file extension; data sources created and saved in Word as part of the Mail Merge process use the .mdb file extension.

2. **Select the Type a new list option button, then click Create**

   The New Address List dialog box opens, as shown in **FIGURE 8-4**. You use this dialog box both to design your data source and to enter records. The column headings in the Type recipient information... section of the dialog box are fields that are commonly used in form letters, but you can customize your data source by adding and removing columns (fields) from this table. A data source can be merged with more than one main document, so it's important to design a data source to be flexible. The more fields you include in a data source, the more flexible it is. For example, if you include separate fields for a person's title, first name, middle name, and last name, you can use the same data source to create an envelope addressed to "Mr. John Montgomery Smith" and a form letter with the greeting "Dear John".

3. **Click Customize Columns**

   The Customize Address List dialog box opens. You use this dialog box to add, delete, rename, and reorder the fields in the data source.

4. **Click Company Name in the list of field names, click Delete, then click Yes in the warning dialog box that opens**

   Company Name is removed from the list of field names. The Company Name field is no longer a part of the data source.

5. **Repeat Step 4 to delete the following fields: Address Line 2, Home Phone, Work Phone, and E-mail Address**

   The fields are removed from the data source.

6. **Click Add, type Project in the Add Field dialog box, then click OK**

   A field called "Project", which you will use to indicate the project location booked by the client, is added to the data source.

7. **Make sure Project is selected in the list of field names, then click Move Up eight times or until Project is at the top of the list**

   The field name "Project" is moved to the top of the list, as shown in **FIGURE 8-5**. Although the order of field names does not matter in a data source, it's convenient to arrange the field names logically to make it easier to enter and edit records.

8. **Click OK**

   The New Address List dialog box shows the customized list of fields, with the Project field first in the list. The next step is to enter each record you want to include in the data source. You add records to the data source in the next lesson.

FIGURE 8-4: New Address List dialog box

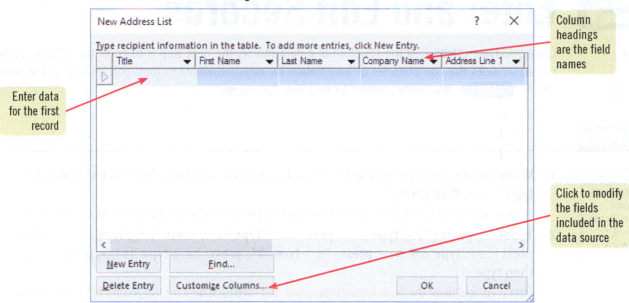

Enter data for the first record

Column headings are the field names

Click to modify the fields included in the data source

FIGURE 8-5: Customize Address List dialog box

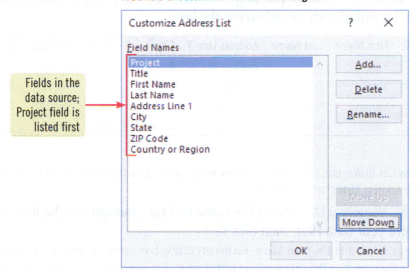

Fields in the data source; Project field is listed first

Merging with an Outlook data source

If you maintain lists of contacts in Microsoft Outlook, you can use one of your Outlook contact lists as a data source for a merge. To merge with an Outlook data source, click the Select from Outlook contacts option button in the Step 3 of 6 Mail Merge pane, then click Choose Contacts Folder to open the Choose Profile dialog box. In this dialog box, use the Profile Name list arrow to select the profile you want to use, then click OK to open the Select Contacts dialog box. In this dialog box, select the contact list you want to use as the data source, and then click OK. All the contacts included in the selected folder appear in the Mail Merge Recipients dialog box. Here you can refine the list of recipients to include in the merge by sorting and filtering the records. When you are satisfied, click OK in the Mail Merge Recipients dialog box.

Enter and Edit Records

Learning
Outcomes
• Add a record
• Edit a record

Once you have established the structure of a data source, the next step is to enter the records. Each record includes the complete set of information for each individual or item you include in the data source. **CASE** *You create a record for each new R2G client.*

STEPS

QUICK TIP
Be careful not to add spaces or extra punctuation after an entry in a field, or these will appear when the data is merged.

1. **Verify the insertion point is in the Project text box in the New Address List dialog box, type China, then press [Tab]**

   "China" appears in the Project field, and the insertion point moves to the next column, the Title field.

2. **Type Ms., press [Tab], type Erica, press [Tab], type Bass, press [Tab], type 62 Cloud St., press [Tab], type Bellevue, press [Tab], type WA, press [Tab], type 83459, press [Tab], then type US**

   Data is entered in all the fields for the first record. You used each field for this record, but it's okay to leave a field blank if you do not need it for a record.

3. **Click New Entry**

   The record for Erica Bass is added to the data source, and the New Address List dialog box displays empty fields for the next record, as shown in **FIGURE 8-6**.

QUICK TIP
You can also press [Tab] at the end of the last field to start a new record.

4. **Enter the following four records, pressing [Tab] to move from field to field, and clicking New Entry at the end of each record except the last:**

Project	Title	First Name	Last Name	Address Line 1	City	State	ZIP Code	Country
Brazil	Mr.	Paul	Beck	23 Plum St.	Boston	MA	02483	US
China	Ms.	Kate	Gans	456 Elm St.	Chicago	IL	60603	US
Mexico	Ms.	Lauren	Miller	48 East Ave.	Vancouver	BC	V6F 1AH	CANADA
Florida	Mr.	Owen	Bright	56 Pearl St.	Cambridge	MA	02139	US

5. **Click OK**

   The Save Address List dialog box opens. Data sources are saved by default in the My Data Sources folder in Microsoft Office Address Lists (*.mdb) format.

TROUBLE
If a check mark appears in the blank record under Owen Bright, click the check mark to eliminate the record from the merge.

6. **Type WD 8-R2G Volunteer Data in the File name text box, navigate to the location where you store your Data Files, then click Save**

   The data source is saved, and the Mail Merge Recipients dialog box opens, as shown in **FIGURE 8-7**. The dialog box shows the records in the data source in table format. You can use the dialog box to sort and filter records, and to select the recipients to include in the mail merge. The check marks in the second column indicate the records that will be included in the merge.

7. **Click WD 8-R2G Volunteer Data.mdb in the Data Source list box at the bottom of the dialog box, then click Edit to open the Edit Data Source dialog box, as shown in FIGURE 8-8**

   You use this dialog box to edit a data source, including adding and removing fields, editing field names, adding and removing records, and editing existing records.

QUICK TIP
If you want to add new records or modify existing records, click Edit recipient list in the Mail Merge pane.

8. **Click Ms. in the Title field of the Kate Gans record to select it, type Dr., click OK in the Edit Data Source dialog box, then click Yes**

   The data in the Title field for Kate Gans changes from "Ms." to "Dr.", and the dialog box closes.

9. **Click OK in the Mail Merge Recipients dialog box**

   The dialog box closes. The file type and filename of the data source attached to the main document now appear under Use an existing list heading in the Mail Merge pane.

FIGURE 8-6: Record in New Address List dialog box

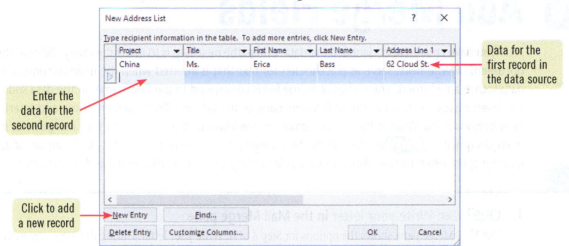

Enter the data for the second record

Click to add a new record

Data for the first record in the data source

FIGURE 8-7: Mail Merge Recipients dialog box

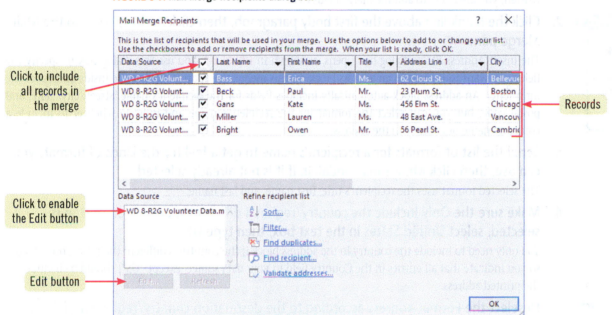

Click to include all records in the merge

Click to enable the Edit button

Edit button

Records

FIGURE 8-8: Edit Data Source dialog box

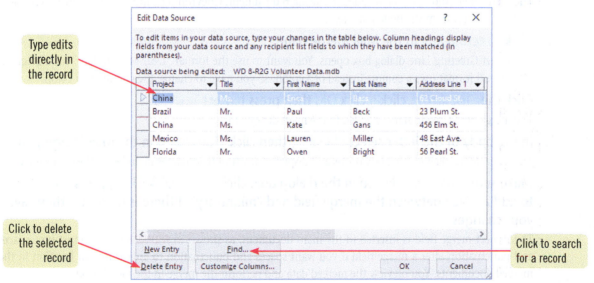

Type edits directly in the record

Click to delete the selected record

Click to search for a record

Add Merge Fields

Learning
Outcomes
• Insert merge fields
• Customize an
  address block or
  greeting field

After you have created and identified the data source, the next step is to insert the merge fields in the main document. Merge fields serve as placeholders for text that is inserted when the main document and the data source are merged. The names of merge fields correspond to the field names in the data source. You can insert merge fields using the Mail Merge pane or the Address Block, Greeting Line, and Insert Merge Field buttons in the Write & Insert Fields group on the Mailings tab. You cannot type merge fields into the main document. **CASE** ▶ *You use the Mail Merge pane to insert merge fields for the inside address and greeting of the letter. You also insert a merge field for the project destination in the body of the letter.*

STEPS

1. **Click Next: Write your letter in the Mail Merge pane**

   The Mail Merge pane shows the options for Step 4 of 6: Write your letter. During this step, you write or edit the boilerplate text and insert the merge fields in the main document. Since your form letter is already written, you are ready to add the merge fields to it.

   QUICK TIP
   You can also click the Address Block button in the Write & Insert Fields group on the Mailings tab to insert an address block.

2. **Click the blank line above the first body paragraph, then click Address block in the Mail Merge pane**

   The Insert Address Block dialog box opens, as shown in **FIGURE 8-9**. You use this dialog box to specify the fields you want to include in an address block. In this merge, the address block is the inside address of the form letter. An address block automatically includes fields for the recipient's name, street, city, state, and postal code, but you can select the format for the recipient's name and indicate whether to include a company name or country in the address.

3. **Scroll the list of formats for a recipient's name to get a feel for the kinds of formats you can use, then click Mr. Joshua Randall Jr. if it is not already selected**

   The selected format uses the recipient's title, first name, and last name.

4. **Make sure the Only include the country/region if different than: option button is selected, select United States in the text box, then type US**

   You only need to include the country in the address block if the country is different than the United States, so you indicate that all entries in the Country field in your data source, except "US", should be included in the printed address.

   QUICK TIP
   You cannot simply type chevrons around a field name. You must insert merge fields using the Mail Merge pane or the buttons in the Write & Insert Fields group on the Mailings tab.

5. **Deselect the Format address according to the destination country/region check box, click OK, then press [Enter] twice**

   The merge field AddressBlock is added to the main document. Chevrons (<< and >>) surround a merge field to distinguish it from the boilerplate text.

6. **Click Greeting line in the Mail Merge pane**

   The Insert Greeting Line dialog box opens. You want to use the format "Dear Mr. Randall:" for a greeting. The default format uses a comma instead of a colon, so you have to change the comma to a colon.

7. **Click the , list arrow, click :, click OK, then press [Enter]**

   The merge field GreetingLine is added to the main document.

   QUICK TIP
   You can also click the Insert Merge Field button or list arrow in the Write & Insert Fields group on the Mailings tab to insert a merge field.

8. **In the body of the letter select PROJECT, then click More items in the Mail Merge pane**

   The Insert Merge Field dialog box opens and displays the list of field names included in the data source.

9. **Make sure Project is selected in the dialog box, click Insert, click Close, press [Spacebar] to add a space between the merge field and "migratory" if there is no space, then save your changes**

   The Project merge field is inserted in the main document, as shown in **FIGURE 8-10**. You must type spaces and punctuation after a merge field if you want spaces and punctuation to appear in that location in the merged documents. You preview the merged data and perform the merge in the next lesson.

Merging Word Documents

FIGURE 8-9: Insert Address Block dialog box

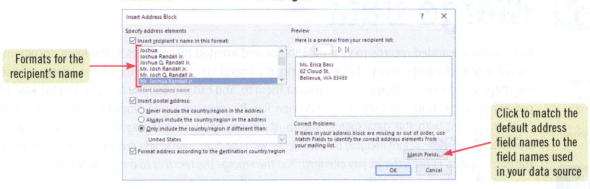

Formats for the recipient's name

Click to match the default address field names to the field names used in your data source

FIGURE 8-10: Merge fields in the main document

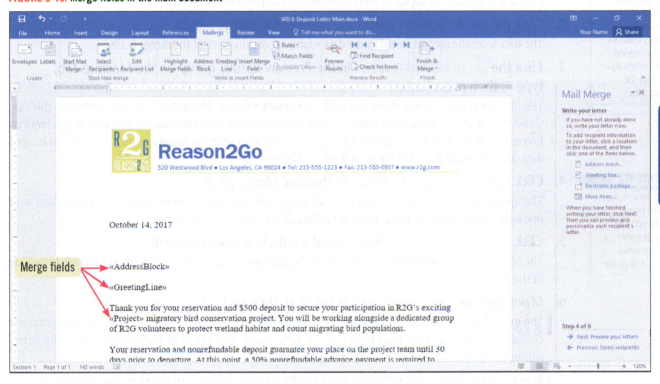

Merge fields

Merge Data

Learning Outcomes
- Preview a merge
- Merge data to a new document
- Customize a merged document

Once you have added records to your data source and inserted merge fields in the main document, you are ready to perform the merge. Before merging, it's a good idea to preview the merged data to make sure the printed documents will appear as you want them to. You can preview the merge using the Mail Merge pane or the Preview Results button in the Preview Results group on the Mailings tab. When you merge the main document with the data source, you must choose between merging to a new file or directly to a printer. **CASE** *Before merging the form letter with the data source, you preview the merge to make sure the data appears in the letter as you intended. You then merge the two files to a new document.*

STEPS

1. **Click Next: Preview your letters in the Mail Merge pane, then scroll down as necessary to see the tour name in the document**

   The data from the first record in the data source appears in place of the merge fields in the main document, as shown in **FIGURE 8-11**. Always preview a document to verify that the merge fields, punctuation, page breaks, and spacing all appear as you intend before you perform the merge.

2. **Click the Next Recipient button `>>` in the Mail Merge pane**

   The data from the second record in the data source appears in place of the merge fields.

3. **Click the Go to Record text box in the Preview Results group on the Mailings tab, type 4, then press [Enter]**

   The data for the fourth record appears in the document window. The non-U.S. country name, in this case CANADA is included in the address block, just as you specified. You can also use the First Record `|◀`, Previous Record `◀`, Next Record `▶` and Last Record `▶|` buttons in the Preview Results group to preview the merged data. **TABLE 8-1** describes other commands on the Mailings tab.

4. **Click Next: Complete the merge in the Mail Merge pane**

   The options for Step 6 of 6 appear in the Mail Merge pane. Merging to a new file creates a document with one letter for each record in the data source. This allows you to edit the individual letters.

5. **Click Edit individual letters to merge the data to a new document**

   The Merge to New Document dialog box opens. You can use this dialog box to specify the records to include in the merge.

6. **Make sure the All option button is selected, then click OK**

   The main document and the data source are merged to a new document called Letters1, which contains a customized form letter for each record in the data source. You can now further personalize the letters without affecting the main document or the data source.

7. **Scroll to the fourth letter (addressed to Ms. Lauren Miller), place the insertion point before V6F in the address block, then press [Enter]**

   The postal code is now consistent with the proper format for a Canadian address.

8. **Click the Save button `🖫` on the Quick Access toolbar to open the Save As dialog box, then save the merged document as WD 8-Deposit Letter Merge to the location where you store your Data Files**

   You may decide not to save a merged file if your data source is large. Once you have created the main document and the data source, you can create the letters by performing the merge again.

9. **Submit the document to your instructor, then close all open Word files without closing Word, saving changes to the files if prompted**

FIGURE 8-11: Preview of merged data

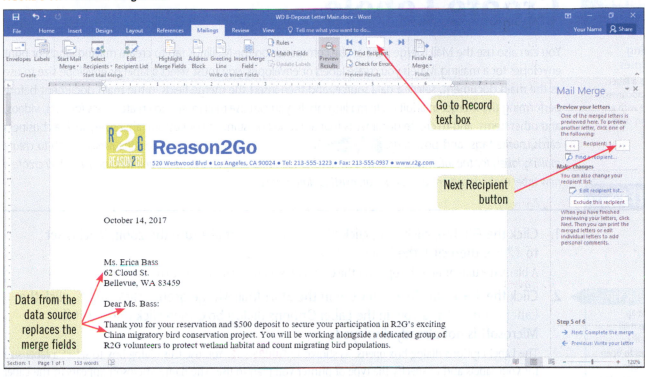

TABLE 8-1: Commands on the Mailings tab

command	use to
Envelopes	Create and print an individual envelope
Labels	Create and print an individual label
Start Mail Merge	Select the type of mail merge document to create and start the mail merge process
Select Recipients	Attach an existing data source to a main document or create a new data source
Edit Recipient List	Edit, sort, and filter the associated data source
Highlight Merge Fields	Highlight the merge fields in the main document
Address Block	Insert an Address Block merge field in the main document
Greeting Line	Insert a Greeting Line merge field in the main document
Insert Merge Field	Insert a merge field from the data source in the main document
Rules	Set rules to control how Word merges the data in the data source with the main document
Match Fields	Match the names of address or greeting fields used in a main document with the field names used in the data source
Update Labels	Update all the labels in a label main document to match the content and formatting of the first label
Preview Results	Switch between viewing the main document with merge fields or with merged data
Find Recipient	Search for a specific record in the merged document
Check for Errors	Check for and report errors in the merge
Finish & Merge	Specify whether to merge to a new document or directly to a printer or to e-mail, then complete the merge

Create Labels

Learning Outcomes
- Create a label main document
- Merge with an existing data source

You can also use the Mail Merge pane or the commands on the Mailings tab to create mailing labels or print envelopes for a mailing. When you create labels or envelopes, you must select a label or envelope size to use as the main document, select a data source, and then insert the merge fields in the main document before performing the merge. In addition to mailing labels, you can use mail merge to create labels for CDs, videos, and other items, and to create documents that are based on standard or custom label sizes, such as business cards, name tags, and postcards. **CASE** ▶ *You decide to use the commands on the Mailings tab to create mailing labels for the information packet you need to send to participants in upcoming R2G projects. You create a new label main document and attach an existing data source.*

STEPS

1. **Click the File tab, click New, click Blank document, make sure the zoom level is set to 120%, then click the Mailings tab**

   A blank document must be open for the commands on the Mailings tab to be available.

   QUICK TIP

   To create an envelope mail merge, click Envelopes to open the Envelope Options dialog box, and then select from the options.

2. **Click the Start Mail Merge button in the Start Mail Merge group, click Labels, click the Label vendors list arrow in the Label Options dialog box, then click Microsoft if Microsoft is not already displayed**

   The Label Options dialog box opens, as shown in **FIGURE 8-12**. You use this dialog box to select a label size for your labels and to specify the type of printer you plan to use. The name Microsoft appears in the Label vendors list box. You can use the Label vendors list arrow to select other brand name label vendors, such as Avery or Office Depot. Many standard-sized labels for mailings, business cards, postcards, and other types of labels are listed in the Product number list box. The type, height, width, and page size for the selected product are displayed in the Label information section.

   QUICK TIP

   If your labels do not match **FIGURE 8-13**, click the Undo button ↺ on the Quick Access toolbar, then repeat Step 3, making sure to click the second instance of 30 Per Page.

3. **Click the second instance of 30 Per Page in the Product number list, click OK, click the Table Tools Layout tab, click View Gridlines in the Table group to turn on the display of gridlines if they are not displayed, then click the Mailings tab**

   A table with gridlines appears in the main document, as shown in **FIGURE 8-13**. Each table cell is the size of a label for the label product you selected.

4. **Save the label main document with the filename WD 8-Volunteer Labels Main to the location where you store your Data Files**

   Next, you need to select a data source for the labels.

5. **Click the Select Recipients button in the Start Mail Merge group, then click Use an Existing List**

   The Select Data Source dialog box opens.

   QUICK TIP

   To create or change the return address for an envelope mail merge, click the File tab, click Options, click Advanced in the left pane of the Word Options dialog box, then scroll down the right pane and enter the return address in the Mailing address text box in the General section.

6. **Navigate to the location where you store your Data Files, open the file WD 8-2.mdb, then save your changes**

   The data source file is attached to the label main document and <<Next Record>> appears in every cell in the table except the first cell, which is blank. In the next lesson, you sort and filter the records before performing the mail merge.

FIGURE 8-12: Label Options dialog box

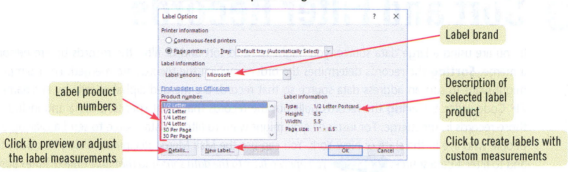

Label brand

Label product numbers

Description of selected label product

Click to preview or adjust the label measurements

Click to create labels with custom measurements

FIGURE 8-13: Label main document

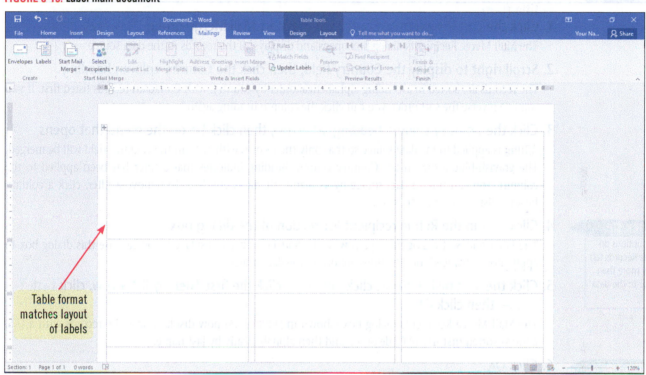

Table format matches layout of labels

Word 2016

Printing individual envelopes and labels

The Mail Merge feature enables you to easily print envelopes and labels for mass mailings, but you can also quickly format and print individual envelopes and labels using the Envelopes or Labels commands in the Create group on the Mailings tab. Simply click the Envelopes button or Labels button to open the Envelopes and Labels dialog box. On the Envelopes tab, shown in **FIGURE 8-14**, type the recipient's address in the Delivery address box and the return address in the Return address box. Click Options to open the Envelope Options dialog box, which you use to select the envelope size, change the font and font size of the delivery and return addresses, and change the printing options. When you are ready to print the envelope, click Print in the Envelopes and Labels dialog box. The procedure for printing an individual label is similar to printing an individual envelope: enter the label text in the Address box on the Labels tab, click Options to select a label product number, click OK, and then click Print.

FIGURE 8-14: Envelopes and Labels dialog box

Sort and Filter Records

Learning Outcomes
• Filter a data source
• Sort records in a data source
• Add merge fields to a label main document

If you are using a large data source, you might want to sort and/or filter the records before performing a merge. **Sorting** the records determines the order in which the records are merged. For example, you might want to sort an address data source so that records are merged alphabetically by last name or in ZIP Code order. **Filtering** the records pulls out the records that meet specific criteria and includes only those records in the merge. For instance, you might want to filter a data source to send a mailing only to people who live in the state of New York. You can use the Mail Merge Recipients dialog box both to sort and to filter a data source. **CASE** ▸ *You apply a filter to the data source so that only United States addresses are included in the merge. You then sort those records so that they merge in ZIP Code order.*

STEPS

1. **Click the Edit Recipient List button in the Start Mail Merge group**

   The Mail Merge Recipients dialog box opens and displays all the records in the data source.

2. **Scroll right to display the Country field, then click the Country column heading**

   The records are sorted in ascending alphabetical order by country, with Canadian records listed first. If you want to reverse the sort order, you can click the column heading again.

3. **Click the Country column heading list arrow, then click US on the menu that opens**

   A filter is applied to the data source so that only the records with "US" in the Country field will be merged. The grayish-blue arrow in the Country column heading indicates that a filter has been applied to the column. You can filter a data source by as many criteria as you like. To remove a filter, click a column heading list arrow, then click (All).

4. **Click Sort in the Refine recipient list section of the dialog box**

   The Filter and Sort dialog box opens with the Sort Records tab displayed. You can use this dialog box to apply more advanced sort and filter options to the data source.

5. **Click the Sort by list arrow, click ZIP Code, click the first Then by list arrow, click Last Name, then click OK**

   The Mail Merge Recipients dialog box (shown in **FIGURE 8-15**) now displays only the records with a U.S. address sorted first in ZIP Code order, and then alphabetically by last name.

6. **Click OK**

   The sort and filter criteria you set are saved for the current merge.

7. **Click the Address Block button in the Write & Insert Fields group, then click OK in the Insert Address Block dialog box**

   The Address Block merge field is added to the first label.

8. **Click the Update Labels button in the Write & Insert Fields group**

   The merge field is copied from the first label to every label in the main document.

9. **Click the Preview Results button in the Preview Results group**

   A preview of the merged label data appears in the main document, as shown in **FIGURE 8-16**. Only U.S. addresses are included, and the labels are organized in ZIP Code order, with recipients with the same ZIP Code listed in alphabetical order by last name.

10. **Click the Finish & Merge button in the Finish group, click Edit Individual Documents, click OK in the Merge to New Document dialog box, replace Mr. Daniel Potter with your name in the first label, save the document as WD 8-Volunteer Labels US Only Zip Code Merge to the location where you store your Data Files, submit the labels, save and close all open files, then exit Word**

FIGURE 8-15: US records sorted in ZIP Code order

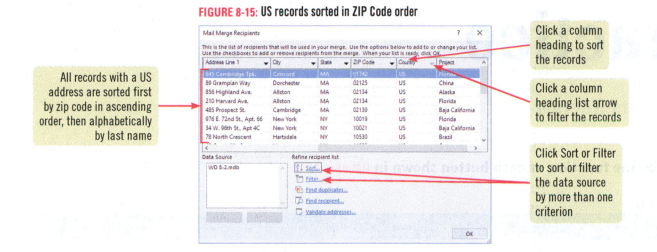

All records with a US address are sorted first by zip code in ascending order, then alphabetically by last name

Click a column heading to sort the records

Click a column heading list arrow to filter the records

Click Sort or Filter to sort or filter the data source by more than one criterion

FIGURE 8-16: Merged labels

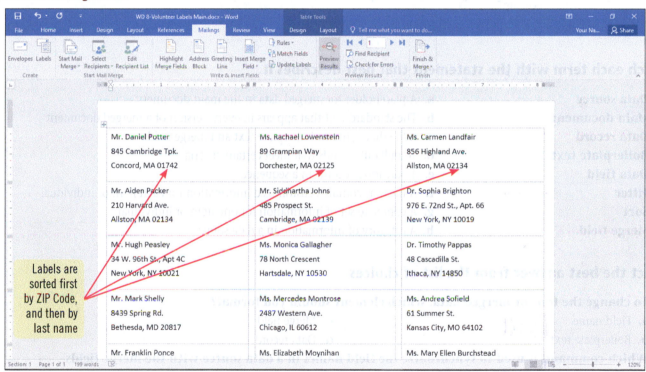

Labels are sorted first by ZIP Code, and then by last name

Inserting individual merge fields

You must include proper punctuation, spacing, and blank lines between the merge fields in a main document if you want punctuation, spaces, and blank lines to appear between the data in the merge documents. For example, to create an address line with a city, state, and ZIP Code, you insert the City merge field, type a comma and a space, insert the State merge field, type a space, and then insert the ZIP Code merge field: <<City>>, <<State>> <<ZIP Code>>.

You can insert an individual merge field by clicking the Insert Merge Field list arrow in the Write & Insert Fields group

and then selecting the field name from the menu that opens. Alternatively, you can click the Insert Merge Field button to open the Insert Merge Field dialog box, which you can use to insert several merge fields at once by clicking a field name in the dialog box, clicking Insert, clicking another field name, clicking Insert, and so on. When you have finished inserting the merge fields, click Close to close the dialog box. You can then add spaces, punctuation, and lines between the merge fields you inserted in the main document.

Practice

Concepts Review

Describe the function of each button shown in FIGURE 8-17.

FIGURE 8-17

Match each term with the statement that best describes it.

8. **Data source**
9. **Main document**
10. **Data record**
11. **Boilerplate text**
12. **Data field**
13. **Filter**
14. **Sort**
15. **Merge field**

a. A placeholder for merged data in the main document
b. The standard text that appears in every version of a merged document
c. A file that contains boilerplate text and merge fields
d. To pull out records that meet certain criteria
e. To organize records in a sequence
f. A file that contains customized information for each item or individual
g. A complete set of information for one item or individual
h. A category of information in a data source

Select the best answer from the list of choices.

16. **To change the font of merged data, which element should you format?**
    a. Field name
    b. Boilerplate text
    c. Merge field
    d. Data record

17. **Which command is used to synchronize the field names in a data source with the merge fields in a document?**
    a. Match fields
    b. Highlight Merge Fields
    c. Rules
    d. Update Labels

18. **In a mail merge, which type of file contains the information that varies for each individual or item?**
    a. Filtered document
    b. Sorted document
    c. Main document
    d. Data source

19. **Which action do you perform on a data source to reorganize the order of the records for a merge?**
    a. Edit records
    b. Sort records
    c. Filter records
    d. Delete records

20. **Which action do you perform on a data source in order to merge only certain records?**
    a. Edit records
    b. Sort records
    c. Filter records
    d. Delete records

Skills Review

1. **Create a main document.**
   a. Start Word, open a new blank document, change the style of the document to No Spacing, then open the Mail Merge pane.
   b. Use the Mail Merge pane to create a letter main document, click Next: Starting document, then select the Use the current document option button.
   c. At the top of the blank document, type **Atlantic Conservation Commission**, press [Enter], then type **1233 Wharf Street, Portsmouth, NH 03828; Tel: 603-555-8457; www.atlanticconservation.org**.
   d. Press [Enter] five times, type today's date, press [Enter] five times, then type **We are delighted to receive your generous contribution of AMOUNT to the Atlantic Conservation Commission (ACC).**
   e. Press [Enter] twice, then type **Whether we are helping to protect the region's natural resources or bringing nature and environmental studies into our public schools, senior centers, and communities, ACC depends upon private contributions to ensure that free public environmental programs continue to flourish in CITY and throughout the REGION region.**
   f. Press [Enter] twice, type **Sincerely,**, press [Enter] four times, type your name, press [Enter], then type **Executive Director**.
   g. Center the first two lines of text, change the font used for Atlantic Conservation Commission to 20 point Berlin Sans FB Demi, then remove the hyperlink in the second line of text. (*Hint*: Right-click the hyperlink.)
   h. Save the main document as **WD 8-Donor Thank You Main** to the location where you store your Data Files.

2. **Design a data source.**
   a. Click Next: Select recipients, select the Type a new list option button in the Step 3 of 6... pane, then click Create.
   b. Click Customize Columns in the New Address List dialog box, then remove these fields from the data source: Company Name, Address Line 2, Country or Region, Home Phone, Work Phone, and E-mail Address.
   c. Add an **Amount** field and a **Region** field to the data source. Be sure these fields follow the ZIP Code field.
   d. Rename the Address Line 1 field **Street**, then click OK to close the Customize Address List dialog box.

3. **Enter and edit records.**
   a. Add the records shown in **TABLE 8-2** to the data source.

   TABLE 8-2

Title	First Name	Last Name	Street	City	State	ZIP Code	Amount	Region
Mr.	John	Sargent	34 Mill St.	Exeter	NH	03833	$250	Seacoast
Mr.	Tom	Jenkins	289 Sugar Hill Rd.	Franconia	NH	03632	$1000	Seacoast
Ms.	Nancy	Curtis	742 Main St.	Derby	VT	04634	$25	North Country
Mr.	Peter	Field	987 Ocean Rd.	Portsmouth	NH	03828	$50	Seacoast
Ms.	Lisa	Juarez	73 Bay Rd.	Durham	NH	03814	$500	Seacoast
Ms.	Willa	Reed	67 Apple St.	Northfield	MA	01360	$75	Pioneer Valley
Ms.	Mia	Suzuki	287 Mountain Rd.	Dublin	NH	03436	$100	Monadnock

   b. Save the data source as **WD 8-Donor Data** to the location where you store your Data Files.
   c. Change the region for record 2 (Tom Jenkins) from Seacoast to **White Mountains**.
   d. Click OK as needed to close all dialog boxes.

4. **Add merge fields.**
   a. Click Next: Write your letter, then in the blank line above the first body paragraph, insert an Address block merge field.
   b. In the Insert Address Block dialog box, click Match Fields.
   c. Click the list arrow next to Address 1 in the Match Fields dialog box, click Street, then click OK.
   d. In the Insert Address Block dialog box, select the Never include the country/region in the address option button, then click OK.

e. Press [Enter] twice, insert a Greeting Line merge field using the default greeting line format, then press [Enter].

f. In the first body paragraph, replace AMOUNT with the Amount merge field.

g. In the second body paragraph, replace CITY with the City merge field and REGION with the Region merge field. (*Note*: Make sure to insert a space before or after each merge field as needed.) Save your changes to the main document.

5. Merge data.

a. Click Next: Preview your letters to preview the merged data, then use the Next Record button to scroll through each letter, examining it carefully for errors.

b. Click the Preview Results button on the Mailings tab, make any necessary adjustments to the main document, save your changes, then click the Preview Results button to return to the preview of the document.

c. Click Next: Complete the merge, click Edit individual letters, then merge all the records to a new file.

d. Save the merged document as **WD 8-Donor Thank You Merge** to the location where you store your Data Files. The fifth letter is shown in **FIGURE 8-18**. Submit the file or a copy of the last letter per your instructor's directions, then save and close all open files but not Word.

6. Create labels.

a. Open a new blank document, click the Start Mail Merge button in the Start Mail Merge group on the Mailings tab, then create a Labels main document.

b. In the Label Options dialog box, select Avery US Letter 5160 Easy Peel Address Labels, then click OK.

c. Click the Select Recipients button, then open the WD 8-Donor Data.mdb file you created.

d. Save the label main document as **WD 8-Donor Labels Main** to the location where you store your Data Files.

7. Sort and filter records.

a. Click the Edit Recipient List button, filter the records so that only the records with NH in the State field are included in the merge, sort the records in ZIP Code order, then click OK as needed to return to the labels document.

FIGURE 8-18

Atlantic Conservation Commission
1233 Wharf Street, Portsmouth, NH 03828; Tel: 603-555-8457; www.atlanticconservation.org

January 19, 2017

Ms. Lisa Juarez
73 Bay Rd.
Durham, NH 03814

Dear Ms. Juarez,

We are delighted to receive your generous contribution of $500 to the Atlantic Conservation Commission (ACC).

Whether we are helping to protect the region's natural resources or bringing nature and environmental studies into our public schools, senior centers, and communities, ACC depends upon private contributions to ensure that free public environmental programs continue to flourish in Durham and throughout the Seacoast region.

Sincerely,

Your Name
Executive Director

b. Insert an Address Block merge field using the default settings, click the Preview Results button, then notice that the street address is missing and the address block includes the region. (*Hint*: To preview all labels, click the Next Record button.)

c. Click the Preview Results button, then click the Match Fields button to open the Match Fields dialog box.

d. Click the list arrow next to Address 1, click Street, scroll down, click the list arrow next to Country or Region, click (not matched), then click OK.

FIGURE 8-19

Ms. Mia Suzuki
287 Mountain Rd.
Dublin, NH 03436

Mr. Tom Jenkins
289 Sugar Hill Rd.
Franconia, NH 03632

Ms. Lisa Juarez
73 Bay Rd.
Durham, NH 03814

Mr. Peter Field
987 Ocean Rd.
Portsmouth, NH 03828

Mr. John Sargent
34 Mill St.
Exeter, NH 03833

e. Click the Preview Results button to preview the merged data, and notice that the address block now includes the street address and the region name is missing.

f. Click the Update Labels button, examine the merged data for errors, then correct any mistakes.

g. Click the Finish & Merge button, then click the Edit Individual Documents to merge all the records to an individual document, shown in **FIGURE 8-19**.

h. Save the merged file as **WD 8-Donor Labels NH Only Merge** to the location where you store your Data Files.

i. In the first label, change Ms. Mia Suzuki to your name, submit the document to your instructor, save and close all open Word files, then exit Word.

Independent Challenge 1

You are the director of the Visual Arts Center (VAC). The VAC is hosting an exhibit of ceramic art titled "Earth and Water" in the city of Cambridge, Massachusetts, and you want to send a letter advertising the exhibit to all VAC members with a Cambridge address. You'll use Mail Merge to create the letter and create an envelope for one letter.

a. Start Word, open a blank document, then using either the Mailings tab or the Mail Merge pane, create a letter main document using the file WD 8-3.docx from the location where you store your Data Files.

b. Replace Your Name with your name in the signature block, then save the main document as **WD 8-Ceramics Letter Main**.

c. Use the file WD 8-4.mdb from the location where you store your Data Files as the data source.

d. Sort the data source by last name, then filter the data so that only records with Cambridge as the city are included in the merge.

e. Insert an Address Block and a Greeting Line merge field in the main document, then preview the merged letters.

f. Merge all the records to a new document, then save it as **WD 8-Ceramics Letter Merge**.

g. Select the inside address in the first merge letter, then click the Envelopes button in the Create group on the Mailings tab to open the Envelopes and Labels dialog box. (*Note*: You will create one envelope and include it as part of the merge document. If you were doing a mailing merge, you would create a separate envelope merge.)

h. On the Envelopes tab in the Envelopes and Labels dialog box, verify that the Omit check box is not selected, then type your name in the Return address text box along with the address **60 Crandall Street, Concord, Massachusetts 01742**.

i. Click Options to open the Envelope Options dialog box, click the Envelope Options tab if it is not the active tab, make sure the Envelope size is set to Size 10, then change the font of the Delivery address and the Return address to Times New Roman.

j. Click the Printing Options tab, select the appropriate Feed method for your printer, then click OK.

k. Click Add to Document, click No if a message box opens asking if you want to save the new return address as the default return address. (*Note*: The dialog box closes without printing the envelope and the envelope is added as the first page of the merge document.)

l. Submit the file or a copy of the envelope and the first merge letter per your instructor's directions, close all open Word files, saving changes, and then exit Word.

Independent Challenge 2

One of your responsibilities at Sustainable Solutions, a growing firm that focuses on sustainability services, resource management, and environmental planning, is to create business cards for the staff. You use mail merge to create the cards so that you can easily produce standard business cards for future employees.

a. Start Word, open a blank document, then use the Mailings tab or the Mail Merge pane to create labels using the current blank document.

b. Select Microsoft North American Size, which is described as Horizontal Card, 2" high x 3.5" wide. (*Hint*: Select the second instance of North American Size in the Product number list box.)

c. Create a new data source that includes the fields and records shown in **TABLE 8-3**: (*Hint*: Customize the Address List fields before adding data.)

TABLE 8-3

Title	First Name	Last Name	Phone	Fax	E-mail	Hire Date
President	Helen	Callaghan	(503) 555-3982	(503) 555-6654	hcallaghan@jad.com	1/12/13
Vice President	Seamus	Gallagher	(503) 555-2323	(503) 555-4956	sgallagher@jad.com	3/18/14

Independent Challenge 2 (continued)

d. Add six more records to the data source, including one with your name as the Administrative Assistant. (*Hint*: Be careful not to add a blank row at the bottom of the data source.)

e. Save the data source with the filename **WD 8-JAD Employee Data** to the location where you store your Data Files, then sort the data by Title.

f. In the first table cell, create the JAD Sustainable Solutions business card.

FIGURE 8-20

JAD Sustainable Solutions

Helen Callaghan
President

984 Grant Street, Portland, OR 97209
Tel: (503) 555-3982
Fax: (503) 555-6654
E-mail: hcallaghan@jad.com
Web: www.JADsustainablesolutions.com

Source: Pixabay

FIGURE 8-20 shows a sample business card, but you should create your own design. Include the company name, a street address, and the website address **www.JADsustainablesolutions.com**. Also include First Name, Last Name, Title, Phone, Fax, and E-mail merge fields. (*Hint*: If your design includes a graphic, insert the graphic before inserting the merge fields. Insert each merge field individually, adjusting the spacing between merge fields as necessary.)

g. Format the business card with fonts, colors, and other formatting features. (*Hint*: Make sure to select the entire merge field, including the chevrons, before formatting.)

h. Update all the labels, preview the data, make any necessary adjustments, then merge all the records to a new document.

i. Save the merge document as **WD 8-JAD Business Cards Merge** to the location where you store your Data Files, submit a copy to your instructor, then close the file.

j. Save the main document as **WD 8-JAD Business Cards Main** to the location where you store your Data Files, close the file, then exit Word.

Independent Challenge 3

You need to create a team roster for the children's baseball team you coach. You decide to use mail merge to create the team roster and mailing labels.

a. Start Word, open a new document, then use the Mailings tab or the Mail Merge pane to create a directory using the current blank document.

b. Create a new data source that includes the following fields: First Name, Last Name, Age, Position, Parent First Name, Parent Last Name, Address, City, State, ZIP Code, and Home Phone.

c. Enter the records shown in **TABLE 8-4** in the data source:

TABLE 8-4

First Name	Last Name	Age	Position	Parent First Name	Parent Last Name	Address	City	State	ZIP Code	Home Phone
Ellie	Wright	8	Pitcher	Kerry	Wright	58 Main St.	Camillus	NY	13031	555-2345
Liam	Jacob	7	Catcher	Bob	Jacob	32 North Way	Camillus	NY	13031	555-9827
Dwayne	Rule	8	Third	Sylvia	Rule	289 Sylvan Way	Marcellus	NY	13032	555-9724
Caroline	Herman	7	Shortstop	Sarah	Thomas	438 Lariat St.	Marcellus	NY	13032	555-8347

Independent Challenge 3 (continued)

d. Add five additional records to the data source using the following last names and positions:

O'Keefe, Second	Goleman, Center	Choy, First
George, Right	Siebert, Left	

Make up the remaining information for these five records.

e. Save the data source as **WD 8-Baseball Team Data** to the location where you store your Data Files, then sort the records by last name.

f. Insert a table that includes five columns and one row in the main document.

g. In the first table cell, insert the First Name and Last Name merge fields, separated by a space.

h. In the second cell, insert the Position merge field.

i. In the third cell, insert the Address and City merge fields, separated by a comma and a space.

j. In the fourth cell, insert the Home Phone merge field.

k. In the fifth cell, insert the Parent First Name and Parent Last Name merge fields, separated by a space.

l. Preview the merged data and make any necessary adjustments. (*Hint*: Only one record is displayed at a time when you preview the data. Click the Next Record button to see more records.)

m. Merge all the records to a new document, then save the document as **WD 8-Baseball Roster Merge** to the location where you store your Data Files.

n. Press [Ctrl][Home], press [Enter], type **Wildcats Team Roster 2017** at the top of the document, press [Enter], type **Coach:** followed by your name, then center the two lines.

o. Insert a new row at the top of the table, then type the following column headings in the new row: **Name**, **Position**, **Address**, **Phone**, **Parent Name**.

p. Format the roster to make it attractive and readable, save your changes, submit a copy to your instructor, close the file, close the main document without saving changes, then exit Word.

Independent Challenge 4: Explore

Mail merge can be used not only for mailings but also to create CD/DVD labels, labels for file folders, phone directories, business cards, and many other types of documents. In this independent challenge, you design and create a data source that you can use at work or in your personal life, and then you merge the data source with a main document that you create. Your data source might include contact information for your friends and associates, inventory for your business, details for an event such as a wedding (guests invited, responses, gifts received), data on one of your collections (such as music or photos), or some other type of information.

a. Determine the content of your data source, list the fields you want to include, and then determine the logical order of the fields. Be sure to select your fields carefully so that your data source is flexible and can be merged with many types of documents. Generally it is better to include more fields, even if you don't enter data in them for each record.

b. Start Word, open a blank document, start a mail merge for the type of document you want to create (such as a directory or a label), then create a new data source.

c. Customize the columns in the data source to include the fields and organization you determined in Step a.

d. Add at least five records to the data source, then save it as **WD 8-Your Name Data** to the location where you store your Data Files.

e. Write and format the main document, insert the merge fields, preview the merge, make any necessary adjustments, then merge the files to a document.

f. Adjust the formatting of the merge document as necessary, add your name to the header, save the merge document as **WD 8-Your Name Merge** to the location where you store your Data Files, submit a copy to your instructor, close the file, close the main document without saving changes, then exit Word.

Visual Workshop

Using mail merge, create the postcards shown in **FIGURE 8-21**. Use Avery US Letter 3263 Postcards labels for the main document, and create a data source that contains at least four records, including your name in the first record. Save the data source as **WD 8-Patient Data**, save the merge document as **WD 8-Patient Reminder Card Merge**, and save the main document as **WD 8-Patient Reminder Card Main**, all to the location where you store your Data Files. (*Hints*: Notice that the postcard label main document is formatted as a table. To lay out the postcard, insert a nested table with two columns and one row in the upper-left postcard; add the text, graphic, and merge field to the nested table; and then remove the outside borders on the nested table. Use a different online image if the image shown is not available to you. The font is Book Antiqua.) Submit a copy of the postcards to your instructor.

FIGURE 8-21

Sylvia C. Ponce, M.D.

124 East 16ᵗʰ Street, Suite 400
New York, NY 10003

Telephone: 212-555-8634

Our records indicate it is time for your annual eye exam. Please call our office to schedule an appointment.

Mr. Philip Pope

3902 Broadway

Apt. 2C

New York, NY 10025

Sylvia C. Ponce, M.D.

124 East 16ᵗʰ Street, Suite 400
New York, NY 10003

Telephone: 212-555-8634

Our records indicate it is time for your annual eye exam. Please call our office to schedule an appointment.

Ms. Zadie Sloan

414 W. 107th St.

Apt. 112

New York, NY 10027

Source: Pixabay

Develop Multipage Documents

CASE ▶ As an assistant to Mary Watson, the VP of Sales & Marketing at Reason2Go (R2G), you have been asked to edit and format a set of guidelines to help R2G managers sponsor events to promote volunteer experiences to prospective customers. You start by working in Outline view to revise the structure for the guidelines, and then you use several advanced Word features to format the document for publication.

Module Objectives

After completing this module, you will be able to:

- Build a document in Outline view
- Work in Outline view
- Navigate a document
- Insert a table of contents
- Mark text for an index
- Generate an index
- Insert footers in multiple sections
- Insert headers in multiple sections
- Finalize a multipage document

Files You Will Need

WD 9-1.docx	WD 9-6.docx
WD 9-2.docx	WD 9-7.docx
WD 9-3.docx	WD 9-8.docx
WD 9-4.docx	WD 9-9.docx
WD 9-5.docx	WD 9-10.docx

Build a Document in Outline View

You work in Outline view to organize the headings and subheadings that identify topics and subtopics in multipage documents. In Outline view, each heading is assigned a level from 1 to 9, with Level 1 being the highest level and Level 9 being the lowest level. In addition, you can assign the Body Text level to each paragraph of text that appears below a document heading. Each level is formatted with one of Word's predefined styles. For example, Level 1 is formatted with the Heading 1 style, and the Body Text level is formatted with the Normal style. **CASE** ▶ *You work in Outline view to develop the structure of the Promotional Event Guidelines.*

STEPS

1. **Start Word, create a new blank document, click the View tab, then click the Outline button in the Views group**

   The document appears in Outline view. Notice that the Outlining tab is now active. **TABLE 9-1** describes the buttons on the Outlining tab.

TROUBLE
If the headings do not appear blue and bold, click the Show Text Formatting check box in the Outline Tools group to select it.

2. **Type R2G Promotional Events**

   FIGURE 9-1 shows the text in Outline view. By default, the text appears at the left margin, is designated as Level 1 and is formatted with the Heading 1 style. You will work more with styles in the next module.

3. **Press [Enter], click the Demote button ➡ in the Outline Tools group to move to Level 2, then type Event Requirements**

   The text is indented, designated as Level 2, and formatted with the Heading 2 style.

4. **Press [Enter], then click the Demote to Body Text button ⇒ in the Outline Tools group**

5. **Type the following text: Three activities relate to the organization of an R2G promotional event: gather personnel, advertise the event, and arrange the physical space.**

   The text is indented, designated as Body Text level, and formatted with the Normal style. Notice that both the Level 1 and Level 2 text are preceded by a plus symbol ⊕. This symbol indicates that the heading includes subtext, which could be another subheading or a paragraph of body text.

6. **Press [Enter], then click the Promote to Heading 1 button ⇐ in the Outline Tools group**

   The insertion point returns to the left margin and the Level 1 position.

7. **Type Personnel, press [Enter], then save the document as WD 9-Promotional Event Outline to the location where you store your Data Files**

   When you create a long document, you often enter all the headings and subheadings first to establish the overall structure of your document.

QUICK TIP
You can press [Tab] to move from a higher level to a lower level, and you can press [Shift][Tab] to move from a lower level to a higher level.

8. **Use the Promote ⬅, Demote ➡, and Promote to Heading 1 ⇐ buttons to complete the outline shown in FIGURE 9-2**

9. **Place the insertion point after R2G Promotional Events at the top of the page, press [Enter], click ⇒, type Prepared by followed by your name, save the document, submit it to your instructor, then close it**

FIGURE 9-1: Text in Outline view

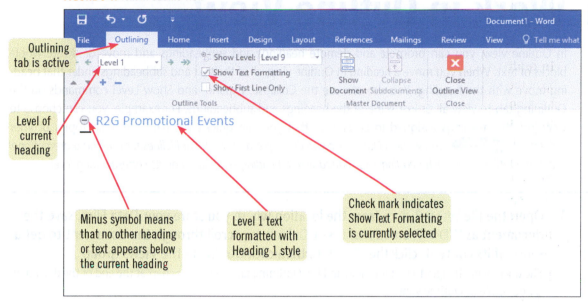

Outlining tab is active

Level of current heading

Minus symbol means that no other heading or text appears below the current heading

Level 1 text formatted with Heading 1 style

Check mark indicates Show Text Formatting is currently selected

R2G Promotional Events

FIGURE 9-2: Completed outline

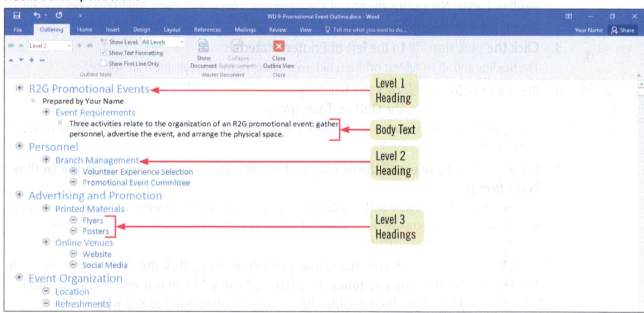

Level 1 Heading

Body Text

Level 2 Heading

Level 3 Headings

R2G Promotional Events
Prepared by Your Name
Event Requirements
Three activities relate to the organization of an R2G promotional event: gather personnel, advertise the event, and arrange the physical space.
Personnel
Branch Management
Volunteer Experience Selection
Promotional Event Committee
Advertising and Promotion
Printed Materials
Flyers
Posters
Online Venues
Website
Social Media
Event Organization
Location
Refreshments

TABLE 9-1: Frequently used outlining buttons in the Outline Tools group on the Outlining tab

button	use to	button	use to
	Promote text to Heading 1		Move a heading and its text up one line
	Promote text one level		Move a heading and its text down one line
	Demote text one level	⊕	Expand text
	Demote to body text	⊖	Collapse text

Work in Outline View

In Outline view, you can promote and demote headings and subheadings and move or delete whole blocks of text. When you move a heading in Outline view, all of the text and subheadings under that heading move with the heading. You also can use the Collapse, Expand, and Show Level commands on the Outlining tab to view all or just some of the headings and subheadings. For example, you can choose to view just the headings assigned to Level 1 so that you can quickly evaluate the main topics of your document. **CASE** ▶ *You work in Outline view to develop a draft of the guidelines for running a promotional event. In Outline view, each heading is formatted with a heading style based on its corresponding level.*

STEPS

1. **Open the file WD 9-1.docx from the location where you store your Data Files, save the document as WD 9-Promotional Event Guidelines, scroll through the document to get a sense of its content, click the View tab, then click Outline in the Views group**

   The document changes to Outline view, and the Outlining tab opens. The chart at the end of the document is not visible in Outline view.

2. **Click the Show Level list arrow in the Outline Tools group, then click Level 1**

   Only the headings assigned to Level 1 appear. All the headings assigned to Level 1 are formatted with the Heading 1 style. Notice that the title of the document Promotional Event Guidelines does not appear because the title text is not formatted as Level 1.

3. **Click the plus sign ⊕ to the left of Printed Materials**

   The heading and all its subtext (which is hidden because the topic is collapsed) are selected.

4. **Press and hold [Shift], click the heading Online Venues, release [Shift], then click the Demote button ➡ in the Outline Tools group**

   You use [Shift] to select several adjacent headings at once. The headings are demoted one level to Level 2, as shown in **FIGURE 9-3**.

5. **Press [Ctrl][A] to select all the headings, then click the Expand button ➕ in the Outline Tools group**

   The outline expands to show all the subheadings and body text associated with each of the selected headings along with the document title. You can also expand a single heading by selecting only that heading and then clicking the Expand button.

6. **Click the plus sign ⊕ next to Advertising and Promotion, click the Collapse button ➖ in the Outline Tools group two times to collapse all the subheadings and text associated with each subheading, then double-click ⊕ next to Personnel to collapse it**

   You can double-click headings to expand or collapse them, or you can use the Expand or Collapse buttons.

7. **Click the Move Up button ▲ in the Outline Tools group once, then double-click ⊕ next to Personnel**

   When you move a heading in Outline view, all subheadings and their associated text also move.

8. **Click the Show Level list arrow, select Level 3, double-click ⊕ next to Printed Materials under the Advertising and Promotion heading, click ⊕ next to Counter Items, then press [Delete]**

   The Counter Items heading and its associated subtext are deleted from the document. The revised outline is shown in **FIGURE 9-4**.

9. **Click the Close Outline View button in the Close group, then save the document**

FIGURE 9-3: Headings demoted to Level 2

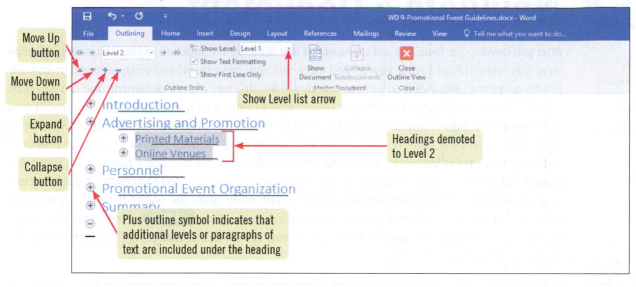

- Move Up button
- Move Down button
- Expand button
- Collapse button
- Show Level list arrow
- Headings demoted to Level 2
- Plus outline symbol indicates that additional levels or paragraphs of text are included under the heading

FIGURE 9-4: Revised outline

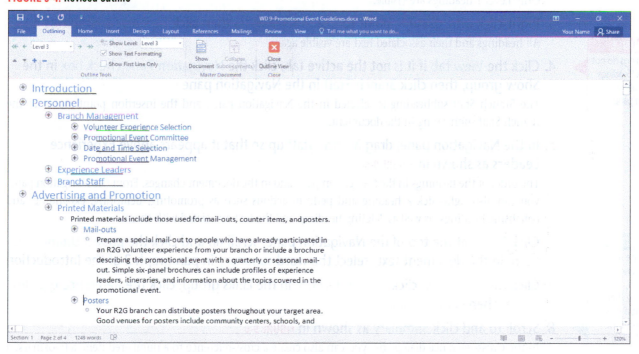

Navigate a Document

After you develop the headings and subheadings that make up the structure of your document in Outline view, you work in Print Layout view to add more text. You can expand and collapse headings and subheadings in Print Layout view so you can quickly see the structure of your document. You can also make adjustments to the document structure in the Navigation pane, which you open from Print Layout view. The **Navigation pane** shows all the headings and subheadings in the document. You can click a heading in the Navigation pane to move directly to it, and you can drag and drop headings to change their order just like you do in Outline view. You can also view thumbnails of the document pages in the Navigation pane. In addition to using the Navigation pane to navigate a document, you can create cross-references in your document. A **cross-reference** is text that electronically refers the reader to another part of the document, such as a numbered paragraph, a heading, or a figure. **CASE** ▶ *You expand and collapse headings in Print Layout view, work in the Navigation pane to make further changes to the document, and then add a cross-reference to a heading.*

STEPS

1. **Press [Ctrl][Home], click Introduction, move the mouse slightly to the left to show the Collapse icon ◢, then click ◢**

   The paragraph under the Introduction heading is hidden. You can click the Expand icon ▷ to expand the heading again so you can read the text associated with that heading.

2. **Right-click Introduction, point to Expand/Collapse, then click Collapse All Headings**

   Only Level 1 headings are visible.

3. **Right-click Introduction, point to Expand/Collapse, then click Expand All Headings**

   All headings and their associated text are visible again.

4. **Click the View tab if it is not the active tab, click the Navigation Pane check box in the Show group, then click Branch Staff in the Navigation pane**

   The Branch Staff subheading is selected in the Navigation pane, and the insertion point moves to the Branch Staff subheading in the document.

5. **In the Navigation pane, drag Branch Staff up so that it appears above Experience Leaders as shown in FIGURE 9-5**

   The order of the headings in the Navigation pane and in the document changes. From the Navigation pane, you can also right-click a heading and perform actions such as promoting, demoting, expanding, and collapsing headings, as well as deleting headings and the text associated with them.

6. **Click Pages at the top of the Navigation pane, scroll up and click the page 1 thumbnail, then, in the document text, select the word summary in paragraph 2 of the Introduction**

7. **Click the Insert tab, click Cross-reference in the Links group, click the Reference type list arrow, then click Heading**

8. **Scroll to and click Summary as shown in FIGURE 9-6**

   In the Cross-reference dialog box, you can also create a cross-reference to a numbered item, a bookmark, a footnote or an endnote, an equation, and a table, as well as a figure such as a chart, a picture, or a diagram.

9. **Click Insert, click Close, then insert a space after Summary if necessary**

   The word "Summary" is now a hyperlink to the Summary heading at the end of the document.

10. **Move the pointer over Summary to show the Click message, press and hold [Ctrl] to show 🖑, click Summary to move directly to the Summary heading, click ✕ to close the Navigation pane, then save the document**

Develop Multipage Documents

FIGURE 9-5: Changing the order of a subheading in the Navigation pane

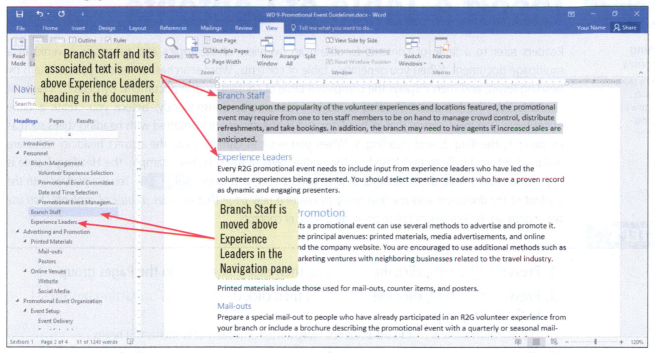

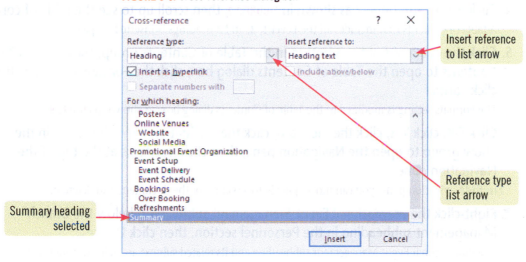

FIGURE 9-6: Cross-reference dialog box

Using bookmarks

A **bookmark** identifies a location or a selection of text in a document. To create a bookmark, you first move the insertion point to the location in the text that you want to reference. This location can be a word, the beginning of a paragraph, or a heading. Click the Insert tab, then click Bookmark in the Links group to open the Bookmark dialog box. In this dialog box, you type a name (which cannot contain spaces) for the bookmark, then click Add. To find a bookmark, press [Ctrl][G] to open the Find and Replace dialog box with the Go To tab active, click Bookmark in the Go to what list box, click the Enter bookmark name list arrow to see the list of bookmarks in the document, select the bookmark you want to go to, click Go To, then close the Find and Replace dialog box. To delete a bookmark you no longer need, click Bookmark in the Links group, click the bookmark you want to remove, then click Delete in the Bookmark dialog box.

Insert a Table of Contents

Learning
Outcomes
• Insert a table of
contents
• Update a table of
contents

Readers refer to a table of contents to obtain an overview of the topics and subtopics covered in a multipage document. When you generate a table of contents, Word searches for headings, sorts them by heading levels, and then displays the completed table of contents in the document. By default, a table of contents lists the top three heading levels in a document. Consequently, before you create a table of contents, you must ensure that all headings and subheadings are formatted with heading styles such as Heading 1, Heading 2, and Heading 3. When you work in Outline view, the correct heading styles are assigned automatically to text based on the outline level of the text. For example, the Heading 1 style is applied to Level 1 text, the Heading 2 style to Level 2 text, and so on. **CASE** ▶ *You are pleased with the content of the document and are now ready to create a new page that includes a table of contents. You use commands on the References tab to generate a table of contents.*

STEPS

1. **Press [Ctrl][Home], click the Insert tab, then click Blank Page in the Pages group**

2. **Press [Ctrl][Home], click the Home tab, then click the Clear All Formatting button 🅰️◆ in the Font group**

   The insertion point is positioned at the left margin where the table of contents will begin.

3. **Click the References tab, then click the Table of Contents button in the Table of Contents group**

   A gallery of predefined styles for a table of contents opens.

4. **Click Automatic Table 2 as shown in FIGURE 9-7, then scroll up to see the table of contents**

   A table of contents that includes all the Level 1, 2, and 3 headings is inserted on page 1.

5. **Click the Table of Contents button in the Table of Contents group, click Custom Table of Contents to open the Table of Contents dialog box, click the Formats list arrow, then click Formal**

   The Formats setting is modified in the Table of Contents dialog box, as shown in FIGURE 9-8.

6. **Click OK, click Yes, click the View tab, click the Navigation Pane check box in the Show group to open the Navigation pane, then click Headings at the top of the Navigation pane**

   In the Navigation pane, you can move quickly to a section of the document and delete it.

7. **Right-click the Promotional Event Management subheading below the Branch Management subheading in the Personnel section, then click Delete**

   The Promotional Event Management subheading and its related subtext are deleted from the document but the heading is not yet deleted from the table of contents.

8. **Scroll to the top of the table of contents, click Update Table, then click OK if prompted**

   The table of contents is updated. The Promotional Event Management subheading is no longer listed in the table of contents.

9. **Move the pointer over the heading Online Venues in the Table of Contents, press [Ctrl], then click Online Venues**

   The insertion point moves to the Online Venues heading in the document. The Navigation pane remains open.

10. **Save the document**

Develop Multipage Documents

FIGURE 9-7: Inserting an automatic table of contents

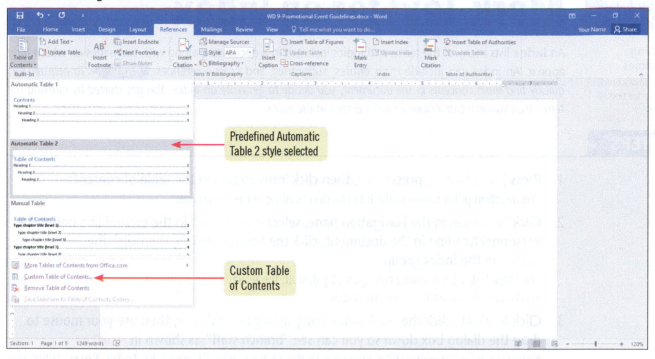

Predefined Automatic Table 2 style selected

Custom Table of Contents

FIGURE 9-8: Table of Contents dialog box

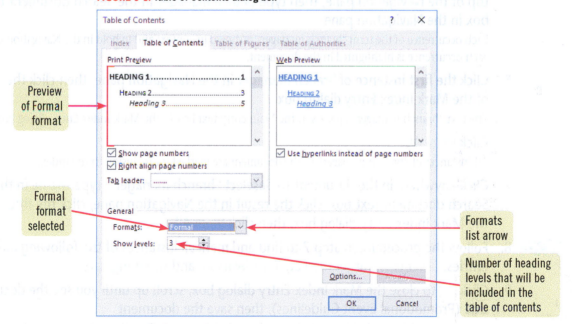

Preview of Formal format

Formal format selected

Formats list arrow

Number of heading levels that will be included in the table of contents

Mark Text for an Index

**Learning
Outcomes**
• Mark index entries
• Search for text to
  index

An **index** lists many of the terms and topics included in a document, along with the pages on which they appear. An index can include main entries, subentries, and cross-references. **CASE** ▶ *To help readers quickly find main concepts in the document, you decide to generate an index. You get started by marking the terms that you want to include as main entries in the index.*

STEPS

1. **Press [Ctrl][Home], press [Ctrl], then click Introduction in the table of contents**

   The insertion point moves to the Introduction heading in the document.

2. **Click Personnel in the Navigation pane, select branch staff in the second line under the Personnel heading in the document, click the References tab, then click the Mark Entry button in the Index group**

   The Mark Index Entry dialog box opens. By default, the selected text is entered in the Main entry text box and is treated as a main entry in the index.

3. **Click Mark All, click the Mark Index Entry dialog box title bar, then use your mouse to drag the dialog box down so you can see "branch staff" as shown in FIGURE 9-9**

   Notice the term "branch staff" is marked with the XE field code. **XE** stands for **Index Entry**. When you mark an entry for the index, the paragraph marks are turned on automatically so that you can see hidden codes such as paragraph marks, field codes, page breaks, and section breaks. These codes do not appear in the printed document. The Mark Index Entry dialog box remains open so that you can continue to mark text for inclusion in the index.

4. **Click anywhere in the document to deselect the current index entry, click Results at the top of the Navigation pane, then type branch manager in the Search document text box in the Navigation pane**

   Each occurrence of the term "branch manager" is shown in context and in bold in the Navigation pane, and each occurrence is highlighted in the document.

5. **Click the first instance of branch manager in the Navigation pane, then click the title bar of the Mark Index Entry dialog box**

   The text "branch manager" appears in the Main entry text box in the Mark Index Entry dialog box.

6. **Click Mark All**

   All instances of "branch manager" in the document are marked for inclusion in the index.

7. **Click anywhere in the document to deselect "branch manager", type theme in the Search document text box, click the result in the Navigation pane, click the title bar of the Mark Index Entry dialog box, then click Mark All**

QUICK TIP
Make sure you click
in the document
to deselect the
currently selected
text before you enter
another search term.

8. **Follow the procedure in Step 7 to find and mark all instances of the following main entries: brochures, target market, Mary Watson, and shopping cart**

9. **Click ☒ to close the Mark Index Entry dialog box, scroll up until you see the document title (Promotional Event Guidelines), then save the document**

   You see two entries marked for the index, as shown in FIGURE 9-10. The other entries you marked are further down the document.

FIGURE 9-9: Selected text in the Mark Index Entry dialog box

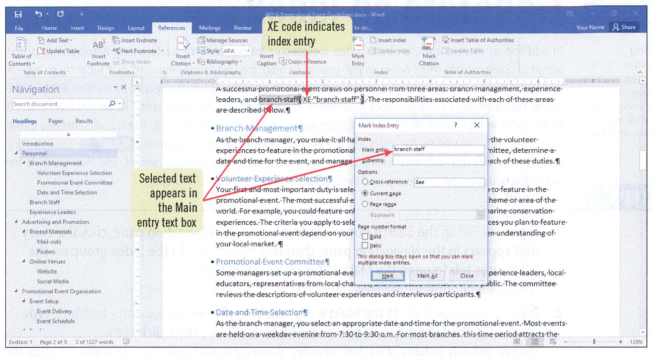

FIGURE 9-10: Index entries on the first page of the document

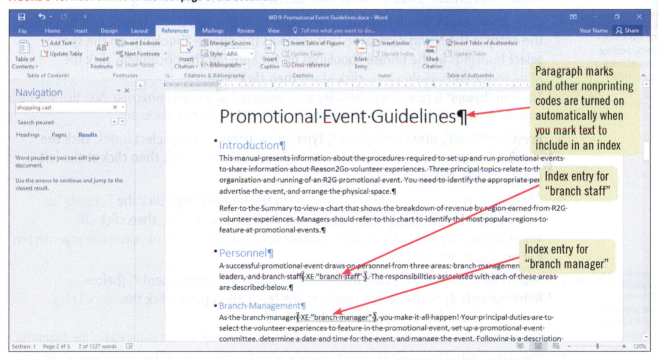

Generate an Index

Learning Outcomes
- Mark index subentries
- Insert a cross-reference in an index
- Generate an index

In addition to main entries, an index often includes subentries and cross-references. A **subentry** is text included under a main entry. For example, you could mark the text "shopping cart" as a subentry to appear under the main entry "website." A **cross-reference** in an index refers the reader to another entry in the index. For example, a cross-reference in an index might read "lecture. *See* events." Once you have marked all the index entries, you select a design for the index, and then you generate it. If you make changes to the document, you can update the index just like you can update a table of contents. **CASE** *You mark one subentry and one cross-reference for the index, create a new last page in the document, and then generate the index. You add one new main entry, and then update the index to reflect this change.*

STEPS

1. **Type charities in the Search document text box in the Navigation pane, click the entry that appears in the Navigation pane, then click Mark Entry in the Index group on the References tab to open the Mark Index Entry dialog box**

    The search term "charities" is already entered into the Mark Index Entry dialog box.

2. **Type Event Committee in the Main entry text box, click in the Subentry text box, type charities in the Subentry text box as shown in FIGURE 9-11, then click Mark**

    The first and only instance of the text "charities" is marked as a subentry that will appear following the Main entry, Event Committee.

3. **Click anywhere in the document, type laptops in the Search document text box, click the Cross-reference option button in the Mark Index Entry dialog box, click after See, type bookings as shown in FIGURE 9-12, then click Mark**

    You also need to mark "bookings" so the Index lists the page number for "bookings."

TROUBLE

Drag the Mark Index Entry dialog box out of the way as needed to see the selected phrase.

4. **Click anywhere in the document, type bookings in the Search document text box, click the entry in the Navigation pane that contains the phrase "bookings on the spot", select bookings in the phrase "bookings on the spot" in the document, click the Mark Index Entry dialog box, click Mark, then click Close**

    The term "laptops" is cross-referenced to the term "bookings" in the same paragraph. Now that you have marked entries for the index, you can generate the index at the end of the document.

5. **Press [Ctrl][End], press [Ctrl][Enter], type Index, press [Enter], select Index, click the Home tab, apply 18 pt, bold, and center alignment formatting, then click at the left margin below Index**

6. **Click the References tab, click Insert Index in the Index group, click the Formats list arrow in the Index dialog box, scroll down the list, click Formal, then click OK**

    Word has collected all the index entries, sorted them alphabetically, included the appropriate page numbers, and removed duplicate entries.

QUICK TIP

The refreshments entry that appears in the table of contents is not included because it appears before the entry you selected.

7. **Search for refreshments, click the second instance of "refreshments" (below Refreshments 4) in the search results in the Navigation pane, click the Mark Entry button in the Index Group, then click Mark All**

    The index now includes each instance of refreshments from the selected text to the end of the document.

8. **Close the dialog box and Navigation pane, scroll to the end of the document, right-click the index, click Update Field, click Index to deselect the index, then save the document**

    The updated index is shown in FIGURE 9-13.

FIGURE 9-11: Subentry in the Mark Index Entry
dialog box

FIGURE 9-12: Cross-reference in the Mark Index Entry
dialog box

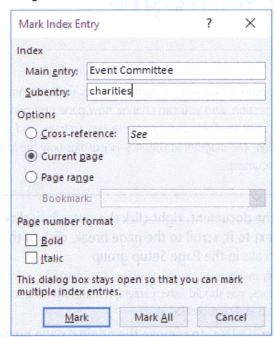

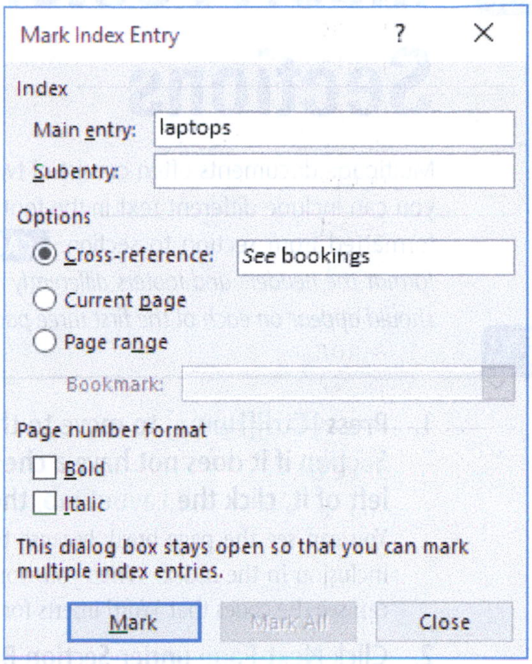

FIGURE 9-13: Completed index

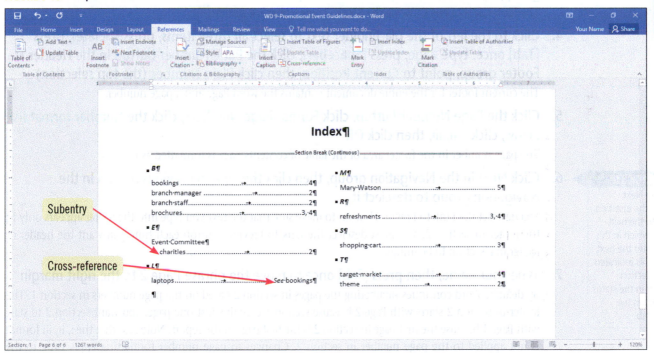

Insert Footers in Multiple Sections

Multipage documents often consist of two or more sections that you can format differently. For example, you can include different text in the footer for each section, and you can change how page numbers are formatted from section to section. **CASE** ▶ *You want to divide the report into two sections, and then format the headers and footers differently in each section. The diagram in* **FIGURE 9-14** *explains how the footer should appear on each of the first three pages in the document.*

STEPS

1. **Press [Ctrl][Home] to move to the top of the document, right-click the status bar, click Section if it does not have a check mark next to it, scroll to the page break, click to the left of it, click the Layout tab, then click Breaks in the Page Setup group**

   You can see the page break because the paragraph marks were turned on when you marked entries for inclusion in the index. When you work with sections, you should leave paragraph marks showing so you can see the codes that Word inserts for section breaks and page breaks.

2. **Click Next Page under Section Breaks, press [Delete] to remove the original page break, then press [Delete] to remove the extra blank line**

   The document is divided into two sections. Section 1 contains the Table of Contents and section 2 contains the rest of the document. Section 2 appears on the status bar.

3. **Press [Ctrl][Home], click the Insert tab, click the Footer button in the Header & Footer group, then click Blank (Three Columns)**

   The footer area opens showing the Blank (Three Columns) format.

4. **Click to the left of the placeholder text to select all three items, press [Delete], press [Tab] once, type Page, press [Spacebar], click the Page Number button in the Header & Footer group, point to Current Position, then click Plain Number (the top selection)**

   The current footer for the entire document contains the word Page and a page number.

5. **Click the Page Number button, click Format Page Numbers, click the Number format list arrow, click i, ii, iii, then click OK**

   The page number in the footer area of the table of contents page is formatted as i.

6. **Click Next in the Navigation group, then click the Link to Previous button in the Navigation group to deselect it**

   You deselect the Link to Previous button to make sure that the text you type into the footer appears only in the footer in section 2. You must deselect the Link to Previous button each time you want the header or footer in a section to be unique.

7. **Type your name, then press [Tab] once to move the phrase Page 2 to the right margin**

   By default, Word continues numbering the pages in section 2 based on the page numbers in section 1. The footer in section 2 starts with Page 2 because section 1 contains just one page. You want section 2 to start with Page 1 because the first page in section 2 is the first page of the report. Note also that the i, ii, iii format is not applied to the page number in section 2. Changes to page number formatting apply only to the section in which the change is made originally (in this case, section 1).

8. **Click the Page Number button, click Format Page Numbers, click the Start at option button, verify that 1 appears, click OK, then compare the footer to FIGURE 9-15**

9. **Click the Close Header and Footer button, then save the document**

FIGURE 9-14: Diagram of section formatting for footers

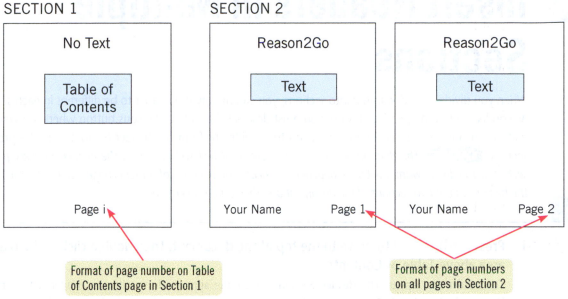

SECTION 1

No Text

Table of Contents

Page i

SECTION 2

Reason2Go

Text

Your Name   Page 1

Reason2Go

Text

Your Name   Page 2

Format of page number on Table of Contents page in Section 1

Format of page numbers on all pages in Section 2

FIGURE 9-15: Completed footer

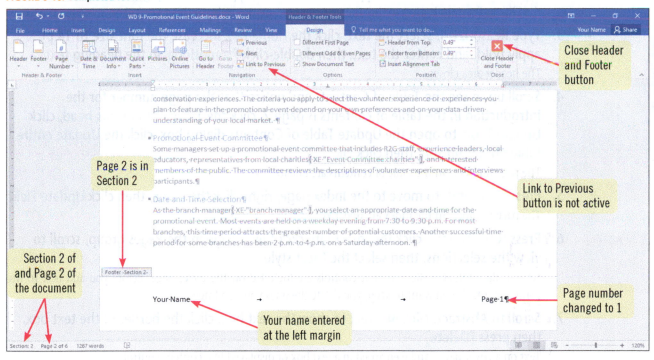

Close Header and Footer button

Page 2 is in Section 2

Link to Previous button is not active

Section 2 of and Page 2 of the document

Page number changed to 1

Your name entered at the left margin

Word 2016

Using text flow options

You adjust text flow options to control how text in a multipage document breaks across pages. To change text flow options, you use the Paragraph dialog box. To open the Paragraph dialog box, click the launcher in the Paragraph group on the Home tab, and then select the Line and Page Breaks tab. In the Pagination section, you can choose to select or deselect four text flow options.

For example, you select the Widow/Orphan control option to prevent the last line of a paragraph from printing at the top of a page (a widow) or the first line of a paragraph from printing at the bottom of a page (an orphan). By default, Widow/Orphan control is active. You can also select the Keep lines together check box to keep a paragraph from breaking across two pages.

Insert Headers in Multiple Sections

Learning Outcomes
• Insert headers in sections
• Add a cover page

When you divide your document into sections, you can modify the header to be different in each section. As you learned in the previous lesson, you must deselect the Link to Previous button when you want the text of a header (or footer) in a new section to be different from the header (or footer) in the previous section. **CASE** ▶ *The diagram in* **FIGURE 9-16** *shows that text will appear in the header on every page in section 2. You do not want any text to appear in the header on the table of contents page (section 1). You modify the headers in the two sections of the document and then add a cover page.*

STEPS

1. **Press [Ctrl][Home] to move to the top of the document, then double-click in the blank area above Table of Contents**
   The header area opens. The Header -Section 1- identifier appears along with the Header & Footer Tools Design tab. Refer to **FIGURE 9-16**. Notice that you do not want text in the header in section 1.

2. **Click Next in the Navigation group, then click the Link to Previous button to deselect it**
   The identifier Header -Section 2- appears. You want text to appear on all the pages of section 2. You deselect the Link to Previous button so that the text you type appears only on this page and on subsequent pages.

3. **Type Reason2Go, select the text, click the Home tab, increase the font size to 14 pt, apply bold, and center the text, then double-click Promotional in the heading text**
   The header area closes.

4. **Scroll up to see the Table of Contents and notice that the page number for the Introduction in the table of contents is page 2, click the Table of Contents head, click Update Table to open the Update Table of Contents dialog box, click the Update entire table option button, then click OK**
   The page numbers in the table of contents are updated.

5. **Press [Ctrl][End] to move to the Index page, right-click the index, then click Update Field**
   The page numbers in the index are updated.

6. **Press [Ctrl][Home], click the Insert tab, click Cover Page in the Pages group, scroll to view the selections, then select the Facet style**
   Several placeholders called content controls are included on the cover page. Before you add text to the content controls you want to keep, you delete the ones you don't need.

7. **Scroll to Abstract, click Abstract to show the text box, click the border of the text box, then press [Delete]**
   Text on a cover page can be enclosed in a text box or displayed in a content control.

8. **Click [Email address] to show the Email content control handle, click the content control handle to select it, then press [Delete]**
   You delete individual content controls that you do not plan to use.

9. **Enter text as shown in** **FIGURE 9-17**, **then save the document**

Develop Multipage Documents

FIGURE 9-16: Diagram of section formatting for headers

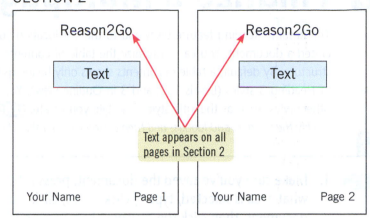

SECTION 1

No Text

Table of Contents

No text appears in the header in Section 1

Page i

SECTION 2

Reason2Go

Text

Reason2Go

Text

Text appears on all pages in Section 2

Your Name   Page 1   Your Name   Page 2

FIGURE 9-17: Text to type in cover page

PROMOTIONAL·EVENT· GUIDELINES¶

R2G·Branch·Management¶

Your·Name¶

¶

Understanding headers, footers, and sections

One reason you divide a document into sections is so that you can modify the page layout and the headers and footers differently in different sections. You can even modify the header and footer within a section because each section consists of two parts. The first part of a section is the first page, and the second part of the section is the remaining pages in the section. This section structure allows you to omit the header and footer on the first page of section 2, and then include the header and footer on all subsequent pages in section 2. To do this, place the insertion point in the section you want to modify, then click the Different First Page check box in the Options group to specify that you wish to include a different header and/or footer (or no header and footer at all) on the first page of a section. In addition, you can also choose to format odd and even pages in a document in different ways by clicking the Different Odd & Even Pages check box in the Options group. For example, you can choose to right-align the document title on odd-numbered pages and left-align the chapter indicator on even-numbered pages.

Finalize a Multipage Document

The Resume Reading feature takes you to the last location you were working on before you saved and closed a document. You can customize the table of contents so that readers can identify the document structure. By default, a table of contents shows only headings formatted with the Heading 1, Heading 2, or Heading 3 styles (Levels 1, 2, and 3 in Outline view). You can also include headings formatted with other styles, such as the Title style or a style you create. **CASE** ▸ *You use the Resume Reading feature, modify the headers and footers, and then customize the table of contents.*

STEPS

QUICK TIP
Including the cover page and table of contents page, the document contains seven physical pages with the text starting on page 3 (designated Page 1).

1. **Make sure you've saved the document, press [Ctrl][G], be sure Page in the Go to what area is selected, type 5, click Go To, click Close, close the document, open the document, then click the Welcome back! notice to go directly to page 5**
   The Resume Reading feature returns you to where you were working before saving and closing the document.

2. **Scroll up to view the page break below the chart, select the page break, click the Layout tab, click Breaks, then click Next Page in the Section Breaks area**

3. **Open WD 9-2.docx, press [Ctrl][A] to select all the text, press [Ctrl][C] to copy all the text, switch to the WD 9-Promotional Event Guidelines document, press [Ctrl][V], click the File tab, click Save As, then save the document as WD 9-Event Guidelines**
   The three pages of the Information Session Guidelines document appear in their own section.

4. **Scroll up to the Table of Contents page, double-click in the header area for section 1, click Next, select Reason2Go, type Promotional Event Guidelines, click Next, click the Link to Previous button in the Navigation group to deselect it, change the header text to Information Session Guidelines, then close the header**

5. **Scroll to the Index page, insert a Next Page section break to the left of Index, double-click in the header area, click the Link to Previous button, delete the header text, then close the header**
   The document now contains four sections, and you have modified the header text in sections 2, 3, and 4.

QUICK TIP
The title of each document is not included in the table of contents so you cannot easily see which headings belong to which documents.

6. **Scroll up to the table of contents page and click the table of contents, click Update Table, click the Update entire table option button, then click OK**

7. **Click the References tab, click the Table of Contents button, click Custom Table of Contents, click Options, select 1 in the TOC level text box next to Heading 1 and type 2, type 3 next to Heading 2, type 4 next to Heading 3 as shown in FIGURE 9-18, scroll down to Title, type 1, click OK until you are returned to the document, then click OK to replace this table of contents**
   The Information Session document starts at page 1 and you want page numbering to be consecutive.

8. **Press [Ctrl], click Information Session Guidelines in the table of contents, scroll to the footer (you'll see Page 1), double-click in the footer, click the Page Number button in the Header & Footer group, click Format Page Numbers, click the Continue from previous section option button, then click OK**

QUICK TIP
Submit files to your instructor as directed.

9. **Click Next in the Navigation group, click the Page Number button, click Format Page Numbers, click the Continue from previous section option button, click OK, exit the footer area, update the table of contents for page numbers only, reduce the zoom to 80% and hide the paragraph marks, compare the revised table of contents to FIGURE 9-19, then save and close all documents and exit Word**

FIGURE 9-18: Table of Contents Options dialog box

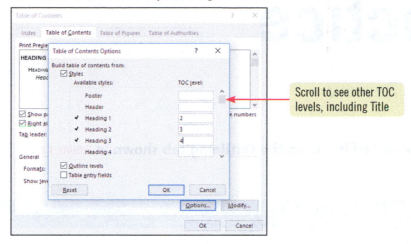

Scroll to see other TOC levels, including Title

FIGURE 9-19: Revised table of contents

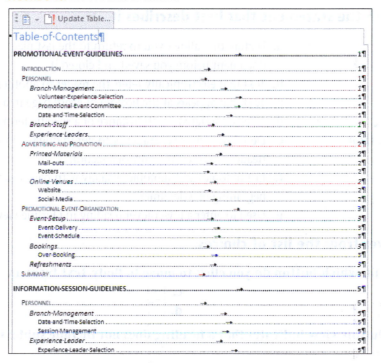

Using Advanced Print Options

With Word 2016, you can scale a document to fit a different paper size and you can choose to print pages from specific sections or a series of sections, even when the page numbering restarts in each section. To scale a document, click the File tab, click Print, click the 1 Page Per Sheet list arrow, then click Scale to Paper Size and view the list of paper sizes available. You can also choose to print a multiple-page document on fewer sheets; for example, you can print the document on two pages per sheet up to 16 pages per sheet. In the Print dialog box, you can also specify how to print the pages of a multiple-section document that uses different page numbering in each section. You need to enter both the page number and the section number for the range of pages you wish to print. The syntax required is: PageNumberSectionNumber-PageNumberSectionNumber which is shortened to p#s#-p#s#. For example, if you want to print from page 1 of section one to page 4 of section three, you enter p1s1-p4s3 in the Pages text box in the Settings area, and then click Print.

Practice

Concepts Review

Label the numbered items on the Outlining tab shown in FIGURE 9-20.

FIGURE 9-20

Match each term with the statement that best describes it.

6. **Demote button**

7. **Table of Contents**

8. **Resume Reading**

9. **Footer**

10. **Cross-reference**

11. **Link to Previous button**

12. **Mark All**

a. Feature that allows you to return to the last place you were working in a document before you saved and closed it

b. Text that electronically refers the reader to another part of the document

c. Text that appears at the bottom of every page in a document or section

d. Click to designate each instance of a specific term for inclusion in an index

e. Deselect to create a header or footer in one section that is different from the header or footer in a previous section

f. List of topics and subtopics usually with page numbers, and shown at the beginning of a document

g. Used to enter a lower-level heading in Outline view

Select the best answer from the list of choices.

13. **On the Outlining tab, which button do you click to move to Body Text from any other level?**
    - a. →
    - b. ←
    - c. →
    - d. ▼

14. **Which symbol in Outline view indicates that a heading does not include subtext such as subheadings or paragraphs of text?**
    - a. ⊕
    - b. «
    - c. ▲
    - d. ⊖

15. **Which of the following options do you select when you want to search for text from the Navigation pane?**
    - a. Headings
    - b. Results
    - c. Find Text
    - d. Search

16. **Which index entry appears subordinate to a main entry?**
    - a. Cross-reference
    - b. Subentry
    - c. Mark place
    - d. Next Entry

17. **Which tab contains the commands used to create an index?**
    - a. References
    - b. Insert
    - c. Layout
    - d. Review

Skills Review

1. Build a document in Outline view.

  a. Start Word, create a new blank document, then switch to Outline view using the View tab.

  b. Type **Introduction** followed by your name as a Level 1 heading, press [Enter], type **Partnership Conditions** as another Level 1 heading, then press [Enter].

FIGURE 9-21

⊖ Introduction by Your Name
⊕ Partnership Conditions
  ○ This section provides background information about Creston Training and discusses how the partnership could benefit both Redfern Communications and Creston Training.
  ⊖ Background
  ⊖ Benefits
  ⊖ Partnership Need
⊕ Products and Services
  ⊖ Creston Training Services
  ⊖ Redfern Communications
  ⊖ Package Opportunities
⊕ Financial Considerations
  ⊖ Projected Revenues
  ⊖ Financing Required
⊖ Conclusion

  c. Type the text shown in **FIGURE 9-21** as body text under the Partnership Conditions heading.

  d. Type **Background**, then use the Promote and Demote buttons to promote the body text to Level 1 and then demote it to a Level 2 heading.

  e. Complete the outline, as shown in **FIGURE 9-21**.

  f. Save the document as **WD 9-Partnership Outline** to the location where you store your Data Files, then close the document.

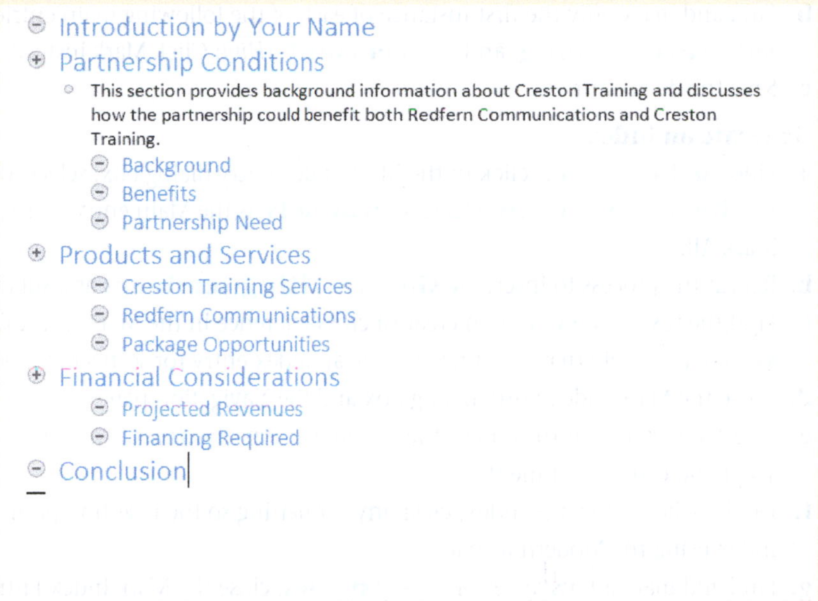

2. Work in Outline view.

  a. Open the file WD 9-3.docx from the location where you store your Data Files, save it as **WD 9-Partnership Proposal**, switch to Outline view, then show all Level 1 headings.

  b. Move the heading Products and Services above Financial Considerations.

  c. Select the Partnership Conditions heading, expand the heading to show all subheadings and their corresponding body text, collapse Benefits, collapse Partnership Need, then move Benefits and its subtext below Partnership Need and its subtext.

  d. Show all levels of the outline, close Outline view, then save the document.

3. Navigate a document.

  a. In Print Layout view, collapse the Introduction heading.

  b. Open the Navigation pane, navigate to Financing Required, then change "six months" to **two years** in the last line of the paragraph below the Financing Required heading.

  c. Right-click the Package Opportunities heading in the Navigation pane, then delete the heading and its subtext.

  d. View the thumbnails of the document pages in the Navigation pane, click the first page, close the Navigation pane, scroll to the Benefits heading, then select the text "Projected Revenues" at the end of the paragraph.

  e. Create a cross-reference from the text Projected Revenues to the PROJECTED REVENUES heading.

  f. Test the cross-reference, then save the document.

4. Insert a table of contents.

  a. Go to the top of the document.

  b. Insert a page break, then return to the top of the document.

  c. Insert a table of contents using the Automatic Table 2 predefined style.

  d. Replace the table of contents with a custom table of contents using the Distinctive format.

  e. Use [Ctrl][click] to navigate to Partnership Need in the document, open the Navigation pane, view the document headings, then right-click and delete the Partnership Need heading from the Navigation pane.

  f. Update the table of contents, then save the document.

Skills Review (continued)

5. **Mark text for an index.**

   a. Show the Results section of the Navigation pane, find the words **computer labs**, then mark all occurrences for inclusion in the index.

   b. Find and mark only the first instance of each of the following main entries: **website design, networking, software training**, and **PowerPoint**. (*Hint*: Click Mark instead of Mark All.)

   c. Save the document.

6. **Generate an index.**

   a. Find **social media**, click in the Mark Index Entry dialog box, select social media in the Main entry text box, type **Redfern Communications Products** as the Main entry and **social media** as the Subentry, then click Mark All.

   b. Repeat the process to insert **business writing seminars** as a subentry of Creston Training.

   c. Find the text **courses**, then create a cross-reference in the Mark Index Entry dialog box to **software training**. Note that you already have an index entry for software training.

   d. Close the Mark Index Entry dialog box and the Navigation pane.

   e. Insert a new page at the end of the document, type **Index** at the top of the page, and format it with bold and 18 pt and center alignment.

   f. Double-click below the index, clear any formatting so the insertion point appears at the left margin, then insert an index using the Modern format.

   g. Find and mark all instances of **Los Angeles**, close the Mark Index Entry dialog box and the Navigation pane, scroll to the index page, update the index so it includes the new entry, then save the document.

7. **Insert footers in multiple sections.**

   a. At the top of the document, select the page break below the Table of Contents, replace it with a Next Page section break, then remove the page break and the extra blank line.

   b. On the table of contents page, insert a footer using the Blank (Three Columns) format.

   c. Delete the placeholders, type your name, press [Tab] twice, type **Page**, press [Spacebar], then insert a page number at the current position using the Plain Number format.

   d. Change the format of the page number to i, ii, iii.

   e. Go to the next section, then deselect the Link to Previous button.

   f. Format the page number to start at 1.

   g. Exit the footer area, scroll through the document to verify that the pages are numbered correctly, scroll to and update the page numbers in the table of contents, then save the document.

8. **Insert headers in multiple sections.**

   a. Move to the top of the document, then double-click to position the insertion point in the header area.

   b. Go to the next section, then deselect the Link to Previous button.

   c. Type **Redfern Communications**, then apply bold and italic.

   d. Exit the header area, then scroll through the document to verify that the header text does not appear on the table of contents and that it does appear on all subsequent pages.

   e. Insert a cover page using the Semaphore style, then delete the Date content control.

   f. Enter **Partnership Agreement Proposal** as the Document title, **Redfern Communications** as the Document subtitle, and your name where indicated.

   g. Delete the Company name and Company address content controls.

   h. Save the document.

9. **Finalize a multipage document.**

   a. Go to the Index page, then save and close the document.

   b. Open the document, then use the Resume Reading feature to return to the last page of the document.

Skills Review (continued)

c. Scroll up to the Page Break after the Conclusion text, then insert a Next Page section break, then delete the page break and paragraph mark following the page break. The insertion point should move to the left of the word Index.

d. Open the file WD 9-4.docx from the drive and folder where you store your Data Files, copy all the text, paste it into the Partnership Agreement Proposal document at the location of the insertion point, insert a Next Page section break, then save the document as **WD 9-Partnership Agreements**.

e. From the table of contents page, access the Header area, move to section 2, replace Redfern Communications with **Creston Training**, move to section 3, deselect the Link to Previous button, replace Creston Training with **Smart Talk Presenters**, move to section 4 (the index page), then deselect the Link to Previous button and remove the header from the index page.

f. Check that the correct headers appear in each of the four sections, then update the table of contents page (select the Update entire table option).

g. Modify the table of contents options so that Heading 1 corresponds to TOC level 2 text, Heading 2 corresponds to TOC level 3 text, Heading 3 corresponds to TOC level 4 text, and Title text corresponds to TOC level 1 text.

h. Modify the footers in sections 3 and 4 so that the page numbering is continuous. You should see page 6 on the index page.

i. Update the index and table of contents pages, compare your document to the pages from the completed document shown in **FIGURE 9-22**, save the document, submit all files to your instructor, close it, then exit Word.

FIGURE 9-22

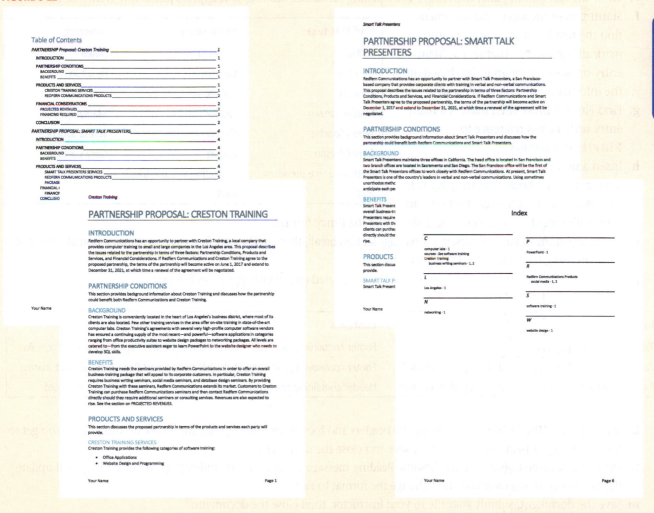

Independent Challenge 1

You work in the Finance Department of Fitness Forever. Recently, the owners began selling franchises. Your supervisor asks you to format a report that details the development of these franchise operations.

a. Start Word, open the file WD 9-5.docx from the drive and folder where you store your Data Files, then save it as **WD 9-Fitness Forever Franchises**.

b. In Outline view, organize the document as shown in the following table, starting with Introduction, followed by Scope of the Report, and then moving column by column. Text that you designate as headings will be formatted with the blue font color.

heading	level	heading	level	heading	level
Introduction	1	Gary Gleeson	2	Phoenix Clientele	3
Scope of the Report	2	Franchise Locations	1	Houston	2
Owner Information	1	Dallas	2	Houston Clientele	3
Marilyn Janzen	2	Dallas Clientele	3	Opening Schedules	2
Teresa Sanchez	2	Phoenix	2		

c. Show level 3, then switch the order of Houston and its subtext so it follows Dallas and its subtext.

d. In Print Layout view, collapse all the headings to show only Level 1 headings, then expand the headings again.

e. Show the Navigation pane, then move the Opening Schedules heading so it appears just below Franchise Locations.

f. Starting from the top of the document, find the text listed in column 1, and mark all instances of that text as Main entry or subentry for an index, based on the information in columns 2 and 3.

find this text	main entry	subentry
Dallas	Location	Dallas
Houston	Location	Houston
Phoenix	Location	Phoenix
Marilyn Janzen	Owner	Marilyn Janzen
Teresa Sanchez	Owner	Teresa Sanchez
Gary Gleeson	Owner	Gary Gleeson
marketing vice president	marketing vice president	
mall	mall	

g. Find Finest Fitness, then make it a main entry with a cross-reference to **Marilyn Janzen**.

h. Insert a new page at the end of the document, type **Index** as the page title, format it with bold, a larger font size, and center alignment, then generate an index using the Fancy format.

i. At the top of the document, insert a Next Page section break, then on the new first page, insert an automatic table of contents using the Automatic Table 1 style.

j. Add and format a header and footer so that the completed document appears as follows:

location	contents
Table of Contents page (section 1)	Footer containing your name at the left margin and Page i at the right margin
Page 1 and the following pages of the report (section 2)	Footer containing your name at the left margin and Page 1 at the right margin
Page 1 and the following pages of the report (section 2)	Header containing the text Fitness Forever Franchises, centered, and bold

k. Scroll through the document to ensure the headers and footers are correct, click the Index heading when you get to the Index page, update the index, then save and close the document.

l. Open the document and click the Resume Reading message to return to the Index page, then scroll up and update the table of contents page and then change the format to Fancy.

m. Save the document, submit your file to your instructor, then close the document.

Independent Challenge 2

As the program assistant at Marchand College in Vermont, you are responsible for creating and formatting reports about programs at the college. You work in Outline view to create a report for a college program of your choice.

a. Start Word, create a new blank document, then save it as **WD 9-Program Information Report**.

b. In Outline view, enter the headings and subheadings for the report as shown in the table starting with **Program Overview**, followed by **Career Opportunities**. You need to substitute appropriate course names for Course 1, Course 2, and so on. For example, courses in the first term of a business studies program could be **Introduction to Business, Accounting Basics**, and so on. You choose the program and courses you want to include in the report.

heading	level	heading	level
Program Overview	1	[Enter name for Course 1]	3
Career Opportunities	2	[Enter name for Course 2]	3
Admission Requirements	2	Second Term	2
Program Content	1	[Enter name for Course 1]	3
First Term	2	[Enter name for Course 2]	3

c. Enter one paragraph of appropriate body text for the following headings: Program Overview, Career Opportunities, and Admission Requirements, then enter short course descriptions for each of the four courses included in the document. For ideas, refer to college websites and catalogs. Collapse all the headings to Level 1.

d. In Print Layout view, add a cover page using the style of your choice. Include the name of the program as the title (for example, **Business Program**), the name of the college (**Marchand College, Vermont**) as the subtitle, and your name where indicated. Remove all other content controls. If the cover page style you choose does not include a content control for a subtitle, enter the information as text and format it attractively.

e. Insert a Next Page section break following the cover page, then insert a page break in the body of the report to spread the report over two pages if it does not already flow to two pages.

f. Format the cover page (section 1) with no header and no footer.

g. Go to the section 2 header and deselect the Different First Page check box in the Options group so that you see Header - Section 2 in the tab below the header area, not First Page Header - Section 2. Format the section 2 header with a right-aligned page number starting with Page 1 using the 1, 2, 3 format. Make sure you deselect Link to Previous.

h. Format the section 2 footer with the name of the program left-aligned in the footer and your name right-aligned. Make sure you deselect Link to Previous.

i. Insert a Next Page section break above the Program Overview heading.

j. Scroll up to the new blank page, then insert an automatic table of contents in either the Automatic Table 1 or Automatic Table 2 format. Replace the table of contents with a custom table of contents that uses the format of your choice (for example, Classic, Fancy, etc.).

k. Customize the table of contents so that it includes only Heading 1 at TOC level 1 and Heading 3 at TOC level 2. None of the Heading 2 headings should appear in the revised table of contents.

l. Double click in the header area on the table of contents page, then delete Page 1.

m. Go to the next section (Section 3), click the Link to Previous button to deselect it, then insert Page 1 right-aligned. Be sure the page number starts at 1. Verify that the header appears on both pages of the section 3 header and that the footer appears on all pages except the cover page.

n. Update the table of contents, save the document, close it, then submit your file to your instructor.

Independent Challenge 3

Many businesses post job opportunities on their websites. You can learn a great deal about opportunities in a wide range of fields just by checking out the job postings on these websites. You decide to create a document that describes a selection of jobs available on an employment website of your choice.

a. Use your favorite search engine and the search phrase **job search** to find websites that post jobs online. Popular sites include glassdoor.com, workopolis.com, and monster.com.

b. On the website you chose, identify two job categories (e.g., Social Media and Online Marketing, or Accounting and Communications) and then find two jobs that appeal to you and that you may even wish to apply for. You can choose to search for jobs in your home town or in another location.

c. Create a new document in Word, then save it as **WD 9-Online Job Opportunities**.

d. In Outline view, set up the document starting with the name of the employment website (e.g., monster.com) and followed by Job Category 1 as shown in the table. (*Note*: You need to enter specific text for headings such as **Marketing** for Job Category 1 and **Marketing Assistant** for Job Posting.)

heading	level
Name of website	1
Job Category 1	2
Job Name	3
Summary of Job Posting	Body Text
Job Category 2	2
Job Name	3
Summary of Job Posting	Body Text

e. Complete the Word document with information you find on the website. Include a short description of each job you select, and list some of the job duties. You do not need to include the entire job posting. If you copy selected text from a website, make sure you clear the formatting so that the text in the document is formatted only with the Normal style. Edit any copied text so that only the most important information is included.

f. Divide the document into two pages so that each job category posting appears on one page.

g. Above the first job posting, enter the following text: **Following is a description of two jobs that interest me. The first job is a[n] [name of job] and the second job is a[n] [name of job]. Information in this report was copied from the [website name or URL] website on [date].** Make sure you substitute the job titles you've identified for [name of job], the name of the website name or its URL for the [website name or URL], and the date you created the report for [date].

h. Make each job title a cross-reference to the appropriate heading in your outline, then test the cross-references.

i. Insert a header that starts on page 1 and includes the text **Online Job Opportunities for** followed by your name, then include a page number on each page of the document in the footer.

j. Save the document and submit the file to your instructor, then close the document.

Independent Challenge 4: Explore

You work for an author who has just written a series of vignettes about her travels in Europe. The author plans to publish the vignettes and accompanying illustrations in a book called *Creative Journeys*. She has written a short proposal to present to publishers. As her assistant, your job is to create a proposal that includes three of the vignettes, each with a unique header. You will further explore the features available in Outline view by using some of the tools available in the Master Document group.

a. Start Word, open WD 9-6.docx, then save it as **WD 9-Creative Journeys Proposal**. Keep the document open.

b. Open WD 9-7.docx, save it as **WD 9-Creative Journeys Venice**, then close it.

c. Open WD 9-8.docx, save it as **WD 9-Creative Journeys Seville Flamenco**, then close it.

d. Open WD 9-9.docx, save it as **WD 9-Creative Journeys Roman Rain**, then close it.

e. From the WD 9-Creative Journeys Proposal document, switch to Outline view, then promote the Creative Journeys Overview heading to Level 1.

f. Click at the end of the outline on the first blank line after the last sentence.

g. Click the Show Document button in the Master Document group.

h. Click the Insert button in the Master Document group, navigate to the location where you saved the files for this challenge, double-click WD 9-Creative Journeys Venice, then click No if prompted.

i. Repeat step h to insert WD 9-Creative Journeys Seville Flamenco as a subdocument, then repeat step h once more to insert WD 9-Creative Journeys Roman Rain as a subdocument. The master document now consists of introductory text and three subdocuments.

j. Click the Collapse Subdocuments button in the Master Document group, then click OK in response to the message. Scroll down as needed to verify that each document is now a hyperlink.

k. Press the [Ctrl] key and click the hyperlink to the Creative Journeys Venice document. View the document, then close it.

l. Click the Expand Subdocuments button, then close Outline view.

m. At the top of the document, add a Next Page section break, then at the top of the new blank page, insert one of an automatic table of contents using the style of your choice.

n. Replace the table of contents with a custom table of contents that uses the Formal format.

o. Insert a footer at the bottom of the table of contents page that includes your name at the left margin and the page number formatted in lower case Roman numerals (i) at the right margin.

p. Go to section 2, deselect Link to Previous, then format the page numbers so they start at 1.

q. Create a header for each section as shown in the table below. Make sure you deselect Link to Previous each time you go to a new section. Enter the text for each header at the left margin and format it with italic. The document contains a total of eight sections and five pages. Note that extra sections are inserted when you insert subdocuments to ensure that each subdocument starts on its own page.

section	contains	header text
1	Table of Contents	no header
2	Overview	Creative Journeys Overview
3	Venice	Venice
5	Seville Flamenco	Seville Flamenco
7	Roman Rain	Roman Rain

r. Update the table of contents, save the document, submit a copy of all four documents to your instructor, then close the document. Note that when you open the document again, the three subdocuments will appear as hyperlinks.

Visual Workshop

Open the file WD 9-10.docx from the drive and folder where you store your Data Files, then save it as **WD 9-Book Marketing Plan**. Modify the outline so that it appears as shown in FIGURE 9-23. You need to change the order of some sections. In Print Layout view, insert a Next Page section break at the beginning of the document, then generate a table of contents using the Automatic Table 2 format and the custom Distinctive format with four levels showing. *Hint*: Click the Show levels list arrow in the Table of Contents dialog box, then click 4. Insert a page break before Promotion in the text, then create a footer in section 2 (remember to deselect Link to Previous) with your name at the left margin and a page number that starts with 1 at the right margin. Make sure no text appears in the footer in section 1. Update the table of contents so that it appears as shown in FIGURE 9-24. Save and close the document, then submit the file to your instructor.

FIGURE 9-23

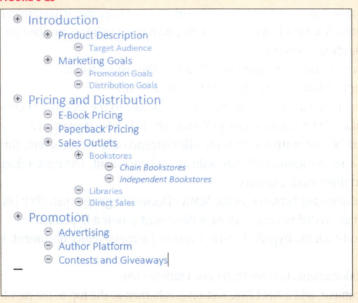

FIGURE 9-24

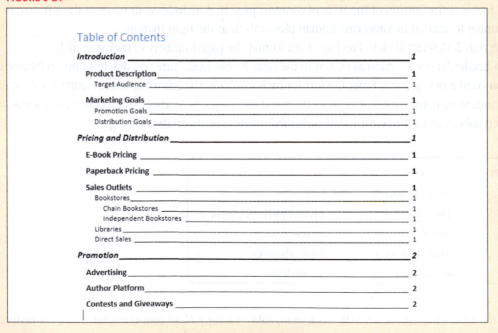

Working with Styles and Templates

CASE ▶ As a special projects assistant at Reason2Go, you've been asked to produce profiles of the top R2G experience leaders for distribution at the company's annual meeting. To save time, you modify styles in an existing profile, create new styles, and then develop a template on which to base the profile for each experience leader.

Module Objectives

After completing this module, you will be able to:

- Explore styles and templates
- Modify built-in styles
- Create paragraph styles
- Create character and linked styles
- Create list styles

- Create table styles
- Create a Style Set
- Manage styles
- Create and attach a template

Files You Will Need

Explore Styles and Templates

Learning Outcomes
- Define why to use styles
- Identify style types
- Define why to use templates

You use styles and templates to automate document-formatting tasks and to ensure consistency among related documents. A **style** consists of formats such as font, font size, and alignment that you name and then save as one set. For example, the settings for a style called Main Head could be Arial font, 14-pt font size, bold, and a bottom border. Each time you apply the Main Head style to selected text, all format settings included in the style are applied. A **template** is a file that contains the basic structure of a document, such as the page layout, headers and footers, styles, graphic elements, and boilerplate text. **CASE** ▶ *You plan to use styles to format an experience leader profile and then create a template for a series of experience leader profiles. You start by familiarizing yourself with styles and templates.*

DETAILS

Information about how you can use styles and templates to help you format documents quickly and efficiently follows:

About Styles

- You apply styles to selected text from the Styles gallery on the Home tab. Using styles helps you save time in two ways. First, when you apply a style, you apply a set of formats all at once. Second, if you modify a style by changing one or more of the formats associated with that style, all text formatted with that style is updated automatically. For example, suppose you apply a style named "Section Head" to each section head in a document. If you then modify the formatting associated with the Section Head style, Word automatically updates all the text formatted with the Section Head style. As discussed in Module 9, default heading styles are applied automatically to headings and subheadings when you work in Outline view to create the structure of a document. For example, the Heading 1 style is applied to text associated with Level 1, the Heading 2 style is applied to text associated with Level 2, and so on. You can modify a default heading style or you can create a new heading style.

- In Word, you can choose from 17 built-in Style Sets on the Design tab or you can create your own Style Set. Each **Style Set** contains **styles** for text elements such as headings, titles, subtitles, and lists. All of the styles associated with a Style Set are stored in the **Styles gallery** on the Home tab.

- Word includes five major style categories. A **paragraph style** includes font formats, such as font and font size, and paragraph formats, such as line spacing or tabs. You use a paragraph style when you want to format all of the text in a paragraph at once. A **character style** includes character formats only, such as font, font size, and font color. You use a character style to apply character format settings only to selected text within a paragraph. A **linked style** contains both a character style and a paragraph style. Either the character style or the paragraph style is applied depending on whether you click in a paragraph to select the entire paragraph or you select specific text. A **table style** specifies how you want both the table grid and the text in a table to appear. A **list style** allows you to format a series of lines with numbers or bullets and with selected font and paragraph formats. **FIGURE 10-1** shows a document formatted with the five style types. These styles have been saved in a new Style Set called R2G Profiles.

About Templates

- Every document you create in Word is based on a template. Most of the time, this template is the **Normal template** because the Normal template is loaded automatically when you start a new document. The styles assigned to the Normal template, such as Normal, Title, Heading 1, Heading 2, and so on, are the styles you see in the Styles gallery on the Home tab when you open a new document.

- Word includes a number of built-in templates. In addition, you can access a variety of templates online. You can also create a template, and then attach that template to an existing document. Once the template is attached to a document, the styles associated with that template become available, which means you can apply the styles included with the template to text in the document.

FIGURE 10-1: A document formatted with five style types

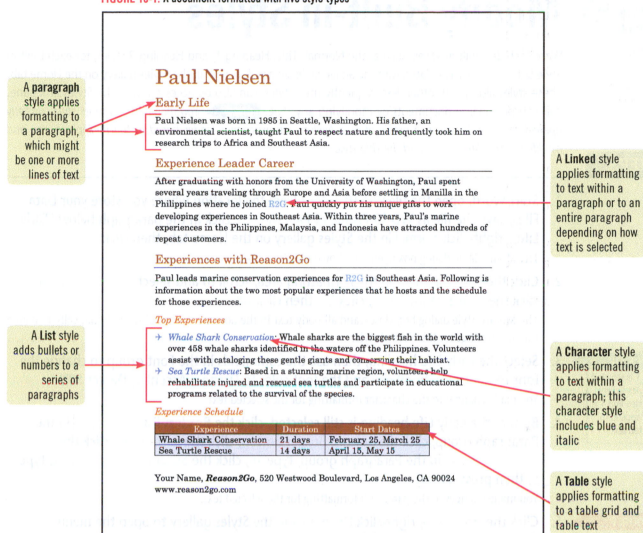

A **paragraph** style applies formatting to a paragraph, which might be one or more lines of text

A **List** style adds bullets or numbers to a series of paragraphs

A **Linked** style applies formatting to text within a paragraph or to an entire paragraph depending on how text is selected

A **Character** style applies formatting to text within a paragraph; this character style includes blue and italic

A **Table** style applies formatting to a table grid and table text

Paul Nielsen

Early Life

Paul Nielsen was born in 1985 in Seattle, Washington. His father, an environmental scientist, taught Paul to respect nature and frequently took him on research trips to Africa and Southeast Asia.

Experience Leader Career

After graduating with honors from the University of Washington, Paul spent several years traveling through Europe and Asia before settling in Manilla in the Philippines where he joined R2G. Paul quickly put his unique gifts to work developing experiences in Southeast Asia. Within three years, Paul's marine experiences in the Philippines, Malaysia, and Indonesia have attracted hundreds of repeat customers.

Experiences with Reason2Go

Paul leads marine conservation experiences for R2G in Southeast Asia. Following is information about the two most popular experiences that he hosts and the schedule for those experiences.

Top Experiences

→ *Whale Shark Conservation*: Whale sharks are the biggest fish in the world with over 458 whale sharks identified in the waters off the Philippines. Volunteers assist with cataloging these gentle giants and conserving their habitat.
→ *Sea Turtle Rescue*: Based in a stunning marine region, volunteers help rehabilitate injured and rescued sea turtles and participate in educational programs related to the survival of the species.

Experience Schedule

Experience	Duration	Start Dates
Whale Shark Conservation	21 days	February 25, March 25
Sea Turtle Rescue	14 days	April 15, May 15

Your Name, **Reason2Go**, 520 Westwood Boulevard, Los Angeles, CA 90024
www.reason2go.com

Understanding Themes, Style Sets, and the Normal style

Style Sets are not the same as themes, but they work with themes to provide you with an almost unlimited range of formatting options. A theme is a set of unified design elements including theme colors, theme fonts for body text and headings, and theme effects for graphics. When you apply a theme to a document, you can further modify the appearance of the text, colors, and graphics in the document by applying one of the 17 built-in Style Sets. You can then modify the appearance even further by changing the settings of the styles associated with the Style Set.

Text that you type into a blank document is formatted with the Normal style from the default Style Set associated with the Office 2016 theme until you specify otherwise. By default, text formatted with the Normal style uses the 11-point Calibri font and is left-aligned, with a line spacing of 1.08 within a paragraph and 8 pt After Paragraph spacing. When you select a new Style Set, the styles associated with that Style Set are applied to the document.

Modify Built-in Styles

Learning Outcomes
• Modify a style
• Update a style

Word includes built-in styles, such as the Normal, Title, Heading 1, and Heading 2 styles, for each built-in Style Set. The styles associated with the active Style Set are displayed in the Styles gallery on the Home tab. These styles along with other, less frequently used styles, can also be accessed from the Styles task pane. You can personalize documents by modifying any style. **CASE** ▶ *You modify the Normal style currently applied to all body text in a profile of Paul Nielsen, an experience leader based in the Philippines. You also modify the Heading 1 style and the Title style.*

STEPS

1. **Start Word, open the file WD 10-1.docx from the location where you store your Data Files, save the file as WD 10-Profile of Paul Nielsen, click in the paragraph below "Early Life," right-click Normal in the Styles gallery on the Home tab, then click Modify**
   The Modify Style dialog box opens, as shown in **FIGURE 10-2**.

2. **Click the Font list arrow in the Formatting area, scroll to and select Century Schoolbook, click the Font Size list arrow, click 12, then click OK**
   The Modify Style dialog box closes, and all body text in the document is modified automatically to match the new settings for the Normal style.

3. **Select the Early Life heading, then use the commands in the Font group to change the font to Century Schoolbook and the font color to Orange, Accent 2, Darker 50%**
   You made changes to the character formatting for the selected text.

4. **Be sure the Early Life heading is still selected, click the Borders list arrow ⊞ ▾ in the Paragraph group, click the Bottom Border button, click the Layout tab, click the Spacing Before text box in the Paragraph group, type 10, click the Spacing After text box, type 6, then press [Enter]**
   You made changes to the paragraph formatting for the selected text.

5. **Click the Home tab, right-click Heading 1 in the Styles gallery to open the menu shown in FIGURE 10-3, then click Update Heading 1 to Match Selection**
   The Heading 1 style is updated to match both the character and the paragraph formatting options you applied to the Early Life heading. All headings in the text that are formatted with the Heading 1 style are updated to match the new Heading 1 style. Notice that the Heading 1 style in the Styles gallery shows a preview of the formatting associated with the Heading 1 style.

6. **Click the launcher ⌃ in the Styles group to open the Styles task pane**
   By default, the **Styles task pane** lists a selection of the styles available in the active Style Set. The Styles task pane also includes options for creating new styles, using the Style Inspector, and managing styles.

7. **Select Paul Nielsen at the top of the page, point to Title in the Styles task pane, click the list arrow that appears, then click Modify**

8. **Change the font to Century Schoolbook, click the Font Color list arrow (currently shows Automatic as the color), select the Orange, Accent 2, Darker 50% color box, then click OK**
   The selected text in the document and the preview of the Title style in the Styles gallery changes to show the new settings.

9. **Save the document**
   You have used three methods to modify the formatting attached to a style. You can modify the style using the Modify Styles dialog box, you can make changes to text associated with a style and then update the style to match the selected text, or you can modify a style from the Styles task pane. You generally use this last method when you need to modify a style that does not appear in the Styles gallery.

FIGURE 10-2: Modify Style dialog box

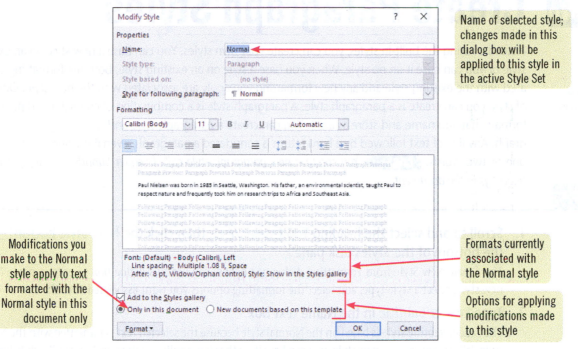

Name of selected style; changes made in this dialog box will be applied to this style in the active Style Set

Modifications you make to the Normal style apply to text formatted with the Normal style in this document only

Formats currently associated with the Normal style

Options for applying modifications made to this style

FIGURE 10-3: Updating the Heading 1 style with new formats

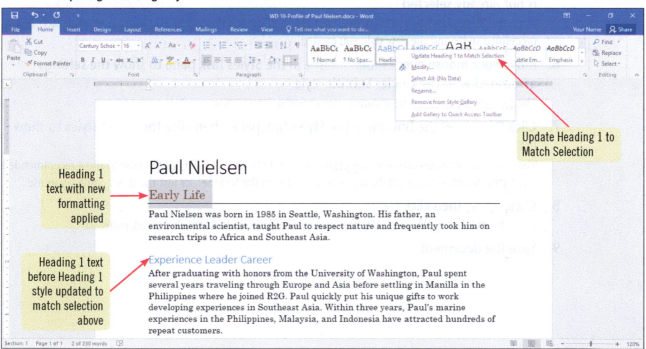

Update Heading 1 to Match Selection

Heading 1 text with new formatting applied

Heading 1 text before Heading 1 style updated to match selection above

Create Paragraph Styles

Learning Outcomes
• Create a paragraph style
• Apply a paragraph style

Instead of using the built-in styles, you can create your own styles. You can base a new style on an existing style or you can base it on no style. When you base a style on an existing style, both the formatting associated with the existing style and any new formatting you apply are associated with the new style. One type of style you can create is a paragraph style. A paragraph style is a combination of character and paragraph formats that you name and store as a set. You can create a paragraph style and then apply it to any paragraph. Any line of text followed by a hard return is considered a paragraph, even if the line consists of only one or two words. **CASE** ▶ *You create a new paragraph style called Leader Subtitle and apply it to two headings in the document.*

STEPS

1. **Scroll to and select the heading Top Experiences, then click the New Style button 🔲 at the bottom of the Styles task pane**

   The Create New Style from Formatting dialog box opens. You use this dialog box to enter a name for the new style, select a style type, and select the formatting options you want associated with the new style.

2. **Type Leader Subtitle in the Name text box**

   The Leader Subtitle style is based on the Normal style because the selected text is formatted with the Normal style. When you create a new style, you can base it on the style applied to the selected text if a style has been applied to that text, another style by selecting a style in the Style based on list box, or no preset style. You want the new style to also include the formatting associated with the Normal style so you leave Normal as the Style based on setting.

3. **Click 12 in the Font Size text box, type 13, click the Italic button, click the Font Color list arrow, click the Orange, Accent 2, Darker 25% color box, then click OK**

4. **Select the heading Experience Schedule (you may need to scroll down), then click Leader Subtitle in the Styles task pane**

   The new Leader Subtitle style is applied to two headings in the document.

5. **Click the Show Preview check box at the bottom of the Styles task pane to select it if it is not already selected**

   With the Show Preview option active, you can quickly see the formatting associated with each of the predefined styles and the new style you created.

6. **Move your mouse over Leader Subtitle in the Styles task pane to show the settings associated with the Leader Subtitle style**

   The Styles task pane and the document are shown in **FIGURE 10-4**.

7. **Click Options at the bottom of the Styles task pane, then click the Select styles to show list arrow**

   The Style Pane Options dialog box appears as shown in **FIGURE 10-5**. You can choose to show recommended styles (the default setting), all the styles associated with the Style Set, or just the styles currently in use.

8. **Click In use, then click OK**

   Only the styles currently applied to the document are displayed in the Styles task pane.

9. **Save the document**

FIGURE 10-4: Formatting associated with Leader Subtitle style

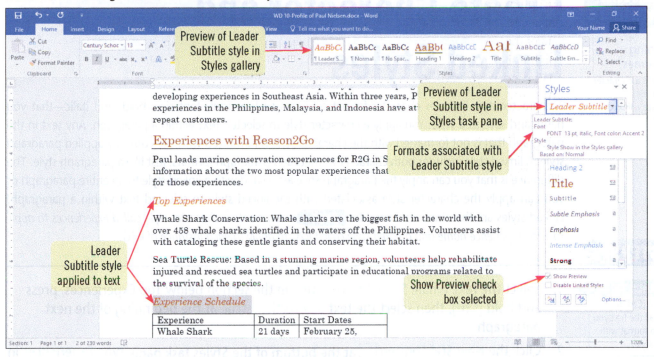

FIGURE 10-5: Style Pane Options dialog box

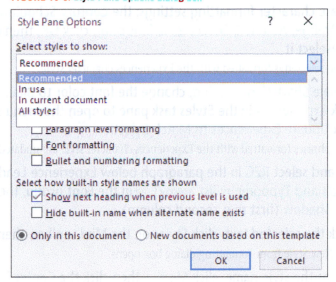

Identifying style formatting

Word includes two ways to quickly determine exactly what styles and formatting are applied to selected text. These methods are useful when you apply a style to text and not all the formatting changes you expect to be made are made. To find out why, use the Style Inspector or the Reveal Formatting task pane. To open the Style Inspector, click the text formatted with the style, then click the Style Inspector button at the bottom of the Styles task pane. The **Style Inspector** lists the styles applied to the selected text and indicates if any extra formats were applied that are not

included in the style. For example, another user could apply formatting such as bold and italic that is not included in the style. You can clear these formats by clicking one of the four buttons along the right side of the Style Inspector or by clicking Clear All to remove all extra formats. If you need to investigate even further, you can click the Reveal Formatting button at the bottom of the Style Inspector to open the Reveal Formatting task pane. The **Reveal Formatting task pane** lists exactly which formats are applied to the character, paragraph, and section of the selected text.

Create Character and Linked Styles

Learning Outcomes
- Create a character style
- Create a linked style

A character style includes character format settings—such as font, font size, bold, and italic—that you name and save as a style. You apply a character style to selected text within a paragraph. Any text in the paragraph that is not formatted with the character style is formatted with the currently applied paragraph style. A linked style includes both character formats and paragraph formats, just like a paragraph style. The difference is that you can apply the paragraph style associated with a linked style to an entire paragraph or you can apply the character style associated with the linked style to selected text within a paragraph. Linked styles are therefore very versatile. **CASE** *You create a character style called Experiences to apply to each Experience name and a linked style called R2G to apply to each instance of R2G.*

STEPS

QUICK TIP
You use [Ctrl] to select all the text you wish to format with a new style.

1. Select the text Whale Shark Conservation in the section below Top Experiences, press and hold [Ctrl], then select the text Sea Turtle Rescue at the beginning of the next paragraph

2. Click the New Style button at the bottom of the Styles task pane, type Experiences in the Name text box, click the Style type list arrow, then click Character

QUICK TIP
You can modify an existing character style in the same way you modify a paragraph style.

3. Select these character formatting settings: the Century Schoolbook font, 12 pt, Italic, and the Orange, Accent 2, Darker 25% font color, click OK, then click away from the text to deselect it

   The text you selected is formatted with the Experiences character style.

4. Select Whale Shark Conservation, change the font color to Blue, Accent 5, Darker 25%, right-click Experiences in the Styles task pane to open the menu shown in FIGURE 10-6, then click Update Experiences to Match Selection

   Both of the phrases formatted with the Experiences character style are updated.

QUICK TIP
Mouse over the options in the Text Effects gallery, then use the ScreenTips to help you make the correct selection.

5. Scroll up and select R2G in the paragraph below Experience Leader Career, click the Text Effects and Typography list arrow in the Font group, then select the Fill – Blue, Accent 1, Shadow (first row, second column)

6. Right-click the selected text, click Styles on the Mini toolbar, then click Create a Style

   The Create New Style from Formatting dialog box opens.

7. Type R2G as the style name, click Modify, then click the Center button

   In the Create New Style from Formatting dialog box, you see that the Linked (paragraph and character) style type is automatically assigned when you create a new style from selected text. The style you created includes character formatting (the text effect format) and paragraph formatting (center alignment).

TROUBLE
Drag the dialog box up as needed until you see the OK button.

8. Click OK, click anywhere in the paragraph under Early Life, then click R2G in the Styles task pane

   The entire paragraph is formatted with the R2G style, as shown in FIGURE 10-7. Both the character formatting and the paragraph formatting associated with the R2G linked style are applied to the paragraph, but only the character formatting associated with the R2G linked style is applied to the R2G text in the next paragraph.

9. Click the Undo button on the Quick Access toolbar, scroll to the paragraph below the Experiences with Reason2Go heading, select R2G in the paragraph, click R2G in the Styles task pane, then save the document

Working with Styles and Templates

FIGURE 10-6: Updating the Experiences character style

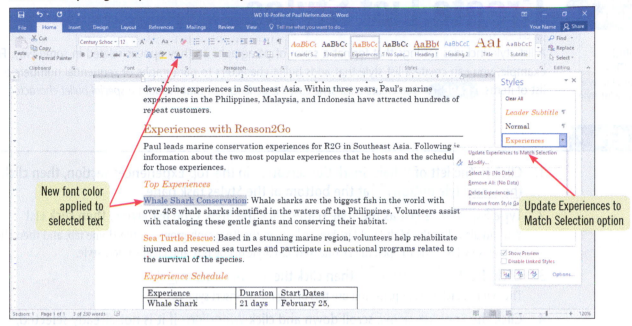

New font color applied to selected text

Update Experiences to Match Selection option

FIGURE 10-7: R2G linked style applied to a paragraph and to selected text

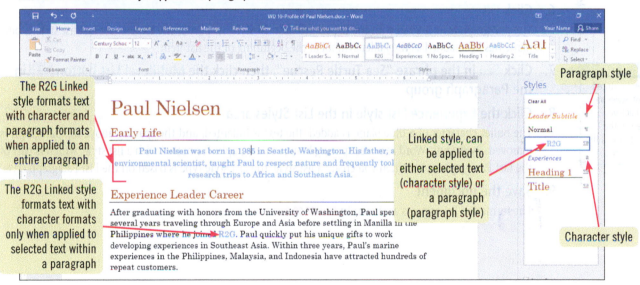

The R2G Linked style formats text with character and paragraph formats when applied to an entire paragraph

The R2G Linked style formats text with character formats only when applied to selected text within a paragraph

Linked style, can be applied to either selected text (character style) or a paragraph (paragraph style)

Paragraph style

Character style

Identifying paragraph, character, and linked styles

Style types are identified in the Styles task pane by different symbols. Each paragraph style is marked with a paragraph symbol: ¶. You can apply a paragraph style just by clicking in any paragraph or line of text and selecting the style. The most commonly used predefined paragraph style is the Normal style. Each character style is marked with a character symbol: a. You apply a character style by clicking anywhere in a word or by selecting a phrase within a paragraph.

Built-in character styles include Emphasis, Strong, and Book Title. Each linked style is marked with both a paragraph symbol and a character symbol: ¶a. You can click anywhere in a paragraph to apply the linked style to the entire paragraph, or you can select text and then apply only the character formats associated with the linked style to the selected text. Predefined linked styles include Heading 1, Title, and Quote.

Create List Styles

Learning Outcomes
• Create a list style
• Modify a list style

A list style includes settings that format a series of paragraphs so they appear related in some way. For example, you can create a list style that adds bullet characters to paragraphs or sequential numbers to a list of items. **CASE** ▶ *You create a list style called Experience List that includes a special bullet character.*

STEPS

1. **Click to the left of Whale Shark Conservation in the Top Experiences section, then click the New Style button** 🔳 **at the bottom of the Styles task pane**

2. **Type Experience List as the style name, click the Style type list arrow, then click List**
   You can also click the Multilevel List button 🔳 in the Paragraph group on the Home tab, and then click Define New List Style to open the Define New List Style dialog box and create a new style.

3. **Click the Bullets button** 🔳**, then click the Symbol button** 🔳
   The symbol dialog box opens. You use this dialog box to insert symbols.

4. **Click the Font list arrow, scroll down and click Wingdings if it is not already selected, double-click the number in the Character code text box, type 81, then click OK**

5. **Click the Font Color list arrow, then click Blue, Accent 5**
   The Create New Style from Formatting dialog box appears as shown in **FIGURE 10-8**.

6. **Click OK**
   The paragraph is formatted with the Experience List list style. As part of the Experience List list style, a blue plane has been added as the bullet symbol at the beginning of the list item.

7. **Click Sea in the phrase "Sea Turtle Rescue", then click the Multilevel List button** 🔳 **in the Paragraph group**

8. **Click the Experience List style in the List Styles area**
   The bullet character of a blue plane is added, the text is indented, and the spacing above the paragraph is removed. By default, Word removes spacing between paragraphs formatted with a list style, which is part of the List Paragraph style. When you create a list style, the List style type is based on the List Paragraph style.

9. **Save the document**
   The formatted list appears as shown in **FIGURE 10-9**.

FIGURE 10-8: List style formatting selections

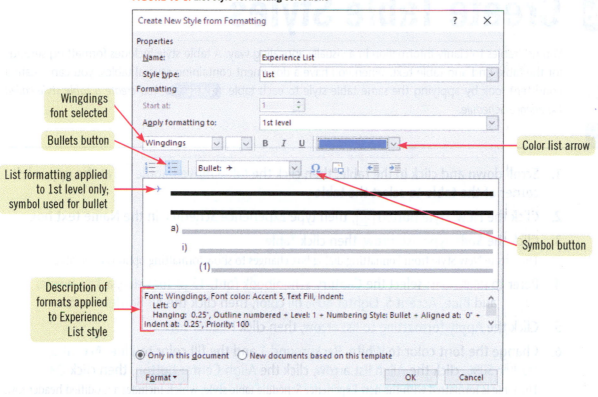

Wingdings font selected

Bullets button

List formatting applied to 1st level only; symbol used for bullet

Description of formats applied to Experience List style

Color list arrow

Symbol button

FIGURE 10-9: Paragraphs formatted with the Experience List style

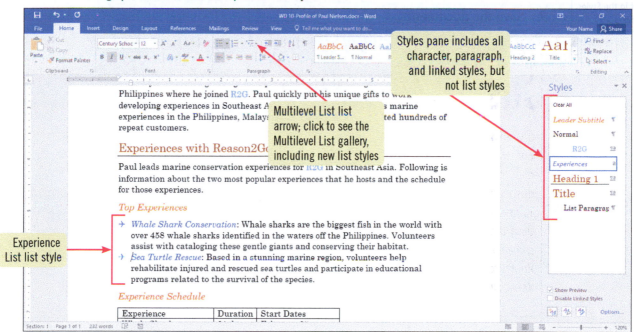

Styles pane includes all character, paragraph, and linked styles, but not list styles

Multilevel List list arrow; click to see the Multilevel List gallery, including new list styles

Experience List list style

Create Table Styles

You use tables to clarify information in a visually appealing way. A table style includes formatting settings for the table grid and table text. When you have a document containing several tables, you can create a consistent look by applying the same table style to each table. **CASE** ▶ *You create a table style called Experience Schedule.*

STEPS

1. **Scroll down and click in the table, then click the table move handle ⊞ at the upper-left corner of the table to select the table**

2. **Click the New Style button 🔲, then type Experience Schedule in the Name text box**

3. **Click the Style type list arrow, then click Table**
   The Create New Style from Formatting dialog box changes to show formatting options for a table.

4. **Refer to FIGURE 10-10: select the Century Schoolbook font, 12 pt font size, a 1 pt border width, and Blue, Accent 5, Lighter 80% fill color, then click the All Borders button**

5. **Click the Apply formatting to list arrow, then click Header row**

6. **Change the font color to White, Background 1 and the fill color to Blue, Accent 5, Darker 50%, click the Align list arrow, click the Align Center button, then click OK**
   The table is formatted with the new Experience Schedule table style, which includes a modified header row.

7. **Double-click one of the column dividers in the table so all text in each row fits on one line**

8. **Click the Table Tools Design tab, right-click the currently selected table style (far-left selection), click Modify Table Style, click the Apply formatting to list arrow, click Header row, change the fill color to Orange, Accent 2, Darker 50%, then click OK**
   The table is modified, as shown in FIGURE 10-11.

9. **Save the document**

FIGURE 10-10: Table style formatting selections

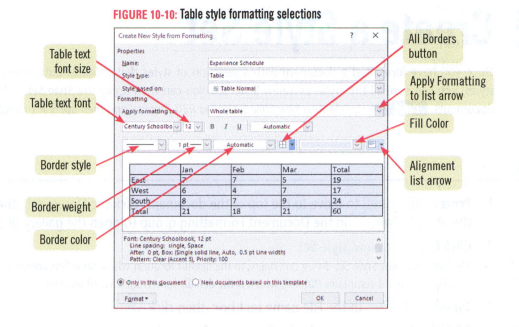

Table text font size

Table text font

Border style

Border weight

Border color

All Borders button

Apply Formatting to list arrow

Fill Color

Alignment list arrow

FIGURE 10-11: Experience Schedule table style applied

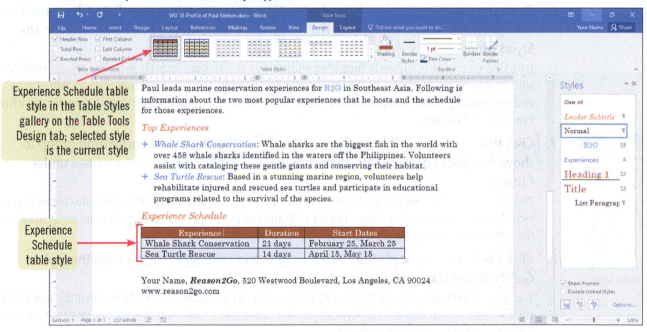

Experience Schedule table style in the Table Styles gallery on the Table Tools Design tab; selected style is the current style

Experience Schedule table style

Create a Style Set

Learning Outcomes
• Create a Style Set
• Apply a color scheme

Once you have formatted a document with a selection of styles that includes both new and existing styles, you can save all the styles as a new Style Set. You can then apply the Style Set to format other documents. **CASE** ▸ *You create a new Style Set called R2G Profiles, and then apply it to another profile.*

STEPS

1. **Press [Ctrl][Home] to move to the top of the document, click the Design tab, then click the More button ⬇ in the Document Formatting group to open the gallery of Style Sets**

2. **Click Save as a New Style Set**

   The Save as a New Style Set dialog box opens to the default location where Style Sets are saved. The Save as type is set to Word Templates (*.dotx), which is the default format for a Word template.

3. **Type R2G Profiles in the File name text box, then click Save**

TROUBLE
If there is more than one thumbnail under Custom, then use the ScreenTips to identify the one associated with the R2G Profiles style set.

4. **Click the More button ⬇ in the Document Formatting group again, move your mouse over the Style Set thumbnail that appears under Custom to show the name of the Style Set as shown in FIGURE 10-12, then click a word in the document to close the gallery**

   The R2G Profiles Style Set is now one of the Style Sets you can use to format other documents.

5. **Click the Colors button in the Document Formatting group, move the mouse over the various color schemes to see how the document changes, scroll to and click Red Violet, then save the document**

   The color scheme for the document has changed.

6. **Open the file WD 10-2.docx from the location where you store your Data Files, save it as WD 10-Profile of Jane Chow, click the Home tab, then click the More button ⬇ in the Styles group**

   Jane Chow's profile is currently formatted with one of the 17 built-in Style Sets. The styles associated with that Style Set are shown in the Styles pane. For example, the Title style is applied to "Jane Chow", and the Heading 1 style is applied to the "Early Life", "Experience Leader Career", and "Experiences with Reason2Go" headings.

QUICK TIP
The styles associated with the R2G Profile Style Set are available. You can apply styles from the Style Set to text in a document. The styles appear in the Styles Gallery on the Home tab and in the Styles task pane.

7. **Click the Design tab, click the More button ⬇ in the Document Formatting group to show the gallery of Style Sets, then click the R2G Profiles Style Set thumbnail under Custom**

   The R2G Profiles Style Set is now available in Jane Chow's profile, and all the new styles you created in previous lessons, except the Experience List list style and the Experience Schedule table style, are available in the Styles gallery and the Styles task pane.

8. **Click the Home tab, apply the Leader Subtitle and Experiences styles from the Styles Gallery to the text as shown in FIGURE 10-13**

   You applied styles associated with the R2G Profiles Style Set to document text. Notice that the Red Violet color scheme you applied to Paul Nielsen's profile is not applied. Color schemes are not saved with a Style Set. You must reapply the color scheme.

9. **Click the Design tab, click the Colors button in the Document Formatting group, click Red Violet, then save the document**

   You will learn more about managing styles and applying the R2G style, the Experience List style, and the Experience Schedule style in the next lesson.

FIGURE 10-12: R2G Profiles Style Set

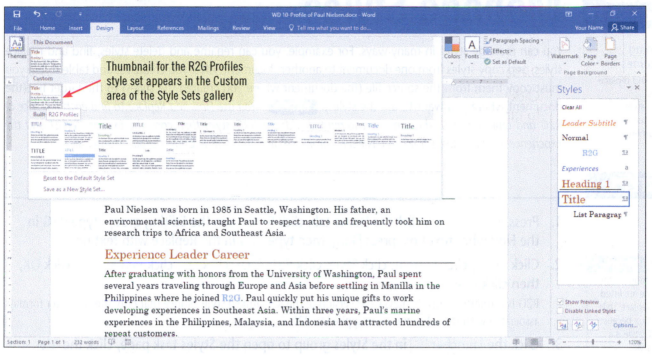

Thumbnail for the R2G Profiles style set appears in the Custom area of the Style Sets gallery

FIGURE 10-13: Applying styles from the R2G Profiles Style Set

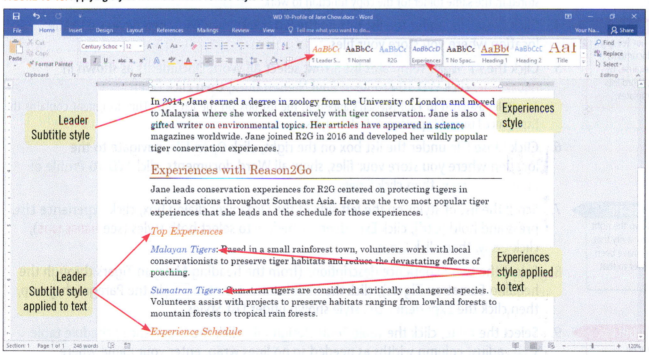

Leader Subtitle style

Experiences style

Leader Subtitle style applied to text

Experiences style applied to text

Manage Styles

Learning Outcomes
• Find and replace styles
• Copy styles between documents

You can manage styles in many ways. For example, you can rename and delete styles, find and replace styles, and copy styles from one document to another document. After you create list and table styles, you must copy them from the source file (the document where you created the styles) to the target file (the document where you want to use the styles). **CASE** ▶ *You use Find and Replace to find each instance of R2G and replace it with the same text formatted with the R2G style, then copy the Experience List and the Experience Schedule styles from Paul Nielsen's profile (source file) to Jane Chow's profile (target file).*

STEPS

1. Press [Ctrl][Home], click the Home tab, click Replace in the Editing group, type R2G in the Find what text box, press [Tab], then type R2G in the Replace with text box

QUICK TIP
Two versions of the R2G style are listed in the Replace Style dialog box because the R2G style is a linked style.

2. Click More, click Format, click Style, click R2G Char, click OK, click Replace All, click OK, then click Close

   R2G is formatted with the R2G Char version of the R2G linked style. Notice that only the character formats associated with the R2G style were applied to R2G.

3. Click the launcher ☞ in the Styles group to open the Styles task pane, click the Manage Styles button ☞ at the bottom of the Styles task pane to open the Manage Styles dialog box, then click Import/Export to open the Organizer dialog box

   You copy styles from the document shown in the left side of the Organizer dialog box (the source file) to a new document that you open in the right side of the Organizer dialog box (the target file). By default, the target file is the Normal template. To copy between files you create, the source and destination files must be stored in the same folder for the copy function to work.

TROUBLE
You do not see any Word documents listed because, by default, Word lists only templates.

4. Click Close File under the list box on the left, click Open File, then navigate to the location where you store your files

5. Click the All Word Templates list arrow, select All Word Documents as shown in FIGURE 10-14, click WD 10-Profile of Paul Nielsen.docx, then click Open

   The styles assigned to Paul Nielsen's appear in the list box on the left side. This document contains the Experience List and Experience Schedule styles.

6. Click Close File under the list box on the right, click Open File, navigate to the location where you store your files, show all Word documents, click WD 10-Profile of Jane Chow.docx, then click Open

QUICK TIP
Scroll down the right list box to verify that the styles have been copied over to that file.

7. Scroll the list of styles on the left side of the Organizer dialog box, click Experience List, press and hold [Ctrl], click Experience Schedule to select both styles (see FIGURE 10-15), click Copy, then click Close

8. Select the two Experience descriptions (from the heading Malayan Tigers through the heading Sumatran Tigers), click the Multilevel List button ☰ in the Paragraph group, then click the Experience List style shown under List Styles

TROUBLE
If your name forces the text to a second line, make adjustments as needed so the contact information is displayed attractively.

9. Select the table, click the Table Tools Design tab, click the Experience Schedule table style, adjust column widths as needed so no lines wrap, enter your name where indicated, then save and close the document

   The file WD 10-Profile of Paul Nielsen is again the active document.

FIGURE 10-14: Selecting All Word Documents as the file type

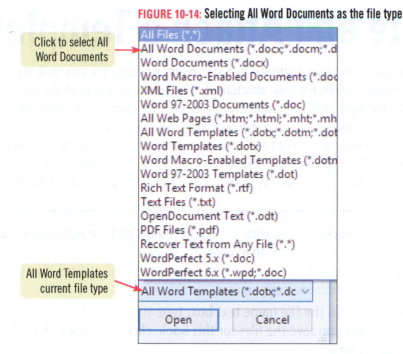

Click to select All Word Documents

All Files (*.*)
All Word Documents (*.docx;*.docm;*.d
Word Documents (*.docx)
Word Macro-Enabled Documents (*.doc
XML Files (*.xml)
Word 97-2003 Documents (*.doc)
All Web Pages (*.htm;*.html;*.mht;*.mh
All Word Templates (*.dotx;*.dotm;*.dot
Word Templates (*.dotx)
Word Macro-Enabled Templates (*.dotn
Word 97-2003 Templates (*.dot)
Rich Text Format (*.rtf)
Text Files (*.txt)
OpenDocument Text (*.odt)
PDF Files (*.pdf)
Recover Text from Any File (*.*)
WordPerfect 5.x (*.doc)
WordPerfect 6.x (*.wpd;*.doc)

All Word Templates current file type

All Word Templates (*.dotx;*.dc ∨

Open   Cancel

FIGURE 10-15: Managing styles using the Organizer dialog box

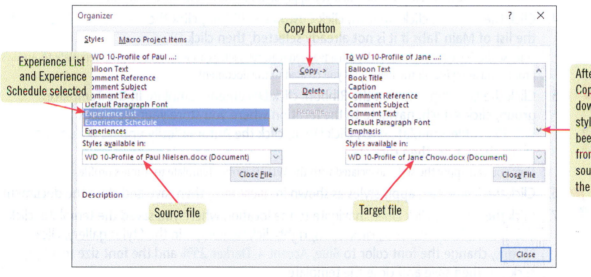

Experience List and Experience Schedule selected

Copy button

Source file

Target file

After clicking Copy, scroll down to verify styles have been copied from the source file to the target file

---

More ways to manage styles

To rename a style, right-click it in the Styles task pane, click Modify, type a new name, then press [Enter]. To delete a style, right-click the style, then click Delete [Style name]. The style is deleted from the Styles task pane, but it is not deleted from your computer. Click the Manage Styles button 🔧 at the bottom of the Styles task pane, select the style to delete, click Delete, then click OK to close the Manage Styles dialog box.

Create and Attach a Template

Learning Outcomes
• Create a template
• Attach a template
• Modify a template

A quick way to use all the styles contained in a document, including list and table styles, is to create a template. A template contains the basic structure of a document, including all the paragraph, character, linked, list, and table styles. You can create a template from an existing document, or you can create a template from scratch. Once you have created a template, you can attach it to a document. The Style Set and all the styles, including the List and Table styles, are then available to format the document to which the template is attached. **CASE** ▶ *You save the Paul Nielsen profile as a template, modify the template, and then attach the template to another leader profile, which you then format using the styles in the attached template.*

STEPS

1. **Click the File tab, click Save As, click This PC in the list of Save As locations, click Browse, click the Save as type list arrow, then click Word Template (*.dotx)**

   When you select Word Template, the save location automatically changes to the Custom Office Templates folder in the My Documents folder on your computer.

2. **Select the filename in the File name text box, type WD 10-Profile Template, navigate to the location where you save the files for this book, click Save, then close the template but do not exit Word**

   The file is saved as WD 10-Profile Template.dotx. The .dotx identifies this file as a template file.

3. **Open the file WD 10-3.docx from the location where you store your Data Files, save the file as WD 10-Profile of Annie Jonson, click the Design tab, then change the color scheme to Red Violet**

   You will see the new color scheme when you apply styles to the text in the document.

4. **Click the File tab, click Options, click Customize Ribbon, click the Developer check box in the list of Main Tabs if it is not already selected, then click OK**

   You use the Developer tab to work with advanced features such as attaching the Profile Template to Annie's profile and applying all the new styles you created to the document.

5. **Click the Developer tab on the Ribbon, click Document Template in the Templates group, click Attach, navigate to the location where you store your files, click WD 10-Profile Template.dotx, click Open, click the Automatically update document styles check box, then click OK**

   Now you can apply the styles associated with the WD 10-Profile Template to Annie's profile.

6. **Click the Home tab, apply styles as shown in FIGURE 10-16, then save and close the document**

7. **Click the File tab, click Open, navigate to the location where you saved the template, click WD-Profile Template.dotx, click Open, right-click Heading 1 in the Styles gallery, click Modify, change the font color to Blue, Accent 4, Darker 25% and the font size to 18 pt, click OK, then save and close the template**

8. **Open WD 10-Profile of Annie Jonson, verify that the font color of the Heading 1 text is now blue and 18 pt, add your name where indicated, then save and close the document**

   The heading style updates automatically because the document is attached to the WD 10-Profile Template that you just modified.

9. **Create a new blank document, click the Design tab, click the More button in the ▾ Document Formatting group, right-click the thumbnail under Custom, click Delete, click Yes, click the File tab, click Options, click Customize Ribbon, click the Developer check box to deselect it, click OK, exit Word, then submit all your files to your instructor**

   You delete the R2G Profiles Style Set from the list of Style Sets so only the default Style Sets appear for the next user of your computer system.

FIGURE 10-16: Annie Jonson's profile formatted with styles

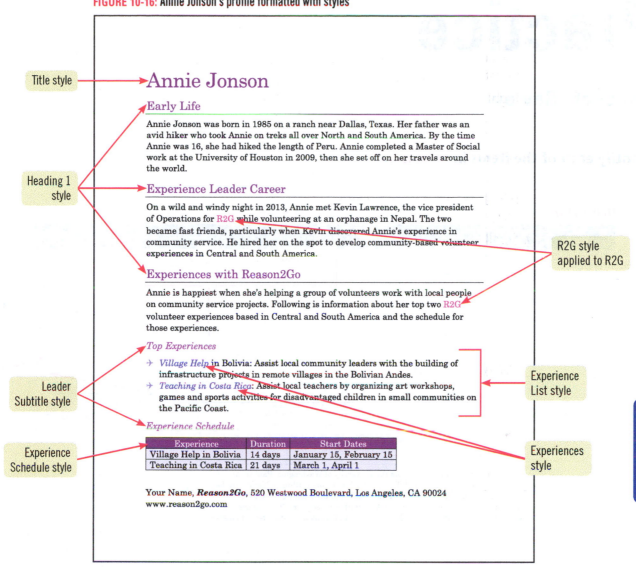

Using Find and Replace to Format Text

You work in the Find and Replace dialog box to replace text formatted with one set of character formats such as bold and italic and replace it with the same or different text formatted with different formatting. Click More, enter the text to find, click Format and specify the formats attached to the text (for example, Font, Bold), click the Replace tab, enter the text to replace and click Format to specify the new formats, then click Replace All.

Practice

Concepts Review

Identify each of the items in FIGURE 10-17.

FIGURE 10-17

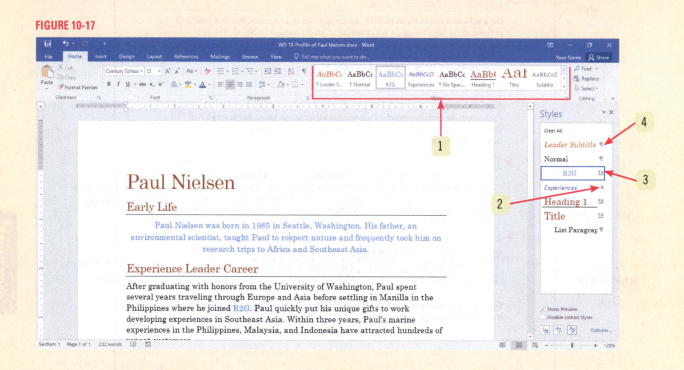

Match each term with the statement that best describes it.

5. **Template**
6. **Organizer dialog box**
7. **Style set**
8. **Character style**
9. **Style**

a. Character formats that you name and store as a set

b. A file that contains the basic structure of a document in addition to selected styles; can be custom made

c. A collection of character, paragraph, and linked styles that is named and available to all documents

d. Used to copy styles from a source document to a target document

e. A collection of saved formats that is used to provide consistent formatting to related items, such as all Heading 1 text

Select the best answer from the list of choices.

10. **What is available in the Style Set gallery?**
    a. Themes associated with the current Style Set
    b. The Developer tab
    c. Styles associated with the current style set
    d. Colors associated with the current Style Set

11. **How do you modify a style?**
    a. Right-click the style in the Styles gallery, then click Modify.
    b. Right-click the style in the Styles gallery, then click Revise.
    c. Double-click the style in the Styles task pane.
    d. Click the style in the Styles task pane, then click New Style.

12. **Which of the following definitions best describes a paragraph style?**
    a. Format settings applied only to selected text within a paragraph
    b. Format settings applied to a table grid
    c. Format settings applied to all text in a paragraph
    d. Format settings applied to the structure of a document

13. **Which of the following style types is not saved with a Style Set?**
    a. Paragraph style
    b. List style
    c. Linked style
    d. Character style

14. **Which dialog box do you use to copy styles from one document to another?**
    a. Reveal Formatting dialog box
    b. Styles dialog box
    c. Organizer dialog box
    d. Modify Styles dialog box

15. **What is the filename extension for a template?**
    a. .dotx
    b. .rtf
    c. .dotc
    d. .dotm

16. **Which tab do you use to attach a template to a document?**
    a. Insert
    b. References
    c. Page
    d. Developer

Skills Review

1. **Modify built-in styles.**
    a. Start Word, open the file WD 10-4.docx from the location where you store your Data Files, save it as **WD 10-Jigsaw Puzzles_Shaped**, then open the Styles task pane.
    b. Modify the Normal style by changing the font to Times New Roman and the font size to 12 pt.
    c. Select the Animal Jigsaw Puzzles heading, then change the font to Bookman Old Style, the font size to 18 pt, and the font color to Green, Accent 6, Darker 50%.
    d. Add a border line below the text.
    e. From the Layout tab, change the Before spacing to 6 pt and the After spacing to 6 pt.
    f. Update the Heading 1 style so that it uses the new formats.
    g. Modify the Title style by changing the font to Bookman Old Style and the color to Green, Accent 6, Darker 50%, then save the document.

2. **Create paragraph styles.**
    a. Scroll to and select the heading "Marketing Plan," then create a new paragraph style called **Operations** that uses the Bookman Old Style font, 14 pt, and italic, and changes the font color to Gold, Accent 4, Darker 25%.
    b. Apply the Operations style to "Summary of New Products."
    c. From the Styles task pane, show only the styles currently in use in the document and make sure the Show Preview check box is selected.
    d. Save the document.

Skills Review (continued)

3. Create character and linked styles.

a. Select "Moose" under Animal Jigsaw Puzzles, then create a new character style named **Jigsaw Puzzle Theme** that uses the Bookman Old Style font, 12 pt, Italic, and the Green, Accent 6, Darker 25% font color.

b. Apply the Jigsaw Puzzle Theme style to "Orca," "Canada," and "France."

c. Select "Puzzle Charm" in the first paragraph, apply the Fill - Gold, Accent 4, Soft Bevel text effect, open the Create New Style from Formatting dialog box, name the style **Company**, and select the Linked style type, then select the option to right-align the paragraph.

d. Apply the Company style to the Moose paragraph, undo the application, then apply the Company style just to the text "Puzzle Charm" in the paragraph above the table.

e. Save the document.

4. Create list styles.

a. Click to the left of "Moose" under Animal Jigsaw Puzzles, then define a new list style called **Jigsaw Puzzle List**. (*Hint:* Click the Multilevel List button in the Paragraph group on the Home tab, then click Define New List Style.)

b. Change the list style to Bullet, open the Symbol dialog box, verify the Wingdings character set is active, type **216** in the Character code text box, then change the symbol color to Green, Accent 6, Darker 50%.

c. Apply the Jigsaw Puzzle List style to each paragraph that describes a jigsaw puzzle: Orca, Canada, and France. (*Hint:* You access the Jigsaw Puzzle List style by clicking the Multilevel List button.)

d. Save the document.

5. Create a table styles.

a. Select the table at the bottom of the document, then create a new table style called **Jigsaw Puzzle Table**.

b. Select Gold, Accent 4, Lighter 80% for the fill color, change the border style to 1/2 pt, verify the border color is set to Automatic, then apply All Borders to the table.

c. Format the header row with bold, the White font color, the Gold, Accent 4, Darker 50% fill color, and Center alignment, then close the Create New Style from Formatting dialog box to apply the new table style to your table.

d. From the Table Tools Design tab, modify the style by changing the fill color for the Header row to Green, Accent 6, Darker 50%, then save the document.

6. Create a Style Set.

a. From the Design tab, save the current Style Set as **Puzzles**, then view the Puzzles Style Set in the Custom section of the Style Sets gallery.

b. Change the color scheme to Green, then save the document.

c. Open the file WD 10-5.docx from the location where you store your Data Files, then save it as **WD 10-Jigsaw Puzzles_3D**.

d. Apply the Puzzles Style Set to the document, then apply the Green color scheme.

e. Apply the Jigsaw Puzzle Theme style to the four jigsaw titles (e.g., Tulips, Palm Trees, and so on).

f. Apply the Operations style to "Marketing Plan," and "Summary of New Products," then save the document.

7. Manage styles.

a. Position the insertion point at the beginning of the document, open the Replace dialog box, enter **Puzzle Charm** in the Find what text box, then enter **Puzzle Charm** in the Replace with text box.

b. Open the More options area, select the Style option on the Format menu, select the Company Char style, then replace both instances of Puzzle Charm with Puzzle Charm formatted with the Company Char style. (*Hint:* If formatting has been previously assigned to either the Find or Replace text, remove the formatting.)

c. Open the Manage Styles dialog box from the Styles task pane, then click Import/Export to open the Organizer dialog box.

d. Close the file in the left pane of the Organizer dialog box, then open the file WD 10-Jigsaw Puzzles_Shaped.docx. Remember to navigate to the location where you save files and to change the Files of type to Word documents.

e. Close the file in the right pane of the Organizer dialog box, then open the file WD 10-Jigsaw Puzzles_3D.docx.

Skills Review (continued)

f. Copy the Jigsaw Puzzle List and Jigsaw Puzzle Table styles from the WD 10-Jigsaw Puzzles_Shaped document to the WD 10-Jigsaw Puzzles_3D document, then close the Organizer dialog box and return to the document.

g. In the file WD 10-Jigsaw Puzzles_3D.docx, apply the Jigsaw Puzzle List style to each of the four jigsaw puzzle descriptions.

h. Select the table, use the Table Tools Design tab to apply the Jigsaw Puzzle Table style to the table, type your name where indicated at the end of the document, save the document, then close it.

8. Create and attach a template.

a. Save the current document (which should be WD 10-Jigsaw Puzzles_Shaped) as a template called **WD 10-Jigsaw Puzzle Template.dotx** to the location where you save files for this book, then close it.

b. Open the file WD 10-6.docx from the location where your Data Files are located, save the file as **WD 10-Jigsaw Puzzles_Landscape**. (*Hint:* Verify that Word document is selected as the file type.) Then, from the Design tab, select the Green color scheme.

c. Show the Developer tab on the Ribbon, open the Templates and Add-ins dialog box, attach the WD 10-Jigsaw Puzzle Template.dotx template, click the Automatically update document styles check box, then click OK.

d. Apply styles from the Jigsaw Puzzles Style Set that are associated with the WD 10-Jigsaw Puzzle Template so that the WD 10-Jigsaw Puzzle_Landscape document resembles the other documents you have formatted for this Skills Review. (*Hint:* Remember to apply the Title, Jigsaw Puzzle Theme, Operations, Jigsaw Puzzle List, and Jigsaw Puzzle Table styles, and to apply the Company style to all three instances of "Puzzle Charm.")

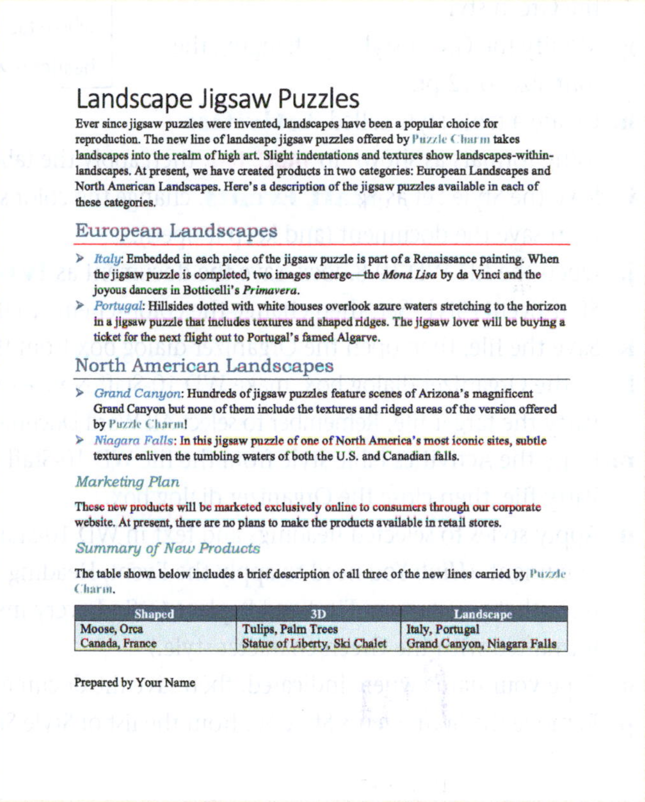

e. Enter your name where indicated, then save and close the document.

f. Open WD 10-Jigsaw Puzzle Template, then modify the Title style so that the font is Century Gothic and the font color is Dark Red in the Standard Colors area. Make sure you update the Title style. Save and close the template.

g. Open WD 10-Jigsaw Puzzles_Landscape, verify that the Title style is updated, compare the document to **FIGURE 10-18**, then close the document.

h. In a new blank document in Word, from the Design tab, delete the Jigsaw Puzzles Style Set, then remove the Developer tab from the Ribbon and exit Word.

i. Submit your files to your instructor.

FIGURE 10-18

Independent Challenge 1

You are the office manager of Green Times, a company that creates educational materials for courses and workshops in environmental studies. The annual company fitness day is coming soon, and you need to inform the employees about the date and time. You have already typed the text of the staff notice and included some formatting. Now you need to modify some of the styles, create new styles, create a new Style Set and copy a style to a new document, and then use the Style Set to format another staff notice about a different event.

Independent Challenge 1 (continued)

a. Start Word, open the file WD 10-7.docx from the location where you store your Data Files, then save it as **WD 10-Staff Notice of Picnic**.

b. Modify and update styles as shown in TABLE 10-1.

TABLE 10-1

style name	changes
Title	Arial Black font; 22-pt font size; Blue, Accent 5, Darker 50%
Heading 1	Arial Black font; 14-pt font size; Blue, Accent 5, Darker 25%

c. Apply the Heading 1 style to the three headings shown in ALL CAPS in the document.

d. Create a new paragraph style called **Event** that uses the Arial font, 20-pt font size, italic, and Blue, Accent 5, Darker 25%, then apply it to "Company Picnic."

e. Create a new character style called **Green** that uses the Arial font, 14-pt font size, italic, and Green, Accent 6, Darker 25%.

f. Find every instance of "Green Times" and replace it with Green Times formatted with the Green style.

TABLE 10-2

table area	changes
whole table	Fill - Green, Accent 6, Lighter 80%; all borders; 1/2 pt border lines
header row	Fill - Green, Accent 6, Darker 50%; White font color and bold

g. Modify the Green style by changing the font size to 12 pt.

h. Create a table style called **Activities** using formats as shown in TABLE 10-2, then apply the table style to the table in the document.

i. Save the Style Set as **Staff Events**, change the color scheme to Blue Green, type your name where indicated, then save the document (and keep it open).

j. Open the file WD 10-8.docx, save the document as **WD 10-Staff Notice of Holiday Party**, apply the Staff Events Style Set, then change the color scheme to Blue Green.

k. Save the file, then open the Organizer dialog box from the Manage Styles dialog box. (*Hint:* Click Import/Export.)

l. In the Organizer dialog box, make WD 10-Staff Notice of Picnic the source file and WD 10-Staff Notice of Holiday Party the target file. Remember to select All Word Documents as the file type when opening the files.

m. Copy the Activities table style from the file WD 10-Staff Notice of Picnic file to the WD 10-Staff Notice of Holiday Party file, then close the Organizer dialog box.

n. Apply styles to selected headings and text in WD 10-Staff Notice of Holiday Party to match the Staff Notice of Picnic document. (*Hint:* You need to apply the Event, Heading 1, and Green styles, as well as the Activities table style. Note that you can use Find and Replace to find every instance of "Green Times" and replace it with Green Times formatted with the Green character style.)

o. Type your name where indicated, then save the document.

p. Remove the Staff Events Style Set from the list of Style Sets, then submit the files to your instructor.

Independent Challenge 2

As the owner of the Pacific Sands Bistro, a vegetarian café in Carmel, California, you need to create two menus—one for spring and one for fall. You have already created unformatted versions of both the spring menu and the fall menu. Now you need to format text in the spring menu with styles, save the styles in a new Style Set called Menus, then use the Menus Style Set to format text in the fall version of the menu. You also need to work in the Organizer dialog box to copy the list and table styles you created for the spring menu to the fall version of the menu.

a. Start Word, open the file WD 10-9.docx from the location where you store your Data Files, then save it as **WD 10-Pacific Sands Bistro Spring Menu**. Apply the Slipstream color scheme.

Working with Styles and Templates

Independent Challenge 2 (continued)

b. Select the title (Pacific Sands Bistro Spring Menu), apply these formats: Berlin Sans FB, 18 pt, a font color of Green, Accent 3, Darker 50%, and Center alignment, then create a new linked style called **Menu Title** based on these formats. (*Hint:* Right-click the formatted text, click the Styles button on the Mini toolbar, click Create a Style, type Menu Title, then click OK. You can verify that the style is a linked style by clicking Modify in the Create New Style from Formatting dialog box.)

c. Select Appetizers, apply the formats Berlin Sans FB, 14 pt, italic, a font color of Green, Accent 3, Darker 25%, then create a new linked style from the selection called **Menu Category**.

d. Apply the Menu Category style to each of the remaining main headings: Soups and Salads, Entrees, Desserts, and Opening Times.

e. Click to the left of Brie cheese (the first appetizer), then create a new list style called **Bistro Menu Item** that includes a bullet character from Wingdings symbol 123 (a stylized flower) that is colored Green, Accent 3, Darker 50%.

f. Click the Multilevel List button, right-click the new Bistro Menu Item style in the List Styles area, click Modify, then in the Modify Style dialog box, click Format (bottom left), click Numbering, click More (bottom left), click the Add tab stop at: check box, select the contents of the text box, type **5.5**, click OK, then click OK.

g. Apply the Bistro Menu Item list style (remember to click the Multilevel List button) to all the menu items in each category.

h. Save the styles in a Style Set called **Menus**.

i. Click anywhere in the table, then create a new table style called **Bistro Times** that fills the table cells with Green, Accent 3, Lighter 80% and includes border lines, and then format the header row with the corresponding dark green fill color and the white font color, bold, and centering.

j. Type your name where indicated at the bottom of the document, then save the document and keep it open.

k. Open the file WD 10-10.docx, save it as **WD 10-Pacific Sands Bistro Fall Menu**, then apply the Menus Style Set.

l. Format the appropriate headings with the Menu Title and Menu Category styles. Note that the Bistro Menu Items list style and the Bistro Times table styles are not saved with the Menus Style Set. You copy them separately in a later step.

m. Change the color scheme to the Red Orange color scheme.

n. Save the file, then open the Organizer dialog box from the Manage Styles dialog box.

o. In the Organizer dialog box, make WD 10-Pacific Sands Bistro Spring Menu the source file and WD 10-Pacific Sands Bistro Fall Menu the target file. Remember to select All Word Documents as the file type when opening the files.

p. Copy the Bistro Menu Item list style and the Bistro Times table style from the file WD 10-Pacific Sands Bistro Spring Menu file to the WD 10-Pacific Sands Bistro Fall Menu file, then close the Organizer dialog box.

q. In the Fall menu document, apply the Bistro Menu Item list style to the first appetizer (Old cheddar cheeses).

r. Click the Multilevel List button, right-click the Bistro Menu Item style, click Modify, then change the bullet symbol for the Menu Item style to Wingdings 124 (a dark flower symbol).

s. Apply the updated Bistro Menu Item list style to all the menu items, apply the Bistro Times table style to the table, type your name where indicated, then remove the Menus style from the list of Style Sets.

t. Save the documents, submit all files to your instructor, then close all files.

Independent Challenge 3

As a student in the marketing program at your local community college, you have volunteered to create a design for a class newsletter and another classmate has volunteered to write text for the first newsletter, which is to be distributed in December. First, you create a template for the newsletter, then you apply the template to the document containing the newsletter text.

a. Open the file WD 10-11.docx, then save it as a template called **WD 10-Newsletter Template.dotx** to the location where you save files for this book.

b. Enter text and create styles as shown in **FIGURE 10-19**. (*Hint:* Use the text in bold for the style names.)

FIGURE 10-19

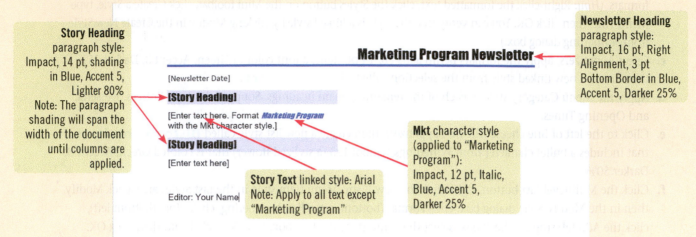

Story Heading paragraph style: Impact, 14 pt, shading in Blue, Accent 5, Lighter 80% Note: The paragraph shading will span the width of the document until columns are applied.

Newsletter Heading paragraph style: Impact, 16 pt, Right Alignment, 3 pt Bottom Border in Blue, Accent 5, Darker 25%

Mkt character style (applied to "Marketing Program"): Impact, 12 pt, Italic, Blue, Accent 5, Darker 25%

Story Text linked style: Arial Note: Apply to all text except "Marketing Program"

Marketing Program Newsletter

[Newsletter Date]

[Story Heading]

[Enter text here. Format *Marketing Program* with the Mkt character style.]

[Story Heading]

[Enter text here]

Editor: Your Name

c. Click to the left of the first [Story Heading], then create two columns from this point forward. (*Hint:* Click the Layout tab, click the Columns button in the Page Setup group, click More Columns, then in the Columns dialog box, click Two in the Presets section, click the Apply to list arrow, select This point forward, then click OK.)

d. Type your name where indicated, then save and close the template.

e. Open the file WD 10-12.docx, save it as a Word document called **WD 10-Newsletter_December**, show the Developer tab on the Ribbon, attach the WD 10-Newsletter Template.dotx to the document, verify that styles will update automatically, then apply styles and formatting as follows: apply the Newsletter Heading style to the newsletter title, the Story Heading style to all four headings, the Story Text style to all paragraphs of text that are not headings, and the Mkt style to Marketing Program (*Hint:* Use the Find Next, not Replace All, Replace feature to replace three instances of Marketing Program in the story text (but do not replace Marketing Program in the Newsletter Heading.)

f. Apply the two-column format starting at the Class Projects heading. (*Note:* You need to apply the two-column format because options related to the structure of a document that are saved with a template are lost when you attach the template to an existing document.)

g. Click at the end of the document (following your name), click the Layout tab, click Breaks, then click Continuous to balance the columns in the newsletter.

h. Save and close the document.

i. Open the file WD 10-Newsletter Template.dotx (*Hint:* Be sure to open the template using the File menu. Do not double-click it.)

j. Modify the Newsletter Heading style so the font size is 20 pt, modify the Mkt character style so the font size is 11 pt and the color is Orange, Accent 2, then save and close the template.

k. Open WD 10-Newsletter_December, verify the changes to the Newsletter Heading and Mtk styles, then close the document.

l. Remove the Developer tab from the Ribbon, then submit all files to your instructor.

Independent Challenge 4: Explore

From Microsoft Word, you can access templates that you can use to create and then customize hundreds of different types of documents from calendars to business proposals to trip itineraries. You use keywords to search for a template, select and create it in Word, and then modify it for your own purposes. You also explore more options in the Styles task pane. (Note: To complete these steps your computer must be connected to the Internet.)

a. Start Word, open a new blank document, click the File tab, click New, click in the Search text box, type **itinerary**, then press [Enter].

b. Select the template Business trip itinerary, click Create, then save the document as **WD 10-Business Trip Itinerary.docx.**

c. Enter your name where indicated above the itinerary table.

d. Select and then delete the Phone number and Travel time columns in the itinerary table, then widen the Comments column so its right edge is even with the border line above the itinerary title.

e. Complete the itinerary table with the information shown in **FIGURE 10-20**.

FIGURE 10-20

Business Trip Itinerary | Your Name

Date	Depart from	Depart time	Destination	Arrival time	Destination address	Comments
June 10	New York, NY	20:00	London, UK	07:00 (June 11)	Hyde Park Hotel	Meet with Jane Harrison for lunch
June 15	London, UK	10:00	Paris, France	14:40	Hotel LeRiche	Train arrives at the Gare du Nord
June 20	Paris, France	9:00	Rome, Italy	11:00	Hotel da Vinci	Fly from Orly airport

f. Open the Styles task pane, then click the Style Inspector button at the bottom of the task pane.

g. Click to the left of Business Trip Itinerary and notice that the Style Inspector lists the Title style as the current paragraph formatting.

h. Click Date and notice that the Style Inspector lists the Normal style with the addition of Bold and the Background 1 color. You can use the Style Inspector to determine exactly what formatting is applied to selected text and then clear the formatting if you wish.

i. Click the Reveal Formatting button at the bottom of the Style Inspector and if necessary, move the Styles task pane so you can see the Reveal Formatting task pane that opens to the right of your screen. The Reveal Formatting task pane lists all the formatting applied to the document.

j. Scroll down the Reveal Formatting task pane to view all the settings. You can click the arrow to the left of any heading to see additional settings.

k. Click TABLE STYLE once under the Table heading to open the Table AutoFormat dialog box. In this dialog box you can quickly select a new built-in table style for the table.

l. Click Grid Table 4 - Accent 2 (orange), then click OK.

m. Close the Reveal Formatting, Styles, and Style Inspector task panes.

n. Select the Orange Red color scheme, save and close the document, exit Word, then submit the file to your instructor.

Visual Workshop

Create a new document, then type the text and create the tables shown in FIGURE 10-21. Save the file as **WD 10-Price List_Flowers Forever**. Do not include any formatting. Select the Green Yellow color scheme, apply the Title style to the title, then modify the Title style so that it appears as shown in FIGURE 10-21. Note that all the colors are variations of the Green Yellow color scheme, Green, Accent 3, and the font style for the title and headings is Comic Sans MS font (or a similar font). Apply the Heading 1 style to the names of the price lists, then modify the Heading 1 style so that it appears as shown in FIGURE 10-21. Create a new Style Set called **Prices**. Create a table style called **Price List** that formats each table as shown in FIGURE 10-21, then modify the column widths as shown. Save the document. Open WD 10-13.docx, save it as **WD 10-Price List_Bundles of Bouquets**, apply the Prices Style Set, copy the Price List table style from WD 10-Price List_Flowers Forever to WD 10-Price List_Bundles of Bouquets, then apply styles and modify column widths so the document resembles the document shown in FIGURE 10-21. Apply the Green Yellow color scheme. Save and close the documents, then submit both files to your instructor.

FIGURE 10-21

Flowers Forever

Gift Basket Price List

Product #	Gift Basket	Price
3300	Thanksgiving Celebration	$65.00
3500	Spring Awakening	$75.00
4000	My Special Valentine	$90.00
4500	New Baby	$60.00

Potted Plants Price List

Product #	Potted Plant	Price
5000	Pink Orchid	$30.00
7780	Mini Peppers	$25.00
7790	Fig Tree	$50.00
7792	Rubber Plant	$40.00
7795	Areca Palm	$30.00

Prepared by Your Name

Working with Styles and Templates

Working with References

CASE ▶ As a special projects assistant at Reason2Go (R2G), you have written an article about a Renaissance artist that will be included in an information package for volunteers on an art restoration experience. The volunteers work with local curators to help restore damaged artwork. You use the AutoCorrect feature to insert text in the article, then modify footnotes and citations, and add figure captions, a bibliography, and a table of figures. You also open a file saved as a Portable Document Format (PDF) file, edit it in Word, and add equations.

Module Objectives

After completing this module, you will be able to:

- Work with AutoCorrect
- Customize footnotes
- Use the Translate feature
- Modify citations and manage sources
- Add and modify captions
- Generate a bibliography and table of figures
- Work with PDF Files in Word
- Work with equations

Files You Will Need

WD 11-1.docx   WD 11-6.docx
WD 11-2.pdf   WD 11-7.docx
WD 11-3.docx   WD 11-8.docx
WD 11-4.pdf   WD 11-9.docx
WD 11-5.docx

Work with AutoCorrect

The AutoCorrect feature is set up to automatically correct most typos and misspelled words. For example, if you type "teh" and press the Spacebar, the AutoCorrect feature inserts "the". The AutoCorrect feature also inserts symbols when you type certain character combinations. For example, if you type (r), the ® symbol appears. You can modify the list of AutoCorrect options, and you can create your own AutoCorrect entries. These entries can be a word, a phrase, or even a paragraph. You set up AutoCorrect to automatically enter the text you specify when you type a certain sequence of characters. For example, you could specify that "San Francisco, California" be entered each time you type "sfc" followed by a space. **CASE** *You need to enter the term "Renaissance" in multiple places in the article. You decide to create an AutoCorrect entry that will insert "Renaissance" each time you type "ren" followed by a space. You also use AutoCorrect to insert symbols, view the AutoFormat settings, and delete an entry from the AutoCorrect list.*

STEPS

1. **Start Word, open the file WD 11-1.docx from the drive and folder where you store your Data Files, save the file as WD 11-Artist Article, click the File tab, click Options, then click Proofing**

   All the options related to how Word corrects and formats text appear in the Proofing section of the Word Options dialog box.

2. **Click AutoCorrect Options**

   The AutoCorrect: English (United States) dialog box opens. By default the AutoCorrect tab is active. In this dialog box, you can specify common tasks such as correcting TWo INitial CApitals, create new AutoCorrect entries, and identify what keystrokes you can use to quickly enter common symbols such as the € or ®.

3. **Scroll through the AutoCorrect list to view the predefined pairs of symbols and words**

   Notice how many symbols you can create with simple keystrokes. The AutoCorrect list is used in all the programs in the Microsoft Office suite, which means that any word you add or delete from the AutoCorrect list in one program is also added or deleted from all other Office programs. On the AutoCorrect tab, you can create a new AutoCorrect entry.

4. **Type ren in the Replace text box, press [Tab], type Renaissance as shown in FIGURE 11-1, click Add, click OK, then click OK**

   When you create an AutoCorrect entry, you need to enter an abbreviation that is not a real word. For example, you should not create an AutoCorrect entry for "Antarctic" from "ant" because every time you type "ant" followed by a space, the word "Antarctic" will appear whether you want it to or not.

5. **Press [Ctrl][F] to open the Navigation pane, type rest of the world, click to the left of world in the document, type ren, then press [Spacebar]**

   The word "Renaissance" is inserted so the phrase is now "Renaissance world."

6. **Press [Ctrl][End] to move to the end of the document, then click in the blank table cell below Cost**

7. **Type (e) to insert the symbol for the Euro currency, type 105.00, then enter €90.00 in the blank cell of the third row and €75.00 in the fourth row as shown in FIGURE 11-2**

8. **Click the File tab, click Options, click Proofing, then click AutoCorrect Options**

   As a courtesy to others who might use the computer you are currently working on, you delete the "ren" Autocorrect entry. If you are the only user of your computer, you can leave the entry so it is available for future use.

9. **Type ren in the Replace text box, click Delete, click Close, click OK, then save the document**

   The "ren" AutoCorrect entry is deleted from Word and all other Office applications.

Working with References

FIGURE 11-1: Creating a new AutoCorrect entry

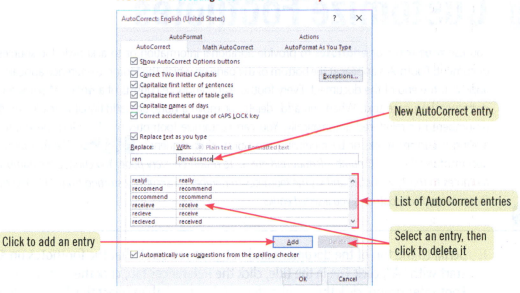

FIGURE 11-1: Creating a new AutoCorrect entry

New AutoCorrect entry

List of AutoCorrect entries

Click to add an entry

Select an entry, then click to delete it

FIGURE 11-2: Completed tour costs

Tour	Description	Cost
Private Tour of the Uffizi	Join a guided tour of the great Uffizi Gallery in Florence.	€105.00
Golden Artisans of Florence	Visit the workshops of three Florentine goldsmiths and marvel at their incredible skill.	€90.00
The Gardens of Florence	Explore the great gardens of Florence, including the famous Boboli Gardens.	€75.00

Symbol added automatically by Autocorrect when (e) is typed

Accessing AutoFormat options in the AutoCorrect dialog box

Two tabs in the AutoCorrect dialog box relate to how Word formats text that you type. From the AutoFormat tab, you can view the list of formats that Word applies automatically to text. The AutoFormat As You Type tab shows some of the same options included in the AutoFormat tab along with some additional options, as shown in **FIGURE 11-3**. Usually, you do not need to change the default options. However, if you do not want an option, you can click the check box next to the option to deselect it. For example, if you decide that you do not want Word to make an ordinal such as 1st into 1st, you can click the Ordinals (1st) with superscript check box to deselect it.

FIGURE 11-3: Options available on the AutoFormat As You Type tab in the AutoCorrect dialog box

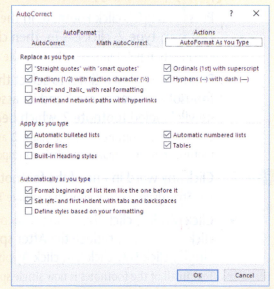

Word 2016

Customize Footnotes

Learning Outcomes
- Change the footnote number format
- Edit a footnote
- Modify the Footnote style

You use **footnotes** or **endnotes** to provide additional information or to acknowledge sources for text in a document. Footnotes appear at the bottom of the page on which the footnote reference appears and endnotes appear at the end of the document. Every footnote and endnote consists of a **note reference mark** and the corresponding note text. When you add, delete, or move a note, any additional notes in the document are renumbered or relettered automatically. You can customize footnotes by changing the number format, by adding a custom mark, or by modifying the numbering sequence. **CASE** *The footnotes in the current document use the A, B, C number format and are set to restart on every page. You change the number format of the footnotes to the 1, 2, 3 style and set the footnotes to number consecutively starting from "1". You then add a new footnote, and edit footnotes you inserted earlier.*

STEPS

1. **Scroll to the top of the document and notice as you scroll that the footnotes on each page start with "A", click The in the title, click the References tab, click the launcher in the Footnotes group, click the Number format list arrow, then select the 1, 2, 3... Number format**

2. **Click the Numbering list arrow, click Continuous, verify Whole document appears next to Apply changes to, compare the Footnote and Endnote dialog box to FIGURE 11-4, click Apply, then scroll to see the renumbered footnotes**

   The footnotes are numbered continuously through the document starting at "1".

3. **Type rigorous training in the Search document text box in the Navigation pane, then click after training in the document**

   The insertion point is positioned where you need to insert a new footnote.

   TROUBLE
   Be sure you are typing in the footnote area.

4. **Click the Insert Footnote button in the Footnotes group, type Artists began training at an early age. They apprenticed with a master, as Cellini did when he was fifteen., then scroll down so you can see all four footnotes on the page**

   FIGURE 11-5 shows the footnote area with the newly inserted footnote (footnote 1).

5. **Click in the line of text immediately above the footnote separator line, click the Next Footnote button in the Footnotes group to move to footnote 5, double-click 5 to move the insertion point to the footnote at the bottom of the page, click after the word Clement, press [Spacebar], type VII, then scroll up and click above the footnote separator**

6. **Press [Ctrl][G], click Footnote in the Go to what list, click in the Enter footnote number text box, type 2, click Go To, then click Close**

   The insertion point moves to the footnote 2 reference mark in the document.

7. **Press [Delete] two times to select the footnote reference mark and then to remove the footnote reference mark and its associated footnote text, then scroll down to see the newly labeled footnote 2, which begins with "Wealthy patrons..."**

   The original footnote reference mark 2 and its corresponding footnote are deleted, and the remaining footnote reference marks and their corresponding footnotes are renumbered starting with 2.

   QUICK TIP
   By default, the Footnote Text style is applied to text in footnotes.

8. **Click any word in one of the footnotes at the bottom of a page, right-click, then click Style**

   The Style dialog box opens with Footnote Text already selected.

9. **Click Modify, click the Format button in the lower left of the Modify Style dialog box, click Paragraph, reduce the After spacing to 6 pt, click the Line spacing list arrow, click Single, click OK, click OK, click Apply, then save the document**

   Text in all of the footnotes is now single spaced with 6 point After spacing.

FIGURE 11-4: Footnote and Endnote dialog box

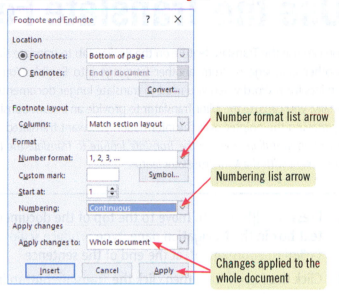

Number format list arrow

Numbering list arrow

Changes applied to the whole document

FIGURE 11-5: Footnote text

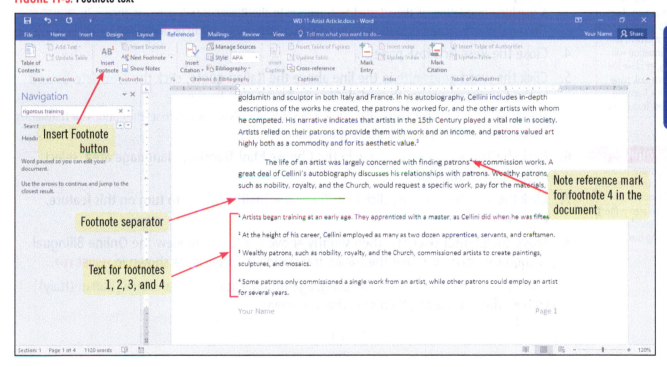

Insert Footnote button

Footnote separator

Text for footnotes 1, 2, 3, and 4

Note reference mark for footnote 4 in the document

Inserting endnotes

Click the Insert Endnote button in the Footnotes group on the References tab to insert a note reference mark for an endnote. When you click the Insert Endnote button, the insertion point moves to the end of your document so that you can enter text for the endnote in the same way you enter text for a footnote. You click above the endnote separator to return to the text of your document. You work in the Footnote and Endnote dialog box to modify options for endnotes.

Use the Translate Feature

You can use the Translate feature on the Review tab to translate single words or short passages of text into another language or from another language into English. You can also access web-based translation services from Word when you need to translate longer documents that require a high degree of accuracy. Finally, you can use the Mini Translator to provide an instant translation of a single word or selected phrase by moving the pointer over the information you want translated. **CASE** ▶ *Some of the text in the article is written in Italian. You use the Translate feature to translate the text from Italian to English, and then you experiment with the Mini Translator feature.*

STEPS

1. Press [Ctrl][Home] to move to the top of the document, click in the Search document text box in the Navigation pane, type produce sculpture, then select the text from Cellini to adornamenti at the end of the sentence

2. Click the Review tab, then click the Translate button in the Language group

   Three translation options are listed.

3. Click Translate Selected Text, click Yes to open the Research task pane, verify that Italian (Italy) appears in the From text box, then if necessary, click the To list arrow and click English (United States)

   A machine translation of the selected text appears in the Research task pane, as shown in **FIGURE 11-6**. The translation is an approximation of the meaning and is not meant to be definitive.

4. Close the Research task pane

5. Click the word goldsmith in the line above the Italian quote, click the Translate button in the Language group, then click Choose Translation Language

   The Translation Language Options dialog box opens. You use this dialog box to set the options for translating the document or the options for the Mini Translator.

6. Click the Translate To: list arrow in the Choose Mini Translator language area, select Italian (Italy), then click OK

7. Click the Translate button, click Mini Translator [Italian (Italy)] to turn on this feature, then click Yes

8. Move the pointer over and then slightly above goldsmith to view the Online Bilingual Dictionary, then note that the Italian translation is "orefice" as shown in **FIGURE 11-7**

9. Click the Translate button in the Language group, click Mini Translator [Italian (Italy)] to turn the feature off, then save the document

FIGURE 11-6: Translating text

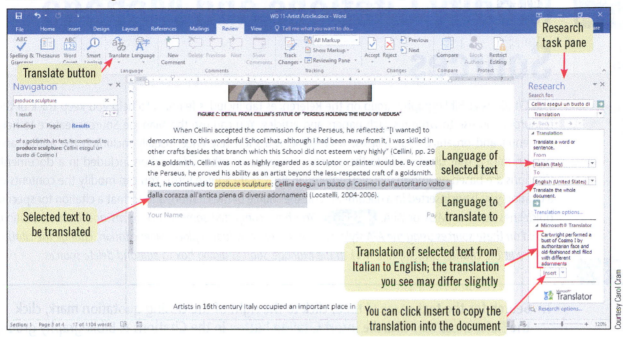

Research task pane

Translate button

Selected text to be translated

Language of selected text

Language to translate to

Translation of selected text from Italian to English; the translation you see may differ slightly

You can click Insert to copy the translation into the document

Courtesy Carol Cram

FIGURE 11-7: Using the Mini Translator

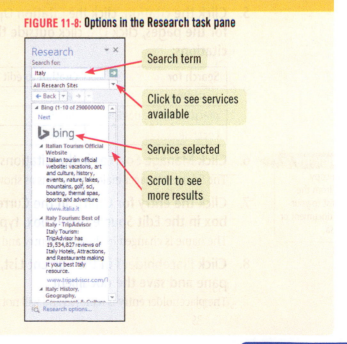

Translation of "goldsmith" into Italian

Online Bilingual Dictionary tools; use ScreenTips to identify tools

Exploring the Research task pane

The Research task pane provides you with a variety of options for finding information. You can open the Research task pane by clicking the Translate button in the Language group on the Review tab, and then clicking Translate Selected Text. Once the Research task pane is open, you can change the settings so you can search for both translations and for information on a specific topic. To find information about a specific topic, you enter keywords into the Search for text box, then click the list arrow for the box under the Search for text box to show the list of services. For example, you can choose to search All Reference Books or All Research Sites, or you can select a specific resource under these broader categories. The services listed under the broader category of All Reference Books include a dictionary, thesauruses, and translation. The services listed under the broader category All Research Sites include Internet research websites. **FIGURE 11-8** shows the results when "Italy" is entered in the Search text box and All Research Sites is selected as the service. You can scroll through the list to find research sites that meet your needs.

FIGURE 11-8: Options in the Research task pane

Search term

Click to see services available

Service selected

Scroll to see more results

Word 2016

Modify Citations and Manage Sources

The Citations & Bibliography group on the References tab includes features to help you keep track of the resources you use to write research papers and articles. You can use the Manage Sources feature to help you enter and organize your sources. A **citation** is a short reference, usually including the author and page number, that gives credit to the source of a quote or other information included in a document. Citations are based on information you entered in the Create Source form. You can modify the contents of a citation you have inserted in a document, edit the source of the citation, and format a citation for specific guidelines such as MLA or APA. **CASE** *You have completed some source forms and inserted citations based on these sources using the APA style. Now you need to include a placeholder citation, change the citation style, edit the citation content, and work in the Manage Sources dialog box to edit and delete sources.*

STEPS

1. Search for the text space of time, click to the right of the closing quotation mark, click the References tab, click the Insert Citation button in the Citations & Bibliography group, click Add New Placeholder, then click OK to add the citation (Placeholder1)

2. Search for Green, click Green in the document, click the field selection handle to select the entire citation (the citation is shaded when it is selected), click the Style list arrow in the Citations & Bibliography group, then click MLA as shown in FIGURE 11-9

   Consistent with the MLA style, the year is removed and the citation includes only the author's name.

3. Click the Citation Options list arrow, click Edit Citation, type 82 in the Pages text box, then click OK

   The citation now shows the author's name and page number reference.

4. Click outside the citation to deselect it, find the text space of time, click (Placeholder1), click the field selection handle to select the entire citation, click the Insert Citation button, then click Cellini, Benvenuto as shown in FIGURE 11-10

5. Click the citation, click the Citation Options list arrow, click Edit Citation, type 324-325 for the pages, click OK, click outside the citation to deselect it, then edit the following citations:

Search for	Citation to edit	Page number to add
apart from	Renfrew	90
precision of the goldsmith	Ogilvie	75
Locatelli	Locatelli	150

6. Click Manage Sources in the Citations & Bibliography group

   The Source Manager dialog box opens as shown in FIGURE 11-11.

7. Click the entry for Ogilvie in the Current List, click Edit, select Ogilvie in the Author text box in the Edit Source dialog box, type O'Connor, click OK, then click Yes if prompted

   The name is changed in the source entry and in the citation in the document.

8. Click Placeholder1 in the Current List, click Delete, click Close, then close the Navigation pane and save the document

   The placeholder entry is removed and will not be included when you generate a bibliography in a later lesson.

FIGURE 11-9: Changing the citation style

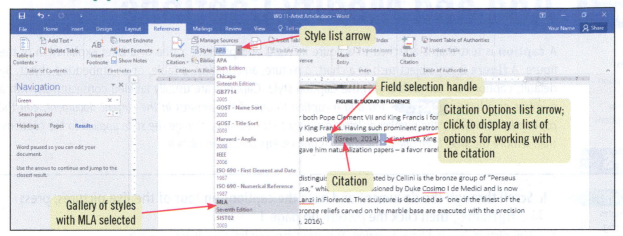

Style list arrow

Field selection handle

Citation Options list arrow; click to display a list of options for working with the citation

Citation

Gallery of styles with MLA selected

FIGURE 11-10: Selecting an existing source

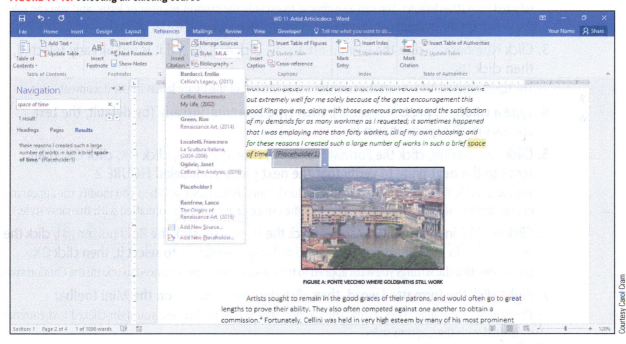

FIGURE A: PONTE VECCHIO WHERE GOLDSMITHS STILL WORK

Courtesy Carol Cram

Word 2016

FIGURE 11-11: Source Manager dialog box

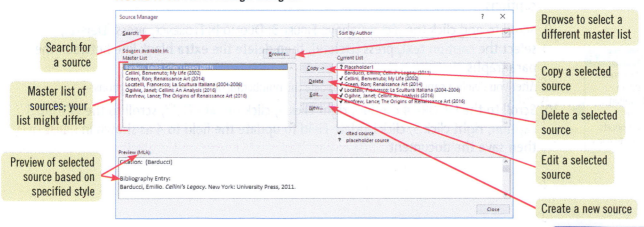

Search for a source

Master list of sources; your list might differ

Preview of selected source based on specified style

Browse to select a different master list

Copy a selected source

Delete a selected source

Edit a selected source

Create a new source

Add and Modify Captions

A **caption** is text that is attached to a figure in Word and provides a title or a brief explanation of the figure. A **figure** is any object such as a chart, a picture, an equation, a table, or an embedded object. By default, captions are formatted with the Caption style. Captions are usually labeled consecutively with a number or a letter. **CASE** ▶ *You add a caption to one of the pictures in the current document, edit the caption label, which is the number or letter assigned to the caption, change the style applied to the captions, then remove the label from one of the captions and update the caption labels.*

STEPS

1. **Scroll through the document and note the captions on four of the five pictures, press [Ctrl][Home], then click the picture on page 1**

   This picture does not have a caption. You insert captions from the References tab.

2. **Click Insert Caption in the Captions group**

   In the Caption dialog box, you can choose to position the caption above the selected item or below the selected item (the default). You can also choose to exclude the caption number or letter, and you can select how you want the captions to be numbered or lettered (for example, FIGURE A).

3. **Click Numbering, click the Format list arrow, click A, B, C,... if it is not already selected, then click OK**

   The figure label FIGURE A uses the same format as the rest of the figure labels in the document.

4. **Type a colon (:), press [Spacebar], then type Beautiful Tuscany (by default, the text appears in all caps as shown in FIGURE 11-12)**

5. **Click Numbering, click the Format list arrow, click 1, 2, 3, ..., click OK, click OK, then scroll to the next page to verify that the next picture is labeled FIGURE 2**

   You can modify the appearance of a figure caption by modifying its style. When you modify the appearance of one caption, all other captions are also modified since each caption is formatted with the same style.

6. **Click WHERE in the FIGURE 2 caption, click the Home tab, click the Bold button [B], click the launcher [⬚] in the Font group, click the Small caps check box to select it, then click OK**

   You've specified the settings you want applied to the Caption style. Now you need to update the Caption style.

7. **Right-click the formatted word, then click the Styles button on the Mini toolbar**

   The gallery of available styles opens. The Caption style is selected because you right-clicked text currently formatted with the Caption style.

8. **Right-click Caption in the gallery, click Update Caption to Match Selection as shown in FIGURE 11-13, then scroll to verify that the updated style is applied to each of the figure captions**

9. **Scroll to and click the picture above FIGURE 3: DUOMO IN FLORENCE, press [Delete], select the caption text, press [Delete], then delete the extra blank line between the paragraphs**

   After you delete a caption, you need to update the numbering of the remaining captions

10. **Scroll to the FIGURE 4 caption, right click 4, click Update Field, scroll to the FIGURE 5 caption, right click 5, click Update Field to update the field to 4 as shown in FIGURE 11-14, then save the document**

FIGURE 11-12: Caption dialog box

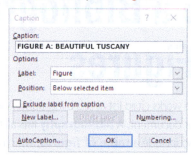

FIGURE 11-13: Caption style selected

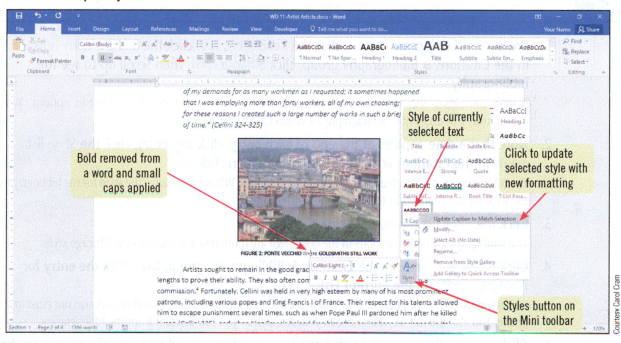

Style of currently selected text

Click to update selected style with new formatting

Bold removed from a word and small caps applied

Styles button on the Mini toolbar

FIGURE 11-14: Caption number updated

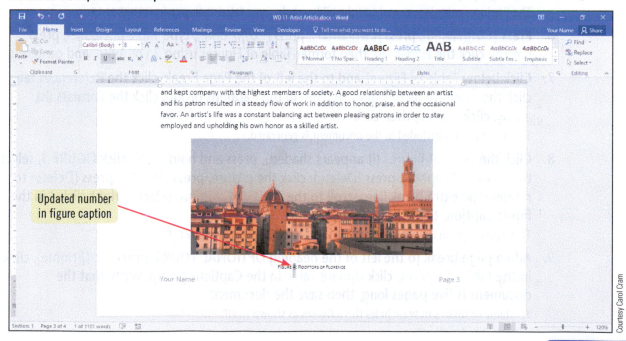

Updated number in figure caption

Word 2016

Courtesy Carol Cram

Learning
Outcomes
• Generate a bibliography
• Update a bibliography
• Generate a table of figures

Generate a Bibliography and Table of Figures

You can document sources in a works cited list or a bibliography. A **works cited** page lists only the works that are included in citations in your document. A **bibliography** lists all the sources you used to gather information for the document. You can also include a **table of figures**, which is a list of all the figures with captions that are used in a document along with the page number on which each figure is found. **CASE** ▶ *You generate a bibliography and a table of figures.*

STEPS

1. **Press [Ctrl][End], press [Enter], click the References tab, click the Bibliography button in the Citations & Bibliography group, click Bibliography, then scroll up to see the bibliography**

   A field containing the bibliography is inserted. When you choose one of the built-in options, Word automatically inserts a title (Bibliography or Works Cited).

2. **Note that a date appears at the end of each entry, click any entry, click the Style list arrow in the Citations & Bibliography group, then click APA**

   The bibliography is formatted according to APA guidelines. When you change the style for the bibliography, the style for the citations in the document is also changed.

3. **Click the Style list arrow, then click Chicago**

   The bibliography and the citations in the document are formatted according to the Chicago style.

4. **Click Manage Sources in the Citations & Bibliography group, then click the entry for Barducci, Emilio in the Current List**

   A check mark does not appear next to Emilio Barducci's name, indicating that this work was not cited in the article. You also did not use the source in your research so you can delete it from the bibliography.

5. **Click Delete, click Close, then click the Update Citations and Bibliography button on the Bibliography tab**

   The Barducci entry is removed and the bibliography is updated as shown in **FIGURE 11-15**

6. **Press [Ctrl][Home], press [Ctrl][Enter], press [Ctrl][Home], type Table of Figures, press [Enter], click the Home tab, then format Table of Figures using 24 pt, bold, and centering**

7. **Click below Table of Figures and to the left of the Page Break, click the References tab, click the Insert Table of Figures button in the Captions group, click the Formats list arrow, click Formal, then click OK**

   The list of figures included in the document is generated.

8. **Click the table of figures (it appears shaded), press and hold [Ctrl], click FIGURE 3, select the FIGURE 3 caption, press [Delete], click the picture, press [Delete], press [Delete] to remove the extra blank line, scroll to the FIGURE 4 caption, select 4, right click 4 in the figure caption, then click Update Field**

   The figure caption number is updated to reflect the deletion of FIGURE 3.

9. **Add a page break to the left of the heading OPTIONAL TOURS, press [Ctrl][Home], click in the table of figures, click Update Table in the Captions group, verify that the document is five pages long, then save the document**

   The table of figures now includes three figures as shown in **FIGURE 11-16**.

FIGURE 11-15: Updated bibliography using the Chicago format

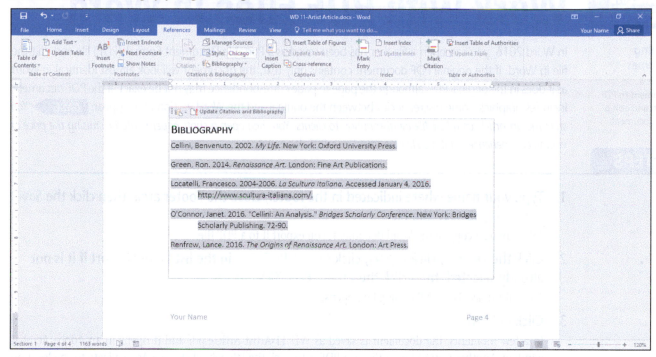

FIGURE 11-16: Updated table of figures

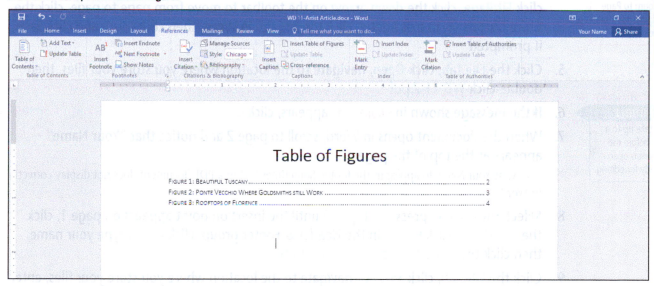

Table of Authorities

A table of authorities lists all the cases, statutes, rules, and other legal references included in a legal document, along with the page on which each reference appears. To create a table of authorities, click the References tab, go to the first reference (called a citation) that you wish to include in the table of authorities, then click the Mark Citation button in the Table of Authorities group. After you have marked all the citations in the document, click the Insert Table of Authorities button in the Table of Authorities group to build the table of authorities. Word organizes and then displays each citation you marked by category.

Work with PDF Files in Word

In Word 2016, you can open a file that has been saved as a Portable Document Format (PDF) file and edit the file in Word. If the original PDF document contains only text, the document will look almost identical in Word as it does in the original PDF, although the page to page correspondence may not be exact. If the PDF document includes graphics, some discrepancies between the original and the Word version may appear. **CASE** ▶ *You save the art article as a PDF file for distribution to clients. You then open a short paper related to raising the price of volunteer experiences that a colleague saved as a PDF document.*

STEPS

1. **Type your name where indicated in the footer, close the Footer area, then click the Save button 🖫 to save the file**

   After saving a copy of the Word document, you export it to a PDF file.

2. **Click the File tab, click Export, click Create PDF/XPS in the list below Export if it is not already selected, then click the Create PDF/XPS button**

   The Publish as PDF or XPS dialog box opens.

3. **Click Publish**

   In a few moments, the document is saved as WD 11-Artist Article.pdf and it opens in an Adobe Acrobat window. Another way to save a file as a PDF is to click the File tab, click Save As, navigate to the location where you want to save the file, click the Save as type list arrow in the Save As dialog box, click PDF as the Save as type, then click Save. The file will be saved as a PDF document.

4. **Maximize the window if it is not maximized, click the Zoom list arrow on the toolbar, click Fit Page, click the down arrow on the toolbar to move from page to page, click the Close button ☒ to exit Adobe, click the File tab in Word, then click Close and click Save if prompted**

5. **Click the File tab, click Open, navigate to the location where you store your files, then double-click WD 11-2.pdf**

6. **If the message shown in FIGURE 11-17 appears, click OK**

7. **When the document opens in Word, scroll to page 2 and notice that "Your Name" appears at the top of the page**

   You want Your Name to appear in the footer. Sometimes text in a PDF document does not display correctly in Word.

8. **Select Your Name, press [Backspace] until the insertion point appears on page 1, click the Insert tab, click Footer in the Header & Footer group, click Blank, type your name, then click the Close Header and Footer button**

9. **Click the File tab, click Save As, navigate to the location where you store your files, enter WD 11-Price Increase as the filename, then click Save**

   The document is saved as a Word document.

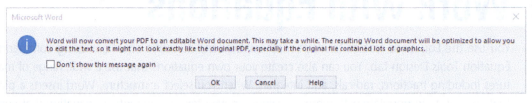

Microsoft Word

Word will now convert your PDF to an editable Word document. This may take a while. The resulting Word document will be optimized to allow you to edit the text, so it might not look exactly like the original PDF, especially if the original file contained lots of graphics.

☐ Don't show this message again

OK   Cancel   Help

Opening non-native files directly in Word

By default, Microsoft Word saves files in one of its proprietary formats. The saved file is called a native Word file because it is saved in a file format that is native to Word, such as .docx for Word documents and .dotx for Word templates. A Word file may not be recognized by other software programs.

Sometimes you may need to open a file in Word that is a non-native file—that is, a file created with a different software program. Depending on the program used to create the original file, you may not be able to open the non-native file in Word.

For example, you will get an error message if you attempt to open an Excel or PowerPoint file in Word.

When you are working with a different program and you want to work with that file in Word, you can save the file as a PDF file, as a txt, or as an rtf file. You can open and work on any of these three non-native file formats in Word. For example, you can save an Excel file as a PDF file, then open and work on the file in Word. **FIGURE 11-18** shows how an Excel file appears after it is saved as a PDF file and then opened in Word.

FIGURE 11-18: Excel file saved as **PDF** and opened in Word

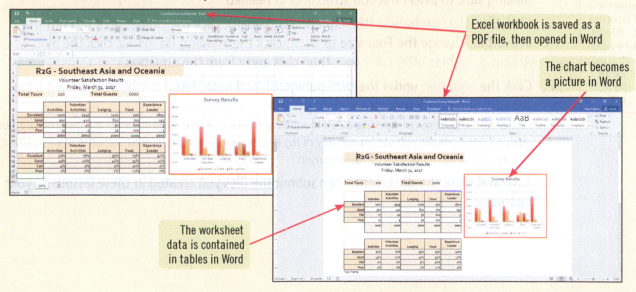

Excel workbook is saved as a PDF file, then opened in Word

The chart becomes a picture in Word

The worksheet data is contained in tables in Word

Work with Equations

Learning Outcomes
- Create an equation
- Format an equation

You use the Equations feature to insert mathematical and scientific equations using commands on the Equation Tools Design tab. You can also create your own equations that use a wide range of math structures including fractions, radicals, and integrals. When you select a structure, Word inserts a placeholder that you can then populate with symbols, values, or even text. If you write an equation that you want to use again, you can save the equation and then access it from a custom equation gallery. **CASE** *The paper on raising the price of volunteer experiences uses the economic concept of elasticity to describe the result of raising the price from $3,400 to $5,000. The paper includes equations to express the economics concepts. You need to create and format one equation from scratch.*

STEPS

1. **Scroll up and delete the text [Equation 1 to be created] below the second paragraph but do not delete the blank line, click the Insert tab, then click Equation in the Symbols group**

   An equation content control is inserted in the document and the Equation Tools Design tab becomes the active tab. This tab is divided into three groups: Tools, Symbols, and Structures. **TABLE 11-1** describes the content of each group.

2. **Click the Fraction button in the Structures group to show a selection of fraction structures, click the first fraction structure in the top row, then increase the zoom to 180%**

   Increasing the zoom helps you see the components of the equation.

3. **Click in the top half of the fraction (the numerator)**

   The box is shaded to indicate it is selected.

4. **Click the More button ⬇ in the Symbols group to expand the Symbols gallery, click the Basic Math list arrow on the title bar, click Greek Letters, then click the Delta symbol (Δ) as shown in FIGURE 11-19**

   You can select commonly used math symbols from eight galleries as follows: Basic Math, Greek Letters, Letter-Like Symbols, Operators, Arrows, Negated Relations, Scripts, and Geometry.

TROUBLE
Follow step 2 to insert the fraction structure each time; use the keyboard arrow keys to move to different parts of the equation. If your insertion point moves outside the equation, click in the equation again.

5. **Type Q, press [↓] to move to the bottom half of the fraction (the denominator), type Q, press [→], type an equal sign (=), then complete the equation as shown in FIGURE 11-20, making sure to insert fraction structures as needed**

6. **Click the selection handle (the equation is shaded), click the Home tab if it is not the active tab, change the Font size to 14 pt, click the Shading list arrow, click the Blue, Accent 5, Lighter 60% color box, then click away from the equation**

7. **Click the equation under the next paragraph and note that it has been imported from the PDF file as a picture, not as an equation**

   One of the challenges of opening a PDF document in Word is that graphics such as equations are not retained. For example, you cannot edit any of the equations. If you want to make a change to an equation, you need to delete it and enter a new equation.

8. **Save and close the document, then submit the files you created in these lessons to your instructor**

FIGURE 11-19: Selecting a symbol

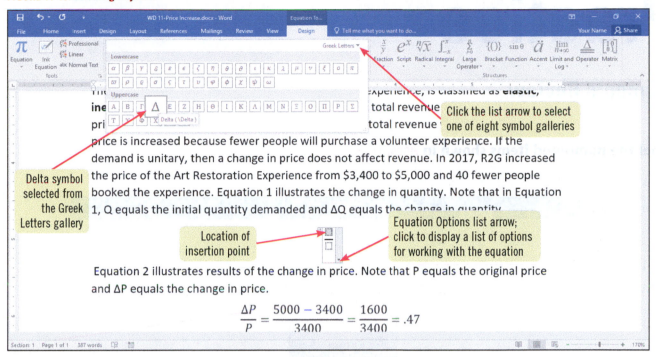

Delta symbol selected from the Greek Letters gallery

Click the list arrow to select one of eight symbol galleries

Location of insertion point

Equation Options list arrow; click to display a list of options for working with the equation

price is increased because fewer people will purchase a volunteer experience. If the demand is unitary, then a change in price does not affect revenue. In 2017, R2G increased the price of the Art Restoration Experience from $3,400 to $5,000 and 40 fewer people booked the experience. Equation 1 illustrates the change in quantity. Note that in Equation 1, Q equals the initial quantity demanded and ΔQ equals the change in quantity.

Equation 2 illustrates results of the change in price. Note that P equals the original price and ΔP equals the change in price.

$$\frac{\Delta P}{P} = \frac{5000 - 3400}{3400} = \frac{1600}{3400} = .47$$

FIGURE 11-20: Completed Equation 1

$$\frac{\Delta Q}{Q} = \frac{100 - 40}{100} = \frac{60}{100}$$

TABLE 11-1: Contents of the Equation Tools Design tab

group	description
Tools	• Use the Equation button to select a built-in equation • Select the equation style: Professional, Linear, or Normal Text • Click the launcher 🔲 to access the Equation Options dialog box where you can specify equation settings and access the Math AutoCorrect list of symbols
Symbols	• Select commonly used mathematical symbols such as (±) and (∞) • Click the More button 🔽 to show a gallery of symbols • Click the list arrow in the gallery to select the group for which you would like to see symbols
Structures	• Select common math structures, such as fractions and radicals • Click a structure button (such as the Fraction button) to select a specific format to insert in the equation for that structure

More equation options

From the Equation Tools Design tab, you can click the Ink Equation button to write an equation using a digital pen or other pointing device. Word converts the written symbols into typed symbols.

From the Shapes menu on the Insert tab, you can select one of the six equation shapes shown in **FIGURE 11-21**.

You modify these shapes in the same way you modify any drawing shape.

FIGURE 11-21:

Equation Shapes
➕ ➖ ✖ ➗ ═ ≠

Practice

Concepts Review

Label the numbered items shown in FIGURE 11-22.

FIGURE 11-22

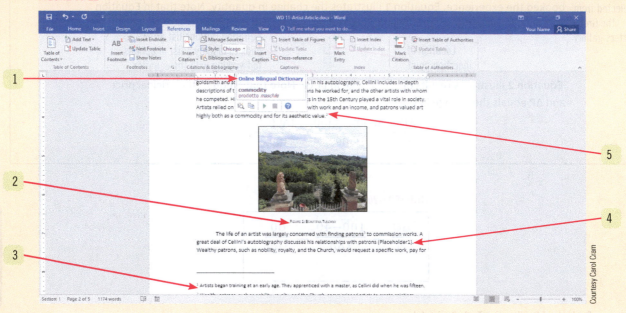

Courtesy Carol Cram

Match each term with the statement that best describes it.

6. Review
7. Footnote
8. Table of Figures
9. Bibliography
10. MLA
11. Citation

a. List of references included in a document, such as an essay or report
b. Provides additional comments on information provided in the text
c. Tab that includes the Translate feature
d. Short reference that credits the source of a quote
e. List of objects, such as charts and pictures, included in a document
f. Example of a style applied to a bibliography and citations

Select the best answer from the list of choices.

12. **Which of the following activities is *not* available in the Manage Sources dialog box?**

a. Copy a source to your document
b. Add a source
c. Change the source style
d. Delete a source

13. **How do you modify the style of a caption?**

a. Right-click the caption, then click Style
b. Edit the formats
c. Click Styles in the Caption dialog box
d. Right-click the caption, then click the Styles button on the Mini toolbar

14. **Which option in the Word Options dialog box do you choose to work with the AutoCorrect feature?**

a. General
b. Display
c. Advanced
d. Proofing

Skills Review

1. Work with AutoCorrect.

  a. Start Word, open the file WD 11-3.docx from the drive and folder where you store your Data Files, then save the file as **WD 11-Social History Term Paper**.

  b. Open the Word Options dialog box, open Proofing, then open the AutoCorrect dialog box.

  c. Verify that the AutoCorrect tab is the active tab, type **sc** in the Replace text box, type **Saint Cyr** in the With text box, click Add, then exit all dialog boxes.

  d. Search for **xx**, use the AutoCorrect keystroke to replace xx with **Saint Cyr**, then adjust the spacing and punctuation as needed. (*Hint*: Select xx, type **sc**, and press [Spacebar] to enter the AutoCorrect text.)

  e. Repeat the process in Step d to replace xx in the next sentence, then check both inserts and delete extra spaces as needed.

  f. Double-click to the left of Your Name in the document footer, type **(c)** to insert the copyright symbol, then replace the "Your Name" placeholder with your name.

  g. Delete the sc entry from the AutoCorrect dialog box.

2. Customize footnotes.

  a. Change the Number format of the footnotes to the 1, 2, 3 number format and select the Continuous option for footnote numbering. Apply the formatting to the whole document.

  b. Find the text "practical skills", then position the insertion point following the period after the word "skills."

  c. Insert a footnote with the following text: **For example, training in textiles enabled girls to obtain employment in the factories**.

  d. Go to footnote 1 and edit it by typing **In the eighteenth century**, before "English girls" at the beginning of the footnote, then click above the separator line.

  e. Go to footnote reference mark **4** in the document text, then delete the footnote reference mark.

  f. Scroll up to page 5, then modify the style of the footnote text in the footnote area by changing the font size to 9 pt, the After spacing to 6 pt, and the line spacing to 1.5.

  g. Click above the separator line, then save the document.

3. Use the Translate feature.

  a. Find the text **This French quote**, then select the text from L'enseignement charitable... to ... à la vie extérieure at the end of the sentence (do not include the period).

  b. Use the Translate feature to view a translation of the selected text from French to English.

  c. Read the English translation, which is an approximate translation of the text.

  d. Close the Research task pane, click the word "schools" in the second line of the next paragraph, then turn on and use the Mini Translator to view the French translation of school (école). Remember to change the Mini Translator Translate to language to French.

  e. Change the Mini Translator language to Spanish (Spain), turn on the Mini Translator, then move the pointer over the word "schools" and note the Spanish translation to escuela.

  f. Turn off the Mini Translator, then save the document.

4. Modify citations and manage sources.

  a. Find the text **popular education in England**, then after the ending quotation mark and before the period, insert a new citation placeholder.

  b. Find the text **roles in society**, then edit the citation so that it includes **28** as the page number. Remember to click the citation to show the Citation Options list arrow.

  c. Find the text **household activities**, then edit the citation so that it includes **93** as the page number.

  d. Change the style to Chicago.

  e. Find the text **Placeholder**, select the (Placeholder1) citation, then replace the placeholder with a citation using the Gabriel Lee source. (*Note*: Be sure to select the citation using the field selection handle; do not edit the citation.)

  f. Edit the citation so that it suppresses the year and displays page **70**. (*Hint*: Click the Year check box to suppress the year.)

g. Open the Source Manager dialog box, edit the entry for Valdez so the name is **Walden**.

h. Delete the Placeholder1 entry from the Source Manager dialog box, then close the dialog box.

5. **Add and modify captions.**

a. Scroll to the picture of the church on page 4, then add a caption with the text **Figure 3: Schools attached to convents and churches educated girls in France** that uses the A, B, C numbering format.

b. Scroll to the next picture and verify that the caption includes Figure D.

c. Modify the Caption style so that the font color is black and the font size is 11 pt.

d. Delete the first picture and caption in the document (the picture of the two girls).

e. Select all the text in the document, use [F9] to update all the captions in the document, then verify that the figure letters have updated. (*Notes:* You may need to use the [Fn] key in conjunction with the [F9] key. If [F9] does not update all captions, scroll through the document and update each caption manually by right-clicking the caption and clicking Update Field.)

f. Save the document.

6. **Generate a bibliography and table of figures.**

a. Move to the end of the document, insert a page break, and clear any formatting.

b. Insert a bibliography, then scroll up to view it.

c. Change the style of the citations and bibliography to MLA.

d. Open the Source Manager dialog box, then change the entry for Josef Hauser to Josef Holbrook.

e. Update the bibliography and confirm that Josef's last name is now Holbrook. The completed bibliography appears as shown in **FIGURE 11-23**.

FIGURE 11-23

f. Go to the top of the document, insert a page break, type **Table of Figures** at the top of the document, then format it with 18 pt, bold, and center alignment.

g. Press [Enter] following "Table of Figures", clear the formatting, then generate a table of figures using the Distinctive format.

h. Use [Ctrl][Click] to go from the entry for Figure D to the figure in the document, then delete Figure D and its caption.

i. Update the table of figures, enter your name in the footer at the bottom of the page, then save the document.

7. **Work with PDF files in Word.**

a. Export the document to a PDF file, then publish the document. The document is saved as **WD 11-Social History Term Paper.pdf**.

b. Fit the document to the page, view the pages of the document, then close it.

c. Open the file WD 11-4.pdf in Word from the location where you store your Data Files.

d. Scroll to the top of page 2, then delete Your Name so the document fits on one page.

e. Insert your name in the footer.

f. Save the file as a Word document called **WD 11-Common Equations.docx**. (*Hint:* Make sure the document is saved as a docx file not as a PDF file.)

8. **Work with equations.**

a. Go to the [Equation 1] placeholder, then replace it with an equation content control.

b. Type **A =**, then select Π (pi symbol) from the uppercase area of the Greek Letters gallery.

c. Click the Script button in the Structures group.

FIGURE 11-24

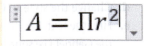

d. Select the first script structure, then type **r** in the large box, and **2** in the small box as shown in **FIGURE 11-24**.

e. Format the new equation by increasing its font size to 14 pt and shading it with Green, Accent 6, Lighter 80%. (*Hint:* Remember to select the equation content control before applying the shading.)

f. Save and close the document, then submit all the files you created for this skills review to your instructor.

Independent Challenge 1

You have finished writing a term paper about Shakespeare's play *Henry IV*: Part 1. Now you use the References features to manage source information. You create a new AutoCorrect entry, insert and modify footnotes, and modify existing citations. You also work in the Source Manager dialog box to organize sources, and then you generate and modify a bibliography.

a. Start Word, open the file WD 11-5.docx from the drive and folder where you store your Data Files, then save it as **WD 11-Literature Term Paper**.

b. Create an AutoCorrect entry that replaces **ssh** with **Shakespeare**, then search for each instance of **xx** and replace it with the **ssh** AutoCorrect entry. Adjust spacing as needed after Shakespeare is inserted. (*Note*: The document contains three instances of "xx.")

c. Go to the top of the document, find the first instance of **chivalric code**, then add the footnote: **Chivalry is associated with the ideals of honor and courtly love held by medieval knights**.

d. Find footnote A, change the date 200 A.D. to **400 A.D.**, then change the number format for all the footnotes to 1, 2, 3.

e. Modify the footnote style so that the footnote text is single spaced and all the text is 9 pt.

f. Find the text **people and situations**, then insert a citation placeholder to the right of the ending quotation mark and before the ending period.

g. Find the text **untouched**, insert a citation after the ending quotation mark and before the period that refers to Quinones, then edit the citation to add the page number **74**.

h. Replace (Placeholder1) with a citation that refers to Quinones and page number **81**.

i. At the end of the document after the last paragraph, insert a new page, and then generate a new bibliography using the MLA style.

j. In the Source Manager dialog box, delete the placeholder, then edit the source by George Aitken so that the last name is **Atkins** instead of Aitken.

k. Update the bibliography.

l. Remove the **ssh** AutoCorrect entry from the AutoCorrect dialog box.

m. Type your name where indicated in the footer, use the (c) code to enter the copyright symbol (©) before your name, submit the file to your instructor, then save and close the document.

Independent Challenge 2

You decide to explore using the Translate feature. You open a document containing a short message in English. You want to determine how accurate a translation is that goes through multiple translations. You translate the passage from English into Italian and then from Italian into German, and finally from German back to English. Then you compare the result of this last translation with the original English text to check the accuracy of the translation. You also work with captions and generate a table of figures.

a. Start Word, open the file WD 11-6.docx from the drive and folder where you store your Data Files, then save it as **WD 11-Translation Practice**.

b. Select the English message (begins "We are delighted…" and ends "beautiful city" but do not select the ending period) at the beginning of the document, then use the Translate Selected Text feature to translate the selected text to Italian.

c. Click in the table cell under From English to Italian, then click Insert in the Research task pane to insert the Italian translation from the Research task pane into the From English to Italian cell in the table. (*Hint*: Scroll down the Research pane to see more of the translation and the Insert button.)

d. Close the Research task pane, select the Italian translation (but do not select the ending period), then use the Translate feature to translate the selected Italian text into German. (*Hint*: You will need to change the entry in the From text box to Italian (Italy) and the entry in the To text box to German (Germany)).

Independent Challenge 2 (continued)

e. Click in the table cell under From Italian to German, then click Insert in the Research task pane to insert the German translation from the Research task pane into the From Italian to German cell in the table.

f. Close the Research task pane, select the German translation in the table cell (but do not include the ending period), use the Translate feature to translate the selected text back into English, insert the English translation from the Research task pane into the table cell under From German to English, then close the Research task pane. (*Hint*: Remember to change the entries in the From and To text boxes to reflect the correct languages: German and English.)

g. Compare the paragraph at the beginning of the document with the translation you just inserted in the last cell of the table. Notice some of the ways in which the syntax of the original English message has changed after two translations.

h. Scroll to Figure b, which is the picture of the prows of two gondolas in Venice. Use the Mini Translator to find the Italian translation for "canals", then type the Italian translation to replace "canals".

i. Add a caption to the first picture (a canal in Venice) that reads: **Figure A: The famous Bridge of Sighs in Venice**. Make sure you select the A, B, C, Numbering style even if it is already selected.

j. Change the style of the captions so they appear in bold with no italics and with After Spacing of 18 pt.

k. Below the last picture, type **Table of Figures**, format it with bold and 14 pt, then generate a table of figures using the Classic format.

l. Delete the picture of the Grand Canal (Figure B) and its caption, then update the figure references and update the table of figures. (*Hint*: Use [Ctrl][A] to select all the text, then press [F9] or update each of the figure references manually.)

m. Type your name in the footer, then save the document.

n. Export the document to a PDF file, scroll through the file after it opens in Adobe Reader, then close the PDF file.

o. Submit your files to your instructor.

Independent Challenge 3

You are helping a teacher to prepare a worksheet showing some of the equations related to circles and spheres for a high school geometry class. The teacher has already entered some of the formulas in Word. She asks you to use the Equation feature to add a new formula and then to create a table of figures to list the formulas used in the document.

a. Start Word, open the file WD 11-7.docx from the drive and folder where you store your Data Files, then save it as **WD 11-Geometry Equations**.

b. Increase the zoom to 150% so you can easily see the formula as you work, then click below the Volume of a Sphere heading and create the Volume of a Sphere equation as follows:

- Click Equation in the Symbols group on the Insert tab, type **V**, then type an equal sign (**=**).
- Click the Fraction button in the Structures group, then select the first fraction style and click in the top box.
- Type **4**, show the Basic Math symbols, then click the Pi (π) symbol (fourth row).
- Click the Script button in the Structures group, select the Superscript style (first selection), then type an **r** in the large box and a **3** in the small box.
- Click in the bottom box in the fraction, type **3**, then compare the completed formula to **FIGURE 11-25**.

FIGURE 11-25

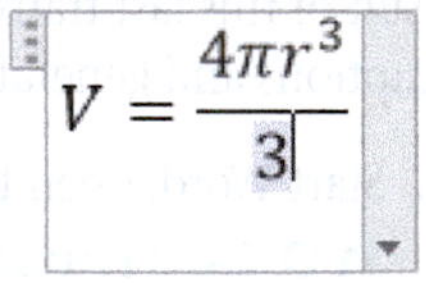

$$V = \frac{4\pi r^3}{3}$$

c. Format the equation for Perimeter of a Circle with the 16 pt font size and the Orange, Accent 2, Lighter 60% shading.

d. Use the Format Painter to apply the same formatting to the other two equations.

e. Click the third equation, click the selection handle, then change the equation to a Linear equation. (*Hint*: Click Linear in the Tools group on the Equation Tools Design tab.)

Independent Challenge 3 (continued)

f. As described below, add captions centered above each of the three equations so that each caption includes the caption number followed by a colon and the name of the equation. For example, caption 1 should be **EQUATION 1: PERIMETER OF A CIRCLE**.

- Make sure you select the entire equation by clicking the selection handle before you insert the caption.
- In the Caption dialog box, you need to select Equation as the label type, and then type a colon and the caption title in the Caption text box in the Caption dialog box. (*Hint*: If Equation is not available as a label type, create a new label. Click New Label in the Caption dialog box, type **Equation**, then click OK.)
- To center the caption, press [Ctrl][e] immediately after you insert the caption.)

g. Modify the Caption style so that the font is 10 point and the font color is Orange, Accent 2.

h. Below the heading SAMPLE EQUATIONS... at the top of the document, insert a table of figures using the Formal style, insert a page break, then update the table of figures.

i. Type your name in the document footer, save the file, submit a copy to your instructor, then close the file.

Independent Challenge 4: Explore

You have just started a job as a research assistant with Data Unlimited, a company that conducts research projects for local businesses. On your first day on the job, your supervisor asks you to demonstrate how you use the Research task pane to find answers to three questions he gives you. He then wants you to use the citation feature in Word to document each of the three websites you accessed to find the answers.

a. Start Word, open the file WD 11-8.docx from the drive and folder where you store your Data Files, then save it as **WD 11-Web Research**.

b. Create an AutoCorrect entry called **pb** that will enter the text **Prepared by** followed by your name.

c. Use pb to enter its associated text under the heading "Web Research Practice" and in the footer, then remove the AutoCorrect entry.

d. Read the first question, then open the Research task pane. (*Hint*: Click anywhere in the document, click the Translate button on the Review tab, then click Translate Selected Text and click Yes. The Research task pane opens.)

e. Click in the Search for text box in the Research task pane, type **Mount K2 first climber**, click the Translation list arrow, then click All Research Sites.

f. Follow one of the links to find the answers to Question 1 in the document: Identify the names of the first team of climbers to scale Mount K2 successfully, the date they did it, and their nationalities.

g. Write a short paragraph in the space provided below the question with the required information.

h. Set the citations and bibliography style to APA, then immediately following the text you typed to answer each question, insert a citation based on a new source you create by entering information about the website you used as a source. (*Hint*: In the Create Source dialog box, set the Type of Source to Web site, click the Show All Bibliography Fields check box, then enter the information about the website you consulted in all fields starred with a red asterisk. If you can't find information for a particular entry, type "unknown". To enter the website address in the URL field, switch to the website, select the website address, press [Ctrl][C], switch back to the Create Source dialog box, click in the URL text box, then press [Ctrl][V].)

i. Use the Research task pane to find an answer to the next question and then provide the appropriate citation based on a source you add. Make sure you consult a different website to find the answer.

j. For the final question, enter your description, then insert a placeholder for the citation. Be sure to modify the font style of all the answers so that it matches the font used in the questions.

k. Following the placeholder, insert a footnote that contains the text: **This information is based on my own observations**.

l. At the end of the document, generate a bibliography.

m. Submit the file to your instructor, then save and close the document.

Visual Workshop

Open the file WD 11-9.docx from the drive and folder where you store your Data Files, then save it as **WD 11-Popular Culture Bibliography**. Open the AutoCorrect dialog box, identify the keystrokes required to enter the ™ symbol, then type the sentence shown in **FIGURE 11-26** and insert the ™ symbol where indicated. Generate a bibliography. Open the Source Manager dialog box, edit the entry for Daniel Larkin so the information appears as shown in **FIGURE 11-26**, update the bibliography, then select the bibliography style so the format of the entries matches **FIGURE 11-26**. Type your name where shown, submit the file to your instructor, then save and close the document.

FIGURE 11-26

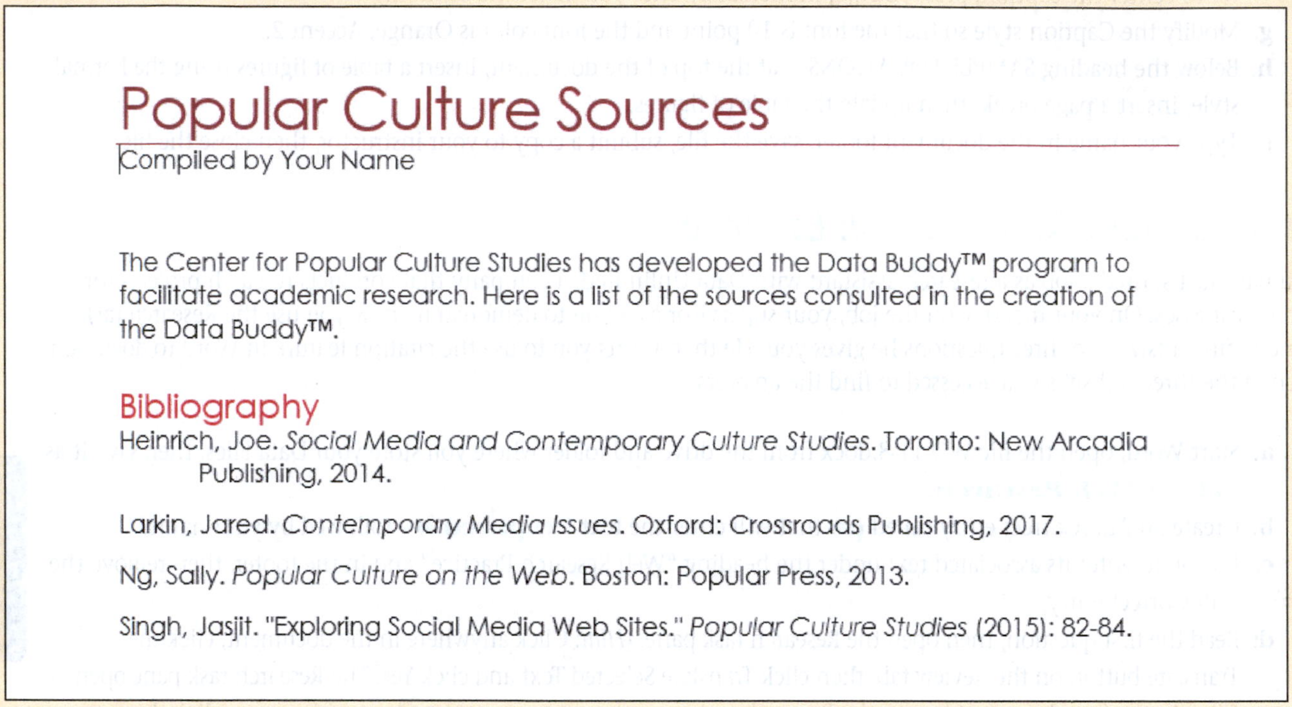

Popular Culture Sources
Compiled by Your Name

The Center for Popular Culture Studies has developed the Data Buddy™ program to facilitate academic research. Here is a list of the sources consulted in the creation of the Data Buddy™.

Bibliography

Heinrich, Joe. *Social Media and Contemporary Culture Studies*. Toronto: New Arcadia Publishing, 2014.

Larkin, Jared. *Contemporary Media Issues*. Oxford: Crossroads Publishing, 2017.

Ng, Sally. *Popular Culture on the Web*. Boston: Popular Press, 2013.

Singh, Jasjit. "Exploring Social Media Web Sites." *Popular Culture Studies* (2015): 82-84.

Glossary

Adjustment handle The yellow square that appears when certain shapes are selected; used to change the shape, but not the size, of a shape.

Anchored The state of a floating graphic that moves with a paragraph or other item if the item is moved; an anchor symbol appears next to the paragraph or item when the floating graphic is selected and formatting marks are displayed.

Bibliography A list of sources that you consulted or cited while creating a document.

Bitmap graphic A graphic that is composed of a series of small dots called "pixels" and often saved with a .bmp, .png, .jpg, .tif, or .gif file extension.

Boilerplate text Text that appears in every version of a merged document.

Bookmark Text that identifies a location, such as the beginning of a paragraph or a selection of text in a document.

Brightness The relative lightness of a photograph.

Building block A reusable piece of formatted content or document part that is stored in a gallery.

Caption Text that is attached to a figure in Word and provides a title or a brief explanation of the figure.

Character style A named set of character format settings that can be applied to text to format it all at once; you use a character style to apply format settings only to select text within a paragraph.

Chart A visual representation of numerical data, usually used to illustrate trends, patterns, or relationships.

Citation A parenthetical reference in the document text that gives credit to the source for a quotation or other information used in a document.

Color saturation The vividness and intensity of color in a photograph.

Color tone The relative warmth or coolness of the colors in a photograph.

Contrast The difference in brightness between the darkest and the lightest areas of a photograph.

Crop To trim away part of a graphic.

Cross-reference (document) Text that electronically refers the reader to another part of the document; you click a cross-reference to move directly to a specific location in the document.

Cross-reference (index) Refers the reader to another entry in the index.

Data field A category of information, such as last name, first name, street address, city, or postal code.

Data record A complete set of related information for a person or an item, such as a person's contact information, including name, address, phone number, e-mail address, and so on.

Data source In a mail merge, the file with the unique data for individual people or items.

Drawing canvas A workspace for creating graphics.

Drawing gridlines A grid of nonprinting lines that appears within the margins in Print Layout view to help you size, align, and position graphics.

Endnote Text that provides additional information or acknowledges sources for text in a document and that appears at the end of a document.

Field name The name of a data field.

Figure Any object such as a chart, a picture, an equation, or an embedded object to which a caption can be added.

Filter In a mail merge, to pull out records that meet specific criteria and include only those records in the merge.

Footnote Text that provides additional information or acknowledges sources for text in a document and that appears at the bottom of the page on which the note reference mark appears.

Index Text, usually appearing at the end of a document, that lists terms and topics that you have marked for inclusion, along with the pages on which they appear.

Link (text box) A connection between two or more text boxes so that the text flows automatically from one text box to another.

Linked style A named set of format settings that are applied either to characters within a paragraph or to the entire paragraph, depending on whether the entire paragraph or specific text is selected.

List style A named set of format settings, such as indent and outline numbering, that you can apply to a list to format it all at once.

Mail merge To merge a main document that contains boilerplate text with a file that contains customized information for many individual items to create customized versions of the main document.

Main document In a mail merge, the document with the boilerplate text.

Merge field A placeholder that you insert in the main document to indicate where the data from each record should be inserted when you perform a mail merge.

Merged document In a mail merge, the document that contains customized versions of the main document.

Navigation pane A pane showing the headings and subheadings as entries that you can click to move directly to a specific heading anywhere in a document. The Navigation pane opens along the left side of the document window.

Normal template Template loaded automatically when you start a new document. Styles assigned to the Normal template are the styles included in the Styles gallery when the document is opened.

Note reference mark A mark (such as a letter or a number) that appears next to text to indicate that additional information is offered in a footnote or endnote.

Nudge To move a graphic a small amount in one direction using the arrow keys.

Paragraph style A named set of paragraph and character format settings that can be applied to a paragraph to format it all at once.

Property control A control that contains document property information or a placeholder, and that can be used to assign or update the document property directly from the document.

Pull quote A text box that contains a quote or an excerpt from an article, formatted in a larger font size, and placed on the same page.

Reveal Formatting task pane Lists exactly which formats are applied to the character, paragraph, and section of the selected text.

Rotate handle A green circle that appears above a graphic when the graphic is selected; drag the rotate handle to rotate the graphic.

Scale To resize a graphic so that its height to width ratio remains the same.

Shape A drawing object, such as a rectangle, oval, triangle, line, block arrow, or other shape that you create using the Shapes command.

Sidebar A text box that is positioned adjacent to the body of a document and contains auxiliary information.

Sizing handles The white circles and squares that appear around a graphic when it is selected; used to change the size or shape of a graphic.

SmartArt A diagram, list, organizational chart, or other graphic created using the SmartArt command.

Style A named collection of character and/or paragraph formats that are stored together and can be applied to text to format it quickly.

Style Inspector Lists the styles applied to the selected text and indicates if any extra formats were applied that are not included in the style.

Style Set A named collection of font and paragraph settings for heading and body text styles, so that when you apply a new style set to a document, all body text and headings that have been formatting with a style change.

Styles gallery Location where all the styles associated with a Style Set are stored; you access the Style Gallery by clicking the More button in the Styles group on the Home tab.

Styles task pane Contains all the styles available to the current document and the buttons to access the Style Inspector, the Reveal Formatting task pane, and the Manage Styles dialog box.

Subentry Text included under a main entry in an index.

Table of Contents Provides a list of the topics and subtopics covered in a multipage document and includes the page number associated with each topic.

Table of figures A list of all the figures used in a document.

Table style A named set of table format settings that can be applied to a table to format it all at once. The Table style includes settings for both the table grid and the table text.

Template A formatted document that contains placeholder text you can replace with new text. A file that contains the basic structure of a document including headers and footers, styles, and graphical elements.

Text box A container that you can fill with text and graphics.

Theme A set of unified design elements, including theme colors, theme fonts for body text and headings, and theme effects for graphics that can be applied to a document all at once.

WordArt A drawing object that contains text formatted with special shapes, patterns, and orientations.

Works cited A list of sources that you cited while creating a document.

XE (index entry) Field code inserted next to text marked for inclusion in an index.

Index